All Over the Place is Sandra's first attempt at writing a memoir. With forty-five years in the travel industry, she started her career with Thomas Cook, before continuing for a number of years with British Airways, then worked for smaller independent travel agencies. For the past twenty-three years, she has built a successful franchise, planning tailor-made trips, from budget to luxury travel, organising business trips for various companies, and gaining a vast font of knowledge along the way. Sandra has been married to the ever-patient Graham for almost as long as her career and has two grown-up daughters.

ALL OVER THE PLACE

Sandra Robinson

_____

ALL OVER THE PLACE

Vanguard Press

VANGUARD PAPERBACK

© Copyright 2023
Sandra Robinson

The right of Sandra Robinson to be identified as author of this work has been asserted by her in accordance with the Copyright, Designs and Patents Act 1988.

All Rights Reserved

No reproduction, copy or transmission of this publication
may be made without written permission.
No paragraph of this publication may be reproduced,
copied or transmitted save with the written permission of the publisher,
or in accordance with the provisions
of the Copyright Act 1956 (as amended).

Any person who commits any unauthorised act in relation to
this publication may be liable to criminal
prosecution and civil claims for damages.

A CIP catalogue record for this title is
available from the British Library.

ISBN 978 1 80016 620 2

Vanguard Press is an imprint of
Pegasus Elliot Mackenzie Publishers Ltd.
www.pegasuspublishers.com

First Published in 2023

Vanguard Press
Sheraton House Castle Park
Cambridge England

Printed & Bound in Great Britain

To Graham, Laura and Hannah —never judge a book by its cover — except this one.

To Sallie for an inspired suggestion for the title of this book, and also to the following people who have given permission to relay incidents involving them: Rosemary, Helen, Mandy, Anne, Vic and Kam. To Steve for checking that my description of Travel Counsellors is accurate. To Graham for painstakingly correcting me on my grammar.

In the Beginning

They say that travel broadens the mind but that was the last thing on my mind when asked, aged eight, what I would like to be when I grew up. At that age, in the 1960s, I could only think of a few choices. I could work in a shop, become a secretary or train as a nurse. This was what my friends thought they would end up doing, but I have never wanted to follow the trend, so quickly thought of what else I could do.

"I'm going to be an air stewardess," I said.

That sounded different. That was it, it sounded different, and thinking about it, it sounded exciting too, but beyond that I had no real idea what an air stewardess did. I had no thoughts about seeing the world either. I just wanted to be different from my friends.

Perhaps unconsciously I was destined for a life in the travel industry because in 1972 my school announced there was a trip on a cruise to the Mediterranean in November of that year. Surprisingly, my parents said I could go and paid the £77 cost. We were to fly out to Venice, board the cruise ship, the SS *Nevassa*, which had dormitory style sleeping arrangements and classrooms on board. From there, we would sail down the Adriatic to Corfu and Athens, through the Corinth Canal, across the Aegean Sea to the Dardanelles to Istanbul, then down to Rhodes for our final stop. On the morning of departure, we met at school excited for our adventure. It was the first time I had travelled abroad and armed with my brand-new blue passport, I felt slightly nervous about taking my first flight. I remember my best friend arriving at school dressed from head to toe in a new outfit, grey Oxford bags, which were tight-fitting trousers with wide legs and turnups. Her black patent platform shoes had a splash of red on either side, and the whole ensemble was topped with a grey zip-up furry cropped jacket — the absolute height of fashion. I felt quite dowdy standing next to her. I found flying a pleasant enough experience. Ears popping when ascending and descending, with a meal served on a plastic tray with plastic cutlery and tiny packets of salt and pepper. (Ah, *that's* what air stewardesses do!) It was all quite natty, I thought. Time passed very quickly as we all chatted excitedly about what was to come. I had my

Kodak Instamatic camera tucked in my bag, with a couple of spare film cartridges to record my adventure.

We arrived at a very foggy Venice Airport and were taken to Venice Island for a quick tour around before boarding the ship. St Mark's Square was virtually empty, so we had free reign to wander around taking in the architecture through the misty gloom, passing the Doge's Palace, with its grand façade and through the narrow streets to the Rialto Bridge, where I bought a nice Murano glass paperweight with my lira to give to my parents. I only ever buy things I like myself. I had to wait another forty-odd years to get it back in my possession after they both passed away. Little did I know that I would return to Venice and get a completely different perspective. No one travels to Venice in November. I always remember the way to remember the climate patterns in the Med from my school days. Hot, dry summers, warm, wet winters. I think we were lucky that we only had fog and we could walk freely around St Mark's Square. The area is often flooded and to get across the square when flooded, they install raised boardwalks, but I didn't know that then.

  Heading down to Corfu I remember the ship dropping anchor on 11th November and attending a Remembrance Day service at eleven a.m. up on deck. Standing on deck, eerily silent in the middle of the ocean, was an unusual experience, in complete contrast to the cacophony of us all singing along to a popular song in the charts some hours later at the top deck disco, but it was one of the first travel memories I have. Arriving in Corfu we had a tour of Corfu Town and then north-west to Paleokastritsa, the prettiest place I had ever seen. I loved the clear turquoise blue sea and pretty, craggy coves. I had only ever seen the greyish-green waters of the Solent so could not believe that the sea came in much better shades of blue. Next stop Athens and time to visit the Acropolis. At that time, the Parthenon was clear of scaffolding, a seemingly rare occurrence in more recent years, so we had an uninterrupted view of the Doric columns and sculpted friezes above them. I nicked a bit of the Acropolis, well, I doubt it was from the actual Acropolis, as I'd picked a bit of stone up from the ground next to it, but it was the same colour as the columns. I needed something to stick into my scrap book that had to be written for homework when we returned. We also paused by the Tomb of the Unknown Soldier to watch the changing of the guard. I was fascinated by the evzone's traditional uniforms with their full white skirts and white wide-sleeved shirts, topped with a colourful waistcoat. They wore red velvet brimless hats with a long tassel attached on the crown, white tights and red leather shoes with a pompom at the front. Their march consisted of a slow high-legged walk, just like John Cleese's silly walk. Maybe, he got the idea from watching them. Of course, my best friend and I just had to buy one of those hats, which we later wore to our local disco, thinking we were the coolest on the dance floor! I have still got that hat, somewhere in the fancy dress bag.

Next stop Istanbul, travelling through the Corinth Canal, where we learnt a bit about the history of the First World War and Gallipoli as we sailed through the Dardanelles. It was certainly better than sitting in a classroom, trying to retain it all from a book. Istanbul was a complete culture shock, and this was where I had a few more firsts - such as my first time in a mosque, at Hagia Sophia, and not really liking the idea of taking my shoes off and leaving them outside. My mum would have had something to say about getting dirty socks or a verruca or something, so it was a good job she wasn't there. It was my first time seeing a priceless diamond, the 86-carat pear-shaped Spoonmaker's Diamond, at the Topkapi Palace Museum; one of the largest in the world. I had my first experience of the bustling Grand Bazaar, where we bartered for gifts, and the first time trying some sickly-sweet baklava. Some of my friends came away with Afghan coats, fashionable at the time and probably full of fleas, but they thought they looked the business. I didn't stand too close to them, just in case! Just imagine returning home to Mum, with fleas *and* dirty socks! Sailing in, under the Galata Bridge, I loved the fact that heading any further east we would be leaving Europe.

Our final port of call was in Rhodes, where we headed south to Lindos, a traffic-free hilltop village full of whitewashed traditional houses, accessed by donkey, or a steep walk uphill. I do not remember riding on a donkey, so we must have puffed our way to the top. The view from the Acropolis at the top was lovely, looking down onto a wide, sweeping, empty, sandy beach. Arriving back in Rhodes Town, we had a bit of time to wander amongst the local traders, who tried to lure us into their shops. One very insistent trader asked me to go into his shop where we could make 'sweet music'. I noticed he had very long thumbnails, so I suppose, he *could* have played the guitar, but I'm sure that wasn't his intention! I could say this first trip abroad was my first educational trip. I did learn a lot, and maybe it did sow a seed.

***

A few years passed without any further thoughts of a future career until it was time to have the required careers interview at school. I had completed my A levels, did not fancy university, but felt I should study something more vocational for one or two years. Being a big fan of the early soap *Crossroads* when I was eleven, which was centred around the Crossroads Motel in the Midlands, I had fancied myself as Miss Diane, who worked on reception in the motel, but quickly dismissed that idea when they said I would have to work shifts and miss celebrating Christmas at home. I remember walking past our local Thomas Cook branch not long after that conversation and having a light-bulb moment. I really liked the idea of booking holidays for people. Mind you, I never went into the shop to find out what exactly the job entailed, as I was too scared, but I found out I could get from Southampton to Bournemouth by train where there was a course for one year to study Travel and Tourism.
That'll do, I thought!

So where do you start learning how to be a travel agent? The first homework we had was to match a long list of resorts to dots on a map of Europe. Suddenly places like Juan le Pins, Genoa, Albufeira, Sitges and Hammamet, places I had never heard of, were on my radar. They all sounded very exotic! I learnt that each airport had a three-letter code. Naturally, we were given another long list, this time to learn hundreds of three-letter codes. These are ingrained into my psyche now, so that looking at car number plates, I read airports. I recently had Nice (NCE) as one of my number plates, but have seen Kathmandu (KTM), Chiang Mai (CNX) and many others over the years. I bet I am not alone doing this! I learnt that all the Canadian airports had codes beginning with Y. Impossible to work out which airports were which, so I just had to learn those. Toronto is YYZ, and Edmonton is YEG. There is no logic to it at all. Some are easier to work out without referring to a manual, such as DUB, Dublin, or FRA, Frankfurt and others relate to the airport name, such as CDG, for Charles de Gaulle, Paris, and LHR for London Heathrow. Others have no rhyme nor reason for the code. The first one of these I learnt at college that was different was AGP for Malaga. Of course, we had to find out if there were any that would make us snigger, to feed our smutty playground humour. We did. We found FUK for Fukuoka in Japan and COK for Cochin, India, all in the name of education!

We learnt how to write air tickets, making sure there were no mistakes, or we would have to 'void' the air ticket by drawing two diagonal lines across it. Written errors were not allowed. The surname had to be shown underlined because in many countries it is difficult to distinguish which is the family name and which is the given name. By the end of each lesson, we always seemed to have red carbon on our fingers. We had role plays planning holidays from brochures, which in those days only offered seven, ten or fourteen nights away, mainly on a beach somewhere and probably in the Mediterranean. We trawled through the Thomas Cook Rail Timetable, a complicated tome full of codes and numbers but apparently a bible for travel agents. I think I only used it a couple of times when I started work. Lessons in law and accounting have faded into the dark recesses of my memory, they were that riveting. We did have a year's introduction to Spanish, which has come in very handy over the years, ordering drinks whilst on holiday, a *'Cuba Libre sin hielo por favor'*, or a *'café con leche señor'*. We had a teacher who took lessons in travel agency practice who was Italian and the only thing I can remember her teaching us, which has stuck, is how to spell itinerary… ee-tin-er-ra-ry. I can hear her saying it now, some forty-five years later. (Go on, say it with an Italian accent!) We had sessions on selling and merchandising too, which explained why products are placed on shelves in certain positions. I found that all very enlightening. For example, we learnt that women take from the hip, and men take from the shoulder, which explains why all the 'dodgy' magazines were placed on the top shelf, although that might not be true! I was in the supermarket the other day picking up some milk, and realised I took the cartons that were at hip level without thinking, even though the same product was on shelves higher up too. I noticed too that the sell-by dates on the products were often shorter at hip level than those higher or lower down. Children's sweets were always on the lower shelves, at their eye level, to add to the stress of shopping with the little darlings. The colour of a product was important too. Generally bright primary colours such red and yellow, were generally eye-catching and would be for lower priced items, and darker colours would indicate a more discerning product. If we relate that to a travel agency the brochures we wanted to push were placed at eye level, and the less popular higher up, or lower down. The lower priced holiday brochures would stand out in bright colours, while the more discerning brochures in muted shades might be nearer the entrance to the shop to draw people in. Even the way the door opened into the shop was significant, opening so the customer naturally walked towards the counter rather than the brochures, which were normally placed on shelves against the wall.

The highlight of the year's course was our trip abroad. It sounds exciting, but to keep the costs to a minimum we travelled in December, to a one star called Hotel Sol Piños, or renamed by us immature students as Hotel Sunny Dick, in Arenal Majorca. It was 1975 and off season, so not hot and not busy. Apart from a fortnight's holiday to Benidorm when I was seventeen, and the cruise on board the school ship *Nevassa*, where I shared a dorm with other girls and a few cockroaches, I had never been much further than Bournemouth or the Isle of Wight for a holiday. So, Arenal in December was, in fact, great, plus I could use my newly acquired proficiency in basic Spanish. I was beginning to enjoy this travelling malarkey. Mr Bull (aka *El Toro*), our course leader, organised various trips across Majorca and part of our challenge was to find our way to the centre of Majorca by public transport. We had to research the bus timetable and work out the best way to travel, with enough time to explore the area and get back without getting lost, with no mobile phones of course to help us. Back in 1975, to a green teenager, this was quite scary, but it sowed a seed and gave me confidence to explore in the future. I am glad to say I did not get lost and discovered what a pretty island Majorca is. New experiences all round: I discovered people disappeared at lunch time for a rest and did not surface again until teatime. I could not imagine doing that at home. I discovered that tomatoes in Spain were enormous, and delicious. I learnt how to drink out of a *porron*, that resembled a cross between a wine bottle and a watering can, without spilling half of it down my front, and I tasted my first olive, which to this day is devil's food. Sangria, on the other hand, well, now you're talking!

When we were approaching the end of the course, it was time to think about getting an actual job. En masse, the class wrote to British Airways to see if they were recruiting, and en masse we all got a Dear John letter saying they were not recruiting at that time but would 'file us away and would be in touch'. So that was that.

After I finished my studies, in the hot summer of 1976, my best friend and I decided to have a week's holiday on the Isle of Wight, but first we had to make the booking. My friend decided as I was the 'travel agent', I should make the booking, and it would be good practice for when I got a job. We had not had a telephone in our house for long, so making a phone call to a hotel was quite a daunting task. So daunting that I got my mum to do it for me! I had been happy enough before we had a phone too go down to the local phone box, and dial 16 to hear the latest pop tunes, or dial 123 to hear the speaking clock, but that was because no one spoke back to you. I would have to gain more confidence to speak to strangers.

At that time, I wanted to move nearer to London, so wrote to a few travel agencies who were advertising jobs in the trade papers. I think I contacted six agencies and received six replies inviting me for an interview. After my break on the Isle of Wight, I travelled up 'north' for my interviews, got offered all of them, and chose the one that paid the most money! It was really that easy! I started working for Thomas Cook in Watford in July 1976 as a junior agent. The first thing my mentor said was, 'Welcome to the real world, and you can forget what you have learnt at college. This is where you will learn what it is really like working in a travel agency.' And I did learn a lot; and much of it remembered to this day.

One of the most important lessons was to be mindful of security. Early on I had taken some cash from a customer for their forthcoming trip. While they were sitting in front of me I counted the money and realised I needed some change. I had to go to the cashier at the end of the shop to get it, so made my way there, leaving the money on the counter. When I returned the money had disappeared. Sweating a bit, I looked around, on the floor, on the shelf behind me, but there was no sign of it. Oh gawd! I had only been there five minutes and already losing the company money. My mentor approached and asked if I had lost something, and with a red face I explained. She opened a drawer and there was the money. She had put it in there for safe keeping, but more importantly to teach me a valuable lesson to secure money once it had been counted. When counting bank notes, I had to make sure all the notes were placed the same way round, so if someone handed cash over there would be no chance of counting the same note twice. It was known that the less than honest customer could try to deceive you by folding notes in half. I have never forgotten these lessons, and these life skills are not something you would learn in a college classroom.

This first job was quite a steep learning curve for me, such as learning how to address the customer correctly. Early on I needed advice on something so asked my colleague, 'This woman wants to know—' and was corrected thus, 'Sandra, the customer is not a *woman*, but a *lady*.' (The *lady* would like to know…)

Further advice followed. Keep your handbag out of sight from customers, so that a stray arm could not reach over and help themselves. Surely, Watford didn't have *that* many criminals? I needed to learn how to answer the phone correctly. 'Hiya' is not the right way! I had to become accustomed to various accents from customers. An Austrian chap came in with a heavy accent asking for a ticket to Eagles. Nope, Eagles? No idea where that was. After a bit of questioning, I found out he meant Igls, a ski resort in Austria. Then we had a lady from somewhere in Asia, who wanted an air ticket. I asked her name, and she replied 'Mmmm'. Thinking she hadn't heard my question, I repeated it, and she gave the same reply. We were getting nowhere. So, I asked how to spell her surname. It was Ng, pronounced Nnnnnn! Years later, I had a call from a lady from one of our business accounts, who worked for the military. She had a strong Northern Irish accent, so when asking her name, I thought she said her name was Copper Kettle, only later realising she was saying Corporal Kettle.

I had only been at Thomas Cook for a few months and had just got used to finding my way there on the bus, when I received a letter from British Airways saying they were now recruiting and inviting me to an interview in London. I could get the tube from where I was living in Northwood and had got used to travelling to the big smoke, so thought it would be worth finding out more. At that stage, I did not really know what the job entailed, but the thought of working for a major airline was like dangling a carrot to a donkey, plus working in London meant a big jump in salary, and because I would get London Weighting, it jumped from £1845 a year to just over £3000 a year. Next year, I'd be a millionaire!

British Airways employed small groups every few months to train and eventually work in their Reservations Department at the old West London Air Terminal. I worked for British Airways for nearly twelve years and loved every minute of it. It was there that I made life-long friends, discovered my love of travel, explored the world and had the training to be the best I could be.

The next Twelve...

So far in my new career I had done every transaction manually. Those were the days when everything was completed in triplicate by filling out various forms. There were forms to complete a booking, forms to take payment, and forms to take personal customer details. Starting a new job introduced me to a whole new world of technology. We had three good months of training, learning how to make flight bookings on BABS, the British Airways Booking System, along with all the travel jargon and codes. It was my first introduction to computerisation. Computers for personal use did not exist then, and the only experience I'd had of using a keyboard was learning to type badly on an ancient typewriter that my dad had brought home from work. It had clunky keys, and everything was typed with carbon paper in between two sheets of A4. I had received weekly lessons in typing at my sixth form college, affectionately known as double bang, but apart from typing line after line of FRF space JUJ space, I didn't gain any proficiency in typing, so it was a good job my chosen career wasn't as a secretary!

Our computer training covered all scenarios and we had to learn the entries to record the information. If I had someone who needed wheelchair assistance, there were three categories to remember, depending on the severity. We had to ask whether the customer had difficulty walking any distance, could manage the aircraft steps, or needed assistance right up to the seat onboard. It was important to know the level of mobility to ensure the traveller had the right assistance.

Sometimes we had to book VIPs under false names to protect their privacy. We, however, could see who the real person was, so it was fun checking who was in first class. My favourite route to check was from London to Los Angeles because there was a good chance that there would be an actor on board flying to Hollywood. GDPR was non-existent in those days. I met a few well-known names over the years and found it interesting to see whether they were full of their own self-importance or not. They were all treated the same by me, whether they were on TV, a famous footballer, a surgeon, head of a company, royalty or Mr & Mrs Ordinary.

We learnt how to book flights for people who needed to lie flat for their journey due to medical reasons by blocking off a row of seats. These were known as stretcher cases. Some people needed to buy two seats as they were simply too large to fit into a single seat, or sometimes we had to book a seat for a cello that was too valuable to go into the aircraft hold. Then there were children who travelled alone, known as unaccompanied minors, who needed a staff member to accompany them from leaving their parents or guardians to handing over to someone at the end of the flight. This involved yet more forms to be completed, with the children being given a red-and-white striped ticket wallet to keep with them throughout their journey so that staff could identify who was travelling alone. To many children it was no big deal to travel thousands of miles, and probably quite annoying too having to be transferred from one person to another along the way, since they were seasoned travellers. But rules were rules and the system worked. The youngsters could be regularly travelling from home abroad to school in the UK, or just a one-off visiting a relative.

We also had to get to grips with the numerous codes for special diets such as vegetarian, kosher, lactose free, Asian vegetarian, baby meals and child meals. — the trend for gluten free was unheard of back then. There were codes for seat requests, including a choice of smoking or non-smoking, and also for linking bookings together, where someone was travelling one way with another person on a separate booking, but not on the return. If someone lost their baggage, there was a form for that too, the PIR, Property Irregularity Report. If one of those had been issued at the airport and was brought to us, we could compensate the passenger if the luggage was lost.

In those early days I remember how nerve-wracking it was to take my first call. Where was my mum when I needed her? We all started off in a department called Agents Telephone Sales. This department would have been the easiest introduction to working live, as we only took calls from travel agents who should know what information they needed to give us, so the transactions were quicker and easier, with fewer questions to ask. This was not always the case of course. It was much easier to quote simple air fares then. The choices were first class, economy class flexible, economy excursion or APEX (advanced purchase excursion) return fares. Return fares were always cheaper than buying two one-way fares, which is not always the case now. Since then, there have been a whole plethora of different fare types, that have been and gone, such as PEX and Super PEX fares, Eurobudget fares and VUSA (Visit USA) fares, all with various rules and regulations to abide by. Back then, there were no financial transactions since the agents took the payments directly from their customers, so we just made the reservations.

After a few months of working in Agents Telephone Sales I moved sections to take calls from the good old British public. This was more challenging because people did not always know what they wanted, so we had to ask the right questions and read everything back to make sure everything was correct. We took payment over the phone, or provisionally held the booking while they sent a cheque in. There was another department that received letters from customers asking for quotes or book flights. With promotion to this department, aptly called the Correspondence Department, I learnt how to write business letters. On one occasion I received a letter from someone asking me to quote a price to Perth, so I duly checked the cost and dashed off a reply. The customer rang to query the price, as it seemed expensive. On investigation, I discovered they were asking about fares to Perth in Scotland, not Australia. Lesson learnt, ask the right questions! (In my defence BA did not fly to Perth in Scotland!) This department was in Buckingham Palace Rd, Victoria in London and one of the highlights, every Thursday, was to watch the troops from our office window, marching down the road to the Mall for the Changing of the Guard. Listening to the marching band always lifted my spirits.

Another busy department, which I moved to for a few months, was the fares department in Agents Enquiries. Here we received calls from travel agents who wanted a more complicated itinerary involving complex fare structures. Although we were working on an automated system, we still had to refer to enormous guidebooks for mileages and routes. There were a couple of these that all the travel industry used called the ABCs. One was red and the other blue, plus another - the OAG, the Overseas Airline Guide, which had more information on overseas airlines and routes. These were our bibles. We employed many tricks to reduce the fares, which took an age to calculate and more new jargon to learn and understand. If someone wanted to travel from A to B, via somewhere along the way, we had to work out the mileage travelled between all points, then compare that mileage to the one from the start place to the end destination. If the trip was not in a straight line as the crow flies, it was likely that the extra stop would incur an additional cost, known as a Higher Intermediate Fare. (e.g.: London — Madrid — Rome, could cost more than a London — Rome.) We were able to reduce fares by adding an extra place at the beginning or end of the trip, which was not flown by the customer. A good example of this was to add Hull at the beginning and Gander, Newfoundland at the end, for someone who wanted to basically travel between London and say Montreal, because the fare from Hull to Gander was lower than that from London to Montreal. This was a legal way of reducing the fare and these were called More Distant Point fares. Amsterdam to anywhere was often a lower fare than from London. Known as cross border selling, this is now banned, but we were able to quote these itineraries back in the late seventies. When Hong Kong was under British rule, there were special air fares called Cabotage fares between London and Hong Kong but sadly they have disappeared too. We had to convert all the fares between countries that had different currencies into Fare Construction Units (FCUs) and then the total was converted into sterling. Fares were complicated structures then and completely different to the automated way things are done now. I cannot say I enjoyed my time in the fares department and was more than ready to meet the public, and of course that meant I got to wear the BA uniform!

In 1979 I got my chance and further promotion. A vacancy arose at the British Airways flagship shop in Regent Street, London. I collected my uniform, practised wearing it in my bedroom, with no idea how to tie the neck scarf, and even took it down to Southampton to show my parents and model for a photo on the front porch. I was that proud!

The Regent Street shop was busy, mainly with foreign travellers coming in to amend their tickets, so I had to learn to recalculate those complicated fares, all in less time, as we had to do this while the customer was waiting. My trick was to tell them to go off shopping for a bit and come back. Thank goodness for Oxford Street around the corner, where there was a vast choice of retail outlets to browse! To ease the constant pressure, we would play a game of Guess the Cabin. Watching people approach, we had to guess whether they wanted first class or economy. Bonus points when you got it right! I was speaking to a good friend of mine recently, whom I worked with at British Airways, and we were remembering situations that arose whilst working in the Regent Street shop. She told me that one day she was in the middle of counting £3000 in cash for a transaction when there was a bomb scare, typical of the time, in the late 1970s to early eighties. Both customers and staff had to stop what they were doing and make a hasty exit from the shop. A quick decision therefore had to be made about the cash, which clearly could not be left on the counter. While everyone trooped outside to safety, she stuffed the £3000 into her pockets, and left the building, with the money safe from the temptation of others. Decisions like these had to be made on the spot, and fortunately for the customer my friend is an honest person, but in the wrong hands, the situation could have ended very differently.

I discovered there were quite a few British Airways travel shops, mainly in and around London, but also further afield. Some were implants, with an office set up within a large company who had the need to send their staff abroad. There was also an office which solely looked after the Foreign and Commonwealth Office staff, and even one inside a London hotel, but most of the travel shops were in places where the public would go. From the Regent Street shop, we had the opportunity to work 'on relief' at other locations when staff were on leave. Working in other places, where people would come to book holidays and flights, gave us new experiences, as this type of work was different from working in Regent Street. Some people became regular customers and to me this was far more personal. I felt this was where I needed to be.

By this time, I was about to get married and move further out of London, so I needed to find a position available closer to home. Luckily for me a vacancy came up in the BA Uxbridge shop, about five miles from Heathrow Airport. I spent the next nine happy years in Uxbridge, with a fabulous team who have become lifelong friends. We have many memories and stories, which I will try to relay. There were four of us in the shop; one manager and three of us girls who worked on the counter. We sold flight tickets and British Airways branded holidays, along with a few other tour operator's holidays that used BA flights. We also sold tickets to staff, as we were able to get excellent discounted flights. This provided the means for many of us to see the world at reduced rates.

We always tried to help our customers if they needed to change their flights. In the days when we wrote air tickets, we were sometimes able to bend the rules a little, unlike today, where everything is done electronically. We had small yellow labels, called revalidation stickers that we would fill in with the new flight details, and then stick it over the flight number that was being changed on the air ticket. We had to add a reason why we were amending or revalidating the ticket, and if we weren't making a charge to amend, we'd put 'res' (reservation) error, as if *we'd* made a mistake. Every ticket had to be validated with an office stamp in the top right-hand corner of the ticket, which showed the IATA number and date of issue. We renamed the validating machine the Bonger, as you had to whack the top of it to make sure the imprint of the details showed on the ticket. Bong! If someone wanted to change their route so they were cutting out a destination, instead of reissuing the ticket, which would have taken time and probably a charge, we would clip the ticket coupons together. In doing so, the intermediate point not required did not show, but using the little yellow revalidation sticker, we could add new flight details to the ticket. None of these things can be done now. Tickets came with two or four coupons, but if the itinerary was longer than four coupons or four journeys, we had to write out more tickets and clip the last page of the first ticket to the front page of the second ticket and so on until we had finished writing on all the coupons for the entire journey. For an extra-long itinerary, it could be that we had a concertina of tickets clipped together, sometimes to the height of a person. One of the items we always carried in our handbags was a pocket-sized stapler. There is a lot to be said for automation!

There were many times when we howled with laughter and the memories still bring a smile to my face.

We had one customer come in just before we were closing who

sidled in and went straight over to the brochure racks, apparently looking for a particular brochure. I was the only one on duty, so asked him if I could help. In a weird, strangled voice, sounding as if he had been set on 33rpm, for a 45rpm record, asked if I had a 'Glooobal' (Global) brochure. I said we didn't but asked what sort of holiday he was looking for. Then he asked for the Yugotours brochure, saying he liked the pictures of the *nude* ladies in the 'Yoogotours' brochure. (There was a section on naturist holidays in there.)

'Okaaaay… well I'm sorry we don't have that one.' Then he asked if I knew what 'stacking' was. On firmer ground, I could answer that one, and said, 'Yes, it was when the planes circled above the airport before landing, waiting for their turn to land.' His reply was that he 'did stacking' too — he stacked cardboard boxes. How do you answer that?

On another occasion we had a gentleman enquiring about the 'job vacancy' we were advertising in our shop window. Trying to work out what he meant, we had a look in the window area. In all BA shop windows we had models of the aircraft artfully displayed on a stand. We had a Concorde, and close by an advert extolling the benefits of travelling supersonic, asking, *'Why not travel by Concorde to New York where you can leave London after breakfast and arrive in time to start your day's meetings?'* On Concorde you could leave Heathrow at say nine a.m. and arrive in New York by about seven a.m. New York time. I am still trying to work out how he translated that into a job opportunity.

There was one extremely hot summer's day when it was dead quiet, doors open, with just me and one other colleague, Rosemary, on duty; we longed to be outside. Time ticked by and we were getting bored with little to do. I had the bright idea of popping out and getting a couple of ice creams. It was so hot, and no one was around. It was completely against the rules to eat whilst sitting at the counter, but it was so quiet we thought it would be safe to risk it. So off I trotted, bought the ice creams and sat down back in my seat, with Rosemary next to me, ready to enjoy the sweet creamy treats. Sod's law, as soon as I had taken the first lick, in came a customer, who went to Rosemary's desk. No problem, she quickly passed her ice cream under the counter to me and started to help them. I was left holding both ice creams, which were hidden from sight. That would have been fine, except another customer appeared, and the only person available to talk to was me! I managed to transfer the ice creams into one hand discreetly under the counter, so I had one spare hand free to use the computer. By this time, the melting ice creams were beginning to run down my hand and then it got worse, as I needed to refer to the ABC Guide. I've no idea what the customer thought as I tried to flick through the hefty tome with one hand, trying to stop the pages turning with my elbow, and all the while I could feel ice cream running down my spare arm. Thankfully, Rosemary's customer left, so I could pass the forbidden treats back to her, but for a moment I was a sticky mess! That was the last time we tried that!

I was usually the first to arrive in the morning and had time for a coffee before opening the shop. One morning I arrived to find the front door unlocked. The front of the shop seemed to be exactly as it should, but I was worried that someone had broken in. We had a safe with our ticket stock and the day's takings out in the back office. I gingerly made my way to the office. The safe was intact, and the TV which we used for training sessions was still there. It appeared that nothing had been taken but I called the police as a precaution. Checking again, I noticed our knitted multicoloured tea cosy had gone. I came to the conclusion that the culprit must have been a Rastafarian, looking for a new hat.

One of my most embarrassing moments happened just outside the shop. I had been over to Heathrow Airport for some work training and had travelled back by bus. The bus stop was right outside the shop front. Indeed, many people used to pop in pretending they were looking for a holiday or picking up brochures just to keep warm instead of waiting outside in the bus queue until their bus came along. That day, it was chilly, so I had the full uniform on, including my heavy navy trench coat. I stuck out like a sore thumb on the bus. When it was time to get off the bus, I took a step down to the pavement, but to my horror my shoe heel on my other foot got caught in the hem of the coat. The momentum of getting off had already begun, and with one foot heading down towards the pavement, and the other still tangled in my coat, there was nowhere to go but down! I ended up flat on my face right outside the shop. Thankfully, it was only my pride that was hurt. I think I pre-empted the pub fall in *Only Fools and Horses*. Seeing that was somehow familiar!

As I said, lots of people came into the shop for reasons other than to enquire about holidays. One day the door swung open, and a couple of people dragged a man in who had collapsed on the pavement outside. He was unconscious. They laid him on the floor in front of the brochures, and then promptly left, but not before leaving the man's broken false teeth on the counter. I suppose they thought we would be fully trained like air stewardesses to administer first aid, since we looked the part, but, in truth, we didn't have a clue. One of us called an ambulance, and another grabbed a rather grubby tea towel that we had in the back office to try to wipe the blood running from a wound. (That probably infected him with more germs.) The man gradually came to and became conscious enough to realise he was without his teeth. We had to placate him as he tried to get up and put the broken teeth back in his mouth. Then we did what all British do in a difficult situation, we put the kettle on. Eventually the ambulance arrived and took him away, and we never heard whether he lived or died. All in a day's work!

To amuse only ourselves, but not customers, we sometimes said we were going down into the basement to get some brochures. The brochure store was accessed from the back office and the shop floor was made of concrete, but we entertained ourselves by doing that pretend comedic thing of walking 'downstairs' behind the counter, bending lower and lower, and then coming back up again. Little things…

It wasn't all fun and games though. We took our jobs very seriously, and on occasion had to take extra care of our customers. I had one regular gentleman who I knew suffered from epilepsy but had never witnessed it until one day when he came in to book a holiday. We had nearly completed the transaction, when midway through writing his cheque for the trip, he suddenly stopped writing, hand shaking with half a word written, which tailed off to nothing. I could see he was struggling. He seemed to be in another world, but really trying to control himself. I wasn't sure if he was aware of what was happening and didn't really know what to do, so busied myself for a few moments.

He stayed like that for quite a few minutes then suddenly without a word he got up and walked out of the shop. I was left with a half-written cheque, and a holiday booked and committed to. He returned the next day and apologised (no need) and we finished the transaction.

On another occasion an elderly lady came in to see us and listening to her, she seemed very educated. We found out she could speak Swahili, and said she wanted to travel first class to Swaziland, where she grew up. When we took her address, we discovered she had come from one of the local care homes. She pulled hundreds of pounds in cash from her handbag to pay, but something was amiss, so we stalled her from completing the transaction. We called the care home to check and found out she had wandered out and wasn't mentally fit to travel. We waited until someone from the home came and collected her and put all her money in an envelope and returned it to her. It was such a shame to see someone so obviously intelligent, but no longer well enough to travel.

Another regular was a single lady, of a timid demeanour, with a bad pasty complexion and lank greasy hair, who always went to the same hotel every year for a fortnight. Never deviating, it had to be the same hotel in Malta. We all thought it was because the five-star hotel was in a great position, and would have great customer service, but we discovered she fancied one of the waiters at the hotel. Simon, a colleague working on relief, made a dry comment that she probably needed a good servicing. Rude!

It was the team that really made the BA Uxbridge shop such a great place to work. Apart from us four, there were other colleagues who regularly came 'on relief' to cover holidays. There was glamorous Pat, perfectly made up, and a real sweetheart. Then there was Simon, who made us laugh all day; Denise, who had some funny stories to tell and was a great mimic, and Anne, one of the loveliest people to work with. My two colleagues on the counter, Rosemary and Sue, made it a real pleasure to go to work. We worked as a strong team, helping each other, and completely on the same wavelength. Later a new girl arrived to take Sue's place, who was leaving to have a baby. I took to Mandy straightaway because she reminded me of myself. In fact, I called her my anagram, because her birth date is an anagram of mine. We all moved on eventually but stayed in the travel industry and have remained friends to this day. We have seen each other marry, have families, and becoming grandparents. Our manager, Janet, ran a tight ship, but we all thought she was a bit eccentric. She would talk to herself in her office, which at the time we thought odd, but now that I am in my senior years, I find myself doing the same thing. For me, repeating information I need to retain out loud is a way of committing it to my memory.

Despite living the nearest, Janet was always the last into the office in the morning. Seemingly abrupt, Janet didn't stand any nonsense and was a bit scary when you first met her. I have learnt over the years that respect has to be earned, but as we all did a good job, I think she really trusted us to do the job properly. Although, maybe not quite trustful enough to leave an open bottle of wine in the office fridge, without marking the level of wine left. Did she think we would be drinking on the job? Us? *Never!* Always thrifty, if we went out together for our Xmas meal, she checked each item on the bill with a tick, instead of just splitting it between us.

I remember a chap coming into the office and asking for the name of the manager.

'It's Janet,' we said, 'but she's at lunch.' He stood there and yelled *'Janet!'*

Janet was in the kitchen preparing her sardines on toast (yes, it stank!) She came dashing out, in her smart BA uniform, but with a pinny on, wielding a knife; truly a comical sight.

She said abruptly, *'Yes?!'* (Basil Fawlty style.) I cannot remember what he wanted, but the sight of her in her uniform in her pinny, dagger in hand, is an image I cannot forget. She used to tell us about ways that she would save money. One of them was reusing old tights. If one leg had a ladder, she would cut that leg off, and wear it with another one-legged tight. Genius! Not sure how comfortable that would have been, but I suppose they would have been the first crotchless tights. When I first met Janet, I thought she was ancient (she was only about forty); she was still single, very independent and opinionated with a loud voice and laugh; well, more of a whoop really. Would she stay single forever? This was a time when people married reasonably young, so not being married in your forties seemed strange to me. A few years later a man started to come into the shop regularly only wanting to speak to her. They ended up getting married. She was still late for work though, and only lived two minutes away, but that was Janet. Sadly, she passed away a few years later; too young really. She gave us a lot to gossip about each day, but I now have very fond memories of her. We all went to her funeral and listened to stories from other friends who had known her from different areas of her life. We realised she was no different with her other friends. Her stepson told us in her eulogy, that when he was going through her clothes, working out what needed to be thrown out and what needed to go to charity, he came across draws full of one-legged tights. She was unique.

Janet had replaced an earlier manager, who shall remain nameless, whom we had to report for fiddling expenses and falsely claiming overtime. We were worried that if someone came to audit the shop, the finger would be pointed at us, so we girls debated what we should do. One of the things we noted was there were claimed expenses for visiting a business account some miles away and taking them out for lunch, but we knew the manager was off work that day, so could not have been wining and dining a client. We checked with the account's company secretary who confirmed the manager had not visited in months. We had a few other grievances, so decided to call our area manager, thinking that nothing would really be done. However, the area manager said he would be down after work that evening, so we should lock up the shop and stay behind.

We got to the end of the day and cleared away as we normally did. While the other two colleagues tidied up out the front, I took the ticket stock and other things back to the safe in the manager's office. The manager knew we were all staying behind and that the area manager was coming but had no idea why. So, when asked if I had any idea why there was a meeting, I felt uncomfortable and wished the ground would swallow me up. I knew we had to get this resolved. When the area manager arrived, we all went out to the back office, and had our grievances aired, along with raising the issue of the false claim for expenses and overtime. Our manager looked dumbstruck. It was all so embarrassing. The upshot was that our manager was demoted and moved to another shop to do the same job as us, then sometime later leaving of their own accord. There is always an amusing end to a story though. Whilst we were having the meeting, our manager's other half came to pick them up. I heard the locked front door rattling, so went out the front to let them in.

'What's going on?' they asked.

I said airily, 'Oh there's a meeting with the area manager.'

The reply was, 'Well, I hope BA are going to pay overtime!'

Irony at its best, I think!

Working in the same place for a few years we got to know many people who came in, including those who loved to bring us gifts. Whilst it was lovely receiving perfume and gift vouchers, we also had some well-intentioned but questionable offerings. One regular visitor was a German lady, who liked to give us some of her homemade St Nicholas biscuits every December. We could never bring ourselves to eat them because we often found stray hairs imbedded in the mixture. Likewise, receiving warm paper bags of homemade samosas with the grease seeping through were graciously accepted, but always ended up in the bin.

There were many airlines that had amusing acronyms, some of which I will list for your amusement:

BOAC — Better On A Camel

BA — Bloody Awful

TWA — Try Walking Across

SABENA — Such A Bloody Experience Never Again

Pakistan International Airlines — Please Inform Allah or Perhaps I'll Arrive

QANTAS — Quite A Nice Take-off, Any Survivors, or Quite A Nice Trip, Awfully Slow

ALITALIA — Always Late In Take-off And Late In Arriving

LIAT — Leaves Island Any Time

DELTA — Doesn't Ever Leave The Airport

EL AL — Every Landing Always Late

LUFTHANSA — Let Us Fondle The Hostess And Not Say Anything (ooh Matron!)

BEA — Back Every Afternoon

SAS — Safe And Sexy
IBERIA — I Bet Every Reject Is Aircrew
LOT — Left On Tarmac
TAROM — Try Another Route Or Method
LAN — Leaves About Now
Air France was known as Air Chance

Then there were airlines that were big in the day, but are no longer with us, such as Pan Am, TWA, Braniff, Eastern, British Caledonian, National, Dan Air, Wardair and more recently, British Midland, Monarch and Flybe. Times were changing. We started checking holiday availability on a small box that whirred and emitted the early computer noises we all remember. The system was called Prestel. I remember waiting for the buffering to stop, the cursor flashing interminably. Gradually, the required information appeared on the screen line by line. I could feel myself going grey waiting for the transaction to complete.

Air fares too were becoming more competitive. A new type of air fare was introduced with the arrival of Freddie Laker, revolutionising the airline industry. He was the first entrepreneur to start an airline that offered standby fares. Suddenly in 1981 it was possible to fly to New York at the last minute for next to nothing. There were no airport taxes in those days, so if you were happy to risk the flight being full, it was a cheap way to travel. British Airways were forced to compete, and then in 1984, along came another rival, Richard Branson, and his new airline Virgin Atlantic. From then on, air fares became more complicated, with many new fares being introduced at various levels to suit requirements. Laker Airways did not survive and went bankrupt in 1982, but Virgin grew and became BA's main rival; no bad thing, as competition kept prices down. Travel was becoming more accessible and more affordable.

British Airways gave me many training opportunities and throughout my time there I attended courses on fare construction, telephone sales and face to face selling techniques. There was also training on how to apply make-up properly, (yes, that was a course!), how to wear our uniforms correctly, and yes, I did learn how that neck scarf was worn! We had courses on psychology, which I found particularly interesting, so that we could recognise the characteristics that make up a personality, and therefore approach the way we sold things in different ways. For example, someone who hated queuing at airports, maybe ran a business, needed to visit an overseas office and was used to delegating would probably be more interested in the cost, the bottom line. It was best to concentrate on the benefits to them, which could mean booking the best flight to get to a meeting, maximising their time for conducting their business. They may need to change flights as business plans change and be able to access an airport lounge so they could work quietly before the flight. Their hotel's location might be important, near a rail station perhaps, or close to an office. These requirements would be based on fact, no messing around with the frilly bits, such as an inviting pool and spa at the hotel or watching a beautiful sunset from the hotel balcony. That sort of thing would be of interest to someone who has an image of themselves sitting by a pool, drink in hand, maybe a romantic dinner; so, we paint emotional pictures, using emotive words. By spending a bit of time with people, we soon get a feel for the type of person they are, and so adapt our behaviour, how we speak and what we say to them. Some people love to chat on the phone, telling us their life story, whilst others just give us the bare minimum of information, and the whole transaction can be over in a few minutes. For me, that's what makes the job so interesting. How many times have you purchased something because you trust and like the person you are dealing with? People buy people first.

After a few years at the Uxbridge shop, I had enough experience to join a small group of colleagues to write and run a residential course, which we entitled New Image, designed to refresh and update the job we were already doing. Basically, this covered everything I had learnt in the customer service environment: How to build customer trust, role play, how to handle difficult customers and address problems, never to Assume (because it makes an *ass* out of *u* and *me*) and ask leading questions to get the right information. We ran these courses from a beautiful old country house in Aldermaston, Hampshire over a four-day period each week. All my BA colleagues from the travel shops had to attend, which as you can imagine presented some issues, as many had been working in their shop for many years and felt they did not need to go on a course to tell them how to do their job. By the end of each week, I think we turned the negatives into positives and at the very least refreshed people's memories on how to be the best they could be. One of the highlights for me though was being collected from home in a limo every Sunday afternoon, with a peak-capped driver, and driven to Aldermaston and back. I felt like royalty!

A major change within British Airways happened around this time. We were advised they were going to close some of the BA shops, and that the few that were staying open were going to be sold to become part of a new Thomas Cook brand called Four Corners. It would have meant a change in contract. Our shop was closing, so we all had to decide what we wanted to do. All this coincided with me about to go on maternity leave, so I decided to freeze my pension and take severance. In August 1988 I said goodbye to British Airways. Sad times, but it marked the end of an era and a new chapter in my life.

New Horizons

I had a brief break from working, but after about eighteen months I had itchy feet and felt ready to juggle family responsibilities and a job. I called in to a tiny travel agency about four miles from my home and asked if they had any vacancies. They nearly bit my arm off offering me a job. This agency was only in its infancy and did not have an ABTA licence. It was owned by local businessman and run by just one person, a young lady who had no travel experience. I can see now that employing someone with my previous experience would have been extremely attractive to them. With no licences to issue air tickets, they relied on another agency to issue them, but in order to stand on its own two feet, the agency needed an ABTA licence, so they would be able to sell package holidays. My expertise was enough to get that licence, but they would have needed myself and another agent trained in fares and ticketing to get the IATA licence to issue air tickets. By this time, I had another daughter so could only work part time. My days were spent selling a broad selection of holidays for locals in the area, and gradually the fledgling company became profitable. Eventually, the owner sold the agency to another businessman, who soon added a few more branches to his portfolio. He has become successful in and around the Chilterns, selling bespoke holidays. One of the people who came into the shop was a charismatic lady, called Helen, who wangled a job working on Saturdays with me. We hit it off, having the same sense of humour. It was never that busy, and so we often spent the morning nattering and getting Danish pastries from the bakery next door (sounds familiar?), which made Saturdays fly by. I stayed for five years, but eventually moved to another local agency, mainly because they offered more money, but also because the new company had a small ski-tour operation.

This added another string to my bow because, in addition to crafting tailored holidays, through other tour operators, selling packages and all other aspects of travel, I learnt how a tour operator works. To become a tour operator, an ATOL licence to sell is required. (Funnily enough, that stands for Air Travel Organiser's Licence.) Our small ski operation sold trips to ski resorts in Europe. We used special air fares, got direct contract rates with the accommodation, had a company who sorted the transfers and ski equipment, and then added our mark up. We sold these trips to other travel agents, paying them a commission, as well as selling directly to the public. This was another learning curve for me as I had no experience in skiing, knew nothing about ski resorts or what equipment was needed to ski. So, I then had more places to learn about in Italy, Austria, Switzerland and France.

At that time, my memory was excellent, and I could recall the telephone numbers and addresses of my clients without having to refer to any data. When I left the first agency, I wrote to a few of the customers who I had personally looked after for the past five years to tell them where I was moving to, only five miles away saying it would be lovely to continue helping them. Imagine my horror, a short while later, when I got a letter from the owner's solicitor accusing me of stealing data from their system. Unbelievable as there wasn't an automated system set up, and all the information was in my head. I later found out that one of the couples who I had written to had popped into the old shop and innocently mentioned they had heard I had left. The manager of the shop, whom I hadn't really gelled with, was worried they were going to lose business, and asked to see the letter I had written. Consequently, the solicitor's letter asked me to return the data I had 'stolen', otherwise further steps would be taken. I took the letter to my new boss and explained there was nothing I could return because I had not stolen anything. We drew up a letter replying that we would not sell anything to anyone who were customers of the other shop for a year. They were happy with this. We only turned one couple away, ironically the couple who copped me. I still maintain that people buy from people, and a company is only as good as the staff that work there. But I now know that moving from one company to another can be difficult if the customer wants to move with you.

During this period too, technology was evolving, and for the first time I heard a new word: email. Not something we had in the office, and I certainly didn't have an email address, but I did understand it was a new way of communicating. This was the beginning of the digital world that would eventually change the way we would work. New terminology became familiar. Around this time, I heard some new terms such as the worldwide web, web addresses, uploading and downloading information on a computer. Not that many people had personal computers at that time, as they were expensive, and cost more than they do nowadays. Mobile phones were not that popular either. I think they were mainly purchased by people working in London and were the size of a house brick. I heard people speaking loudly on their mobiles on the London tube, hearing their life story, and the 'importance' of their public conversation. 'Oh, hi Giles. Yah blah blah blah.'

Another five years had passed since returning to work after the birth of my children, but all this time I felt guilty. Guilty I was not there all the time for my two young daughters when I could not always go to school events like Sports Day and guilty if I had to let my colleagues down if the children were ill. It was like juggling balls, trying to please everyone. I was beginning to tire of the parochial gossip too which was rife in a village environment. We would see someone walking past the shop window and get comments from a colleague about an affair that person was having for example. I was not interested in stuff like that and did not know any of them anyway. I regularly read the travel trade papers that were delivered each week, and in the back of them there were always adverts from a company about a new concept in travel. The company was looking for people with travel industry experience who could run their own business from home. Computer, printer and licences to operate would be provided by the company but we would have to find our own clients. Earning potential if you were good was massive. In a normal agency, the staff would be paid a salary and the commissions paid by the airlines and tour operators were paid to the shop. It did not matter whether you booked a ferry or a massive tailor-made trip round the world, the salary would be the same, only the agency's profits would differ. This new working-from-home concept meant being self-employed and anything sold would have the commission split between the agent and the head office. The higher the value trip you booked, the more money you could potentially earn. The monthly commission paid to the head office would be invested to employ staff there, who would in turn negotiate better commissions for those at the sharp end, process all the administration and pay for the licences to operate. I really liked the sound of this, as I could see my guilty days could be at an end, as I could work around my family and commitments, and perhaps have a higher earning potential as a bonus.

I contacted the number in the advert and was invited to meet with them, so I travelled up to Atherton, Greater Manchester in the summer of 1999. The company was called Travel Counsellors. My first impression on entering their offices was that they were in a disorganised mess. There seemed to be lots of boxes all over the place, all a bit messy, but they were a friendly group of people, and as I would be working from home, the mess was not a concern, and as I found out later, they were already outgrowing the office. They explained more about how the concept worked. The idea was that I would find my own customers and be their point of contact for anything they booked from the start to their return, making it a very personal experience. I would get to know my customers, speak with them regularly, with updates, or just keep in touch to see how things were. I met with the owner, David Speakman, who had come up with the idea. He had successfully run an agency in Atherton with a few staff and thought the future lay in remote working and could see a decline in travel agencies on the high street. I remember saying to him at my interview that it would be good if somehow in the future we could have virtual brochures that we could look at online rather than having piles of brochures like they had on the high street. Storing all the brochures whilst working from home could be difficult. David thought this may happen in the future.

I took my computer and printer and a lot of notes away with me and became the 50th person to join this new venture. I think at that stage too there were only about six people working at the head office in Atherton, including the girls who worked with David in his shop. For me I had yet another steep learning curve. How do you start a business with no clients? You have no shop, so no passing footfall or visual presence for potential clients. I gave lots of business cards to friends and family, contacted people I had got to know over the years to tell them about my new venture. I was working on the maxim I had learnt earlier that people buy people first, and that I could be trusted to make new bookings and really look after my new customers. All the training and experience I had had over the past twenty-three years would stand me in good stead.

At first business was slow, as expected, but gradually I started making bookings for the company my husband worked for, involving travel to Europe and beyond, together with a few bookings from people I had looked after in my previous jobs. Then someone I knew at the school gate told me her husband ran a company and was looking for an agent to look after their travel arrangements. That business grew and with it their travel requirements. Their business was my bread and butter as I only got paid when people travelled, and business travellers usually book last minute. I am still looking after their business over twenty years later. I asked every person I booked to pass my name onto any friends, colleagues and relatives, and gradually my contacts grew. I enjoyed people saying they would like to 'try me', to see if I was any good. Some of these are still loyal clients and have become friends. I have watched them marry, have children, and now book those children who have grown up with families of their own. Many of them I have never met because networking means you will be getting enquiries countrywide.

My business gradually grew organically, just by referrals from other people, or by talking to people. My cousin started a small company from his kitchen, making organic baby meals for his children. As the company grew, they moved to proper offices and needed someone to organise their trips abroad, so I was asked to step up to the plate. That company is called Ella's Kitchen and is now one of the biggest baby food manufacturers in the country. Repeat business became evident after about two years, and from then on, my business grew and grew. I was beginning to find a niche in the type of holidays I booked. Whilst I could book anything from a ferry to a fortnight on a beach, I became very adept at tailor-making personalised trips to far-flung places, mainly because I enjoyed that type of holiday myself. I combined that with organising trips for business travellers as well, which gave me a broad spread of incoming business and utilised all the skills I had built on previously.

When I started working from home, I had my office set up in my dining room, with a small desk in the corner next to the dining room table. We have an open plan layout, so that room leads into the lounge. When the girls came in from school, they wanted to watch TV, but that meant I was continually asking them to turn down the volume if my phone rang. As I got busier, it was clear that we had to do something to make my workspace more private. I often had people calling in to discuss their trips, and I felt this was encroaching on the family's privacy. We decided to convert our garage into an office space, as it had not been used for its purpose for years. This meant I would go 'out' to work every day, basically out of the kitchen door, walk under the carport in my slippers to the new office, separate to the house. It could be locked at night, and I could have private conversations about travel with my customers. We had room for two comfortable chairs and a couple of desks, in case I decided to employ someone to do my admin. It has worked a treat. For a short period, I had an assistant to keep the database updated, send out information and tickets for my clients, and generally let me get on with the job of selling.

Head office grew too, and soon they moved to larger offices in Bolton with various new departments; a department for IT, for Marketing, for Operations, Sales, Corporate, Administration and Accounting. All the commission being earned paid for all of this, and eventually outside investors helped increase the size of the company. Gradually International Offices were opened operating in the same way, so there were now Travel Counsellors working from home in Ireland, The Netherlands, South Africa, Australia and the UAE.

As a company we went from no one in the industry having heard of us and having to spell 'Travel Counsellors' phonetically to becoming one of the most highly respected companies in the business. We have won numerous awards for Customer Service, Enterprise and Innovation including the Queens Award on three occasions. On a personal level, I have become one of the top selling Travel Counsellors in the company. Now in its 27th year, Travel Counsellors has over 1200 people working (as I do) from their home office, and head office has recently moved again to even larger offices, reminiscent of the BBC's offices, with a shiny glass exterior, open plan hot desking and a few hundred staff to look after us all. I feel immensely proud to have contributed to the company's success.

David Speakman hit on a winning formula when he started a company where like-minded travel people came together. If you were good at your job, success was inevitable, and the rewards were far reaching. Not only financial rewards, but the opportunities to travel were enormous. The more successful the company became, the more invitations to visit foreign resorts were offered. One might think working from home would be isolating, given that you are working alone, but this proved to be inaccurate. To me working alone meant I would get no distractions and would get far more done in a day, yet technology allowed instant communication with head office and other colleagues, so there was always someone to chat to, brainstorm, ask questions, and I never felt alone. The most innovative way head office communicates with us all is through TCTV. They have a purpose-built TV studio within the head office building, where regular broadcasts are made to us while we tune in on our laptops. It is the best way of giving us company updates and help us all uniformly follow procedures for all travel related information.

The whole company meets for conferences a few times a year, giving us updates of new innovations being introduced to make our working life easier. The highlight of these has always been the annual conference, a three-day extravaganza, where we have been inspired by various guest speakers, who are high achievers in their own field, such as Sir Chris Hoy, Nicola Adams, Joanna Lumley and Bear Grylls to name a few. In addition to this we are treated to a fabulous weekend of celebrations, and a chance to meet up with friends within the company, enjoy a sparkling Gala Dinner, where the year's outstanding achievers within the company are acknowledged and rewarded. The top sellers have won cars; suppliers offer fabulous travel prizes and we have been entertained by top acts, such as Gary Barlow. Peter Kay, Michael McIntyre, Ronan Keating and many others. My highlight was celebrating my 20th year as a Travel Counsellor and being wined and dined on the top table at the Gala Dinner, and then meeting Gary Barlow personally for a photo before he went on stage. As I was already a fan, I count myself lucky that it was him performing that year. The top selling Travel Counsellors, known as Gold Travel Counsellors, are treated twice a year to a weekend or few days away with partners. I am one of the fortunate few to be a Gold Travel Counsellor and have been lucky enough to attend quite a few of these over the past twelve years.

In winter there is always a 'Gold Dinner' organised somewhere high end in the UK as a thank you to those achieving 'Gold' status. We have travelled on the Northern Belle, stayed at Gleneagles, dined at the Dorchester Hotel, had a private tour of Harry Potter World at Leavesden where we dined in the Great Hall and have also enjoyed a private tour and dinner at Madame Tussauds, to name a few. The highlight for us though is the annual trip abroad. Normally a few days away, we have partied on a Danube River Cruise, (unbelievably, they ran out of alcohol and had to restock! Oops!) We have flown out to Mauritius, staying in five-star luxury, visited some of the Middle Eastern resort hotels, in Dubai, Abu Dhabi, and Muscat. We have cruised the Mediterranean, enjoyed the delights of Las Vegas and Orlando, and been treated to luxury trips to Barbados and Jamaica. All the hard work and hours spent building up my business has really paid off. All those thoughts of having an easier work/life balance have not worked out that way. I have worked far more hours that I thought I would, thinking I would be spending more time relaxing with my family. Building a successful business is not a nine-to-five job. I have always made sure I have been there for my clients, but without the understanding of my husband and family that would not have been possible.

Working long hours has had many benefits though. Financial rewards have enabled us to give our daughters a good education. We have travelled the world, and learnt so much about different cultures, history, architecture, but have also observed poverty and wealth at first hand. I feel strongly that education comes from all around and not just in the classroom. It broadens horizons and instils empathy and understanding. Seeing the real thing instead of reading about it in a book can build memories.

Sitting in my office alone over the past twenty plus years has not presented as many anecdotes worth recounting as in my years in the shops. My sense of humour has not diminished, and I still find it in many things. Not many people come to my office as most of my clients do not live locally. There are a few though. I have had builders visiting to book holidays wanting to pay in cash. It always amused me to see them delving into various pockets and pulling out wads of cash, £500 here and another £1000 there, reminding me of a magician pulling rabbits from a hat. On another occasion, I had a call from a local pig farmer who wanted help booking something that I was unable to book on the Travel Counsellors' system. I said I would go over to his farm and give him a hand with his booking as he was not sure of what he was doing. It wasn't long before I sorted his request, and he asked me if he owed me anything for my time. Not sure how to respond, I was a bit hesitant in my reply. To my surprise he suggested half a pig as payment, butchered into small cuts for my freezer. Now, I do like pork, but not so much that I would be eating it for the next six months! Besides, I was supposed to split anything I earned between myself and my head office. I'm not sure they would have appreciated a few pork chops in the post! I declined his offer, and gratefully received £100 for my time.

Early one morning, I had a chap knocking on my front door to book a trip. It was too early to open the office, and I had, in fact, only just got out of the shower. Dressing gown, slippers and hair wrapped in a towel; it was a far cry from my days of wearing my smart BA uniform. Being the conscientious soul that I am, I swallowed my pride and inhibitions and got stuck into making his booking. I wonder how many other travel agents work in a state of undress. I made a nice booking though! Another couple of regulars, arriving unannounced were two elderly gents who liked cruise holidays. They were both in their late eighties and enjoyed some fabulous banter together. I always said I would love to have been a fly on the wall in their cabin. They travelled all over the place, much to the concern of their families. I really made sure they were looked after and made everything run as smoothly and as easily as possible for them.

Fortunately, there have not been many complaints from customers but there was one occasion when I was away on holiday with the family. One of my colleagues was looking after my business and she called me apologetically, whilst I was away, to say she had taken a call from one of my clients, a surgeon, who had arrived in Mauritius for his holiday. He was aggressive and rude. He had chosen the five-star resort and had been there before with a previous girlfriend. As one would expect from a five-star hotel, the staff greeted him and his partner by name, and said it was lovely to welcome them both again. That all sounded complimentary except this girlfriend was a new model… awkward! His main complaint was that it was raining, and the temperature was too low. My colleague was very sympathetic and professional and asked him what he wanted us to do. This was a time when large swathes of the UK were underwater because of some extreme storms in the height of our summer. Climate change had clearly affected any guarantees of weather, and even our powers of persuasion could not arrange for the weather to change.

He wanted me to pay for them to fly back home immediately in business class. Checking the weather forecast for their remaining ten days, the weather was forecast to be much better. Out of the twelve days they were away, he had in total two days of inclement weather. My colleague told him we would not pay for them to fly back in business class but if he really wanted to fly home, we could rebook his flights at the cost to amend. Unsurprisingly, he decided to stay put. The weather did improve, and the remaining days were hot and sunny. I did feel concerned that he had missed a couple of days in the sun, so I ordered a couple of bottles of wine and some chocolates to be delivered in time for his arrival home. His response to my gesture was a rather curt email saying if I thought some wine and chocolates solved everything, I was very much mistaken. He never took the complaint any further, so it could not have been that bad, but it left a bad taste. I heard nothing more from him but did hear a few years later that he had been struck off as a surgeon for some misdemeanour, and not long after had died.

I relayed the story to the colleague he had spoken to, whose response was, 'I bet he's in a hot place now!' Is that karma?

Of the early memories I have when I started working as a Travel Counsellor, I remember my mum calling me up for chats, thinking I had all the time in the world. Working from home was not the norm in 1999, and many people thought the job was a little something I did in my spare time, not realising I was doing the same work as 'going out to work'. Much more actually, because now I was self-employed, and running my own business. I think people imagined I would be out at coffee mornings with friends, taking time off as and when I wanted to, and just played at my new job. In fact, I worked over forty hours a week, starting at nine a.m. and often working well into the evening, sometimes weekends too. It might be that I could only speak to a client after they got back from their work, or if I was checking something for someone in the States, I would need to speak to them on USA time. As I became more established, I needed to set some boundaries, to try and get the work/life balance back on track. Overall, most of my clients did not bother me at weekends or in the evenings, although many a time I have answered emails whilst watching TV in an evening. The customer service training was so ingrained, it was addictive.

In the past thirty-odd years there have been a few natural and man-made disasters that have affected travel. First there were a couple of Gulf wars, where flights were rerouted to avoid Middle East air space, followed by the 9/11 World Trade Centre terrorist attacks. I can clearly remember watching this unfold from my desk in the dining room, not grasping the enormity of it all. This transformed the way we travel. I think we will all remember what we were doing the day the world changed. From a travel perspective, gone were the days of going up to the flight deck for a look around on board a plane. Luggage had more thorough security checks. This was the start of limiting the carriage of liquids to 100ml in hand luggage, which had to be carried in a clear plastic bag. Gradually more and more security measures have been introduced.

The next upset was the eruption of the unpronounceable volcano in Iceland, Eyjafjallajökull, emitting tons of volcanic ash high into the atmosphere, grounding all airlines across western and northern Europe. People were stranded for days on end. I spent hours rebooking clients and rebooking again trying to get them on flights which were subsequently cancelled. I heard stories of colleagues driving over to places in Europe to pick up stranded people. Ferries and trains were chock full. It seemed never ending, but eventually planes began to fly again and life got back to normal. Hurricanes stranded people holidaying in the Caribbean. One family I booked had got to the end of their two-week, all-inclusive holiday, in a five-star resort in Grenada, when a hurricane grounded all the flights. They were able to stay in the same resort until flights resumed and ended up having another week or so at no expense. Every cloud!

Nothing even came close to the situation that started in early 2020. In my experience, after forty-five years of being in the industry, the Covid-19 virus has without doubt been the most devastating, putting even erupting volcanoes and terrorism into the shade. Covid-19 decimated businesses worldwide. It was as if a light had been switched off. I had just had my most successful year ever and in February 2020 we started hearing about a mysterious deadly airborne virus in China that seemed to be spreading. Suddenly, it was all systems go to get people back to the UK before borders closed. I contacted people on holiday in places such as India, Australia and New Zealand. who were unaware of the growing pandemic. I had held flights for them and explained the urgency to get them home. I even received a few calls from people who had made their own arrangements and were seeking assistance and had reached out to ask if I could help.

Having got everyone home, I spent the next eighteen months refunding or rebooking imminent bookings. We all thought it would be over by Christmas, but bookings made for early 2021 and beyond had to be rebooked again, and again. The way our commissions worked is that we got paid when the customer travelled. This meant that I had to return some paid commissions so that we could refund those affected customers. Given the uncertainty of travel, those new bookings had to be made so that they were as flexible as possible and could be cancelled if travel became impossible.

As this was a situation no one had ever been in before, there were many new directives and things to check before we could start booking anything. A simple transaction that before would have taken maybe thirty minutes, had tripled because there were so many checks to make before booking anything imminent, such as checking which governments allow entry to their country. Were there any tests and forms that need to be completed? Did travellers need to quarantine on arrival? Did they have insurance which covered the virus? Did they need to be fully vaccinated in order to be allowed entry into a country?

Were they travelling via a transit point, and was that permitted, and did they need a test do to this? What type of test could they take? There was a whole new vocabulary to learn, such as PCR and antigen testing, lamp tests, Passenger Locator Forms, QR codes, Fit to Fly forms, traffic light systems; none of which had been heard of before 2020. Were there any children in the party, and what were the rules for those? Then having to check the current advice to return to the UK, or their country of origin, which kept changing regularly. So, it was not a question of reading the Government advice once but keeping track of the updates for all the places the customer would be travelling to. I had to keep the office open to administer the changes, even though by this time I was working for no income.

Gradually towards the end of 2021, there were glimmers that the travel industry was recovering, but still some nervousness about taking a flight to another country. I think the virus is something that we will all have to learn to live with. But again, just as with the 2011 terrorist attacks, the way we travel has changed.

Cooks Perks

One of the major benefits of working in the travel industry are the numerous opportunities to travel and experience the hospitality of foreign resorts and airlines. The biggest perk was the opportunity to travel on standby, for next to nothing, on all the British Airways' routes, and the longer we worked for the company the better the benefits. After ten years we were able to travel on a confirmed basis in business class, all subject to availability of course. This extended to our immediate family too. Consequently, I had to become very adept at being flexible with my travel arrangements as there was always the constant chance of being offloaded if the flights became full. Fortunately, working in sales and reservations I had access to flight availability, so could plan my trips around the less busy flights. We were also allowed to travel on standby on other airlines, but much further down the list of priority to board the plane. Those that had worked for the airline for a long time would be higher up the confirmed list for a flight than those with fewer years' service. I will always be incredibly grateful for the opportunities I have had, and they have led to some fantastic trips. The massive perks of travelling at a reduced rate on my British Airways concessions were mostly successful, but there were times when I could not travel on the day I had planned or could not get a seat in business class if the flights were busy.

One of the more recent trips was a flight back from Singapore to London with my husband. It is always a popular route so often difficult to plan accurately. The flight we had chosen looked almost full in all the cabins, but nevertheless we went to the desk to check in. They told us that we might not get on the flight, and we should wait until everyone had checked in and then return to the check-in desk. There are always people who do not arrive in time for their flight or cancel at the last minute. Whilst we were waiting my husband and I discussed the options. If we were able to get on the flight, but had to be separated in different cabins, I said I would like to have the better seat as I would be going straight into the office when I got home, so I needed to be able to sleep on board. When it was time to check the availability again, I was advised they could get us both on the flight, but one of us would sit in economy and the other in premium economy. No business class unfortunately, but frankly we were just thankful we could get on the flight. As discussed, I opted for the premium economy seat with my husband in economy; I was hoping he did not mind too much.

When we arrived back at Heathrow, we met up at the baggage claim section and I asked him if he had managed to sleep. He said that he had had a great flight. Apparently just before take-off the cabin stewardess approached my husband and asked him to follow her with his cabin bag. She took him into the business class section, as there was one last spare seat. Lucky! Arriving at his seat, he nodded to the chap sitting next to him, thinking he looked vaguely familiar. His neighbour was having trouble with his seat, so the crew were busy helping him. My husband struck up a conversation with him.

'Have you been on holiday?'

'No, I'm in the cheese business and was visiting some contacts looking for marketing opportunities,' answered his neighbour.

'Have you far to travel when you arrive in the UK?'

'No, not really, we are in Oxfordshire,' came the reply. It was at that moment the penny dropped and my husband realised he was sitting next to a guitarist from a well- known band and now a cheesemaker. The point of retelling this is if I had not jumped in and said I wanted to be in the upgraded cabin and let my husband take the premium economy seat instead, I would have been sitting in that seat. That'll teach me!

All Part of the Job

While working for British Airways we had many chances to view aircraft interiors, often in a different way to how one would expect. An idea from someone senior within BA thought it would be good for various departments to see how other parts of the airline worked. For myself, that gave me the opportunity to shadow an airline pilot for a day. We met outside the Uxbridge travel shop early one morning and drove to Heathrow, as this particular pilot was scheduled to fly a plane full of passengers to Amsterdam. Before boarding the aircraft, we had to go to a debriefing including checking weather charts, which could have affected the route and flying altitude. Nothing untoward showed for our trip but it was interesting to see the route on a chart that showed the aircraft registration number rather than the BA flight number. We boarded the Boeing 737, turned left and entered the tiny cabin at the front. I sat behind the captain in a jump seat, strapped myself in and watched while they did their final checks. I wore headphones, so could hear air traffic control giving the all-clear to start taxiing. Once we took off, the plane basically flew itself, as it was all automated, and in no time we started our descent into Schiphol Airport. The landing was smooth, and we began our taxi to the gate. The captain then turned round to me and asked if I could drive.

Wondering why, I said, 'Yes.'

Then he asked if I would like to taxi the aircraft along the runway. There was a small metal handwheel to one side forward of my seat, which controlled the nose wheel. He told me to take hold of it and keep an eye on the central line running along the length of the taxiway. I had to keep the nose wheel on that line, which meant the aircraft was in the right position. I remember thinking of all the passengers strapped in behind me, unaware of a novice guiding them in! Sadly, we had no time to spend in Amsterdam, but turned around immediately and repeated the experience on a return home to Heathrow. I do feel fortunate to have had the opportunity to experience a few hours in the life of an airline pilot.

When Concorde was first built, we were able to go on board and look around, but I never had the opportunity to take a flight. I remember thinking how narrow the cabin was compared to any of the other aircraft. It felt quite claustrophobic. In front of the first seat was a screen that showed the speed when the aircraft was in flight. For many people, flying on Concorde would have been a pipe dream since the cost was so high. However, for a while, to attract business, British Airways marketed flights out into the Atlantic, where the aircraft would reach Mach 1 and customers could experience the sonic boom. These flights to nowhere were advertised at £399 each. I told my parents about it, and my father said he would love to go, something that would be so special for him, because he was wheelchair bound and very much restricted in what he could manage. My father had been diagnosed with MS, and it was becoming increasingly difficult for him to remain mobile. He did drive a three-wheeled turquoise-blue mobility car to and from work, and is, indeed, the only person I know to be stopped by the police for speeding in one! I bought them two tickets, booked the wheelchair status (he was in need of the highest assistance since he could not walk at all), and organised preboarding for them. My ice-cream colleague, Rosemary, had also sold two tickets to her parents. We were told that there was a spare ticket free for someone in our office, and obviously both me and Rosemary wanted to go. We tossed a coin, and Rosemary won, so she got to go. I was allowed to go to Heathrow to see them all off, but not before having a photo taken of us girls in our uniform and my parents pre-boarding. As my father had to be first on and given the lack of space to help him from his wheelchair, he was put in the aisle seat 1C, with my mother next to him in 1A by the window. This of course was the front row with a clear view of the speed data screen and probably the best seats on the aircraft. I think the flight was one of Dad's highlights.

The only time I have been in first class on a BA airliner was when the aircraft cleaners went on strike. To keep the flights operating we were asked if we wanted to earn some overtime and help clean the aircraft. I drove one of the transit vans to the aircraft with the cleaners and equipment on board. I had to follow a route following lines on the road to get to the plane so that I avoided driving in the path of any moving aircraft. Our designated plane was a 747 and having travelled in economy on a long flight myself, I knew what state those toilets could be in, so I made a beeline for first class! We had to take any leftover food and alcohol back to the office - not for staff consumption! A shame because there were plenty of miniature bottles of alcohol just begging to be used, and trays of unused foodstuff. So that was my only first-class experience.

Years later I heard that a new fifth airport terminal was being opened at Heathrow, and they were looking for guinea pigs to try out the systems and procedures before the grand opening. I volunteered, along with my friend and colleague Mandy. We were each given a scenario as passengers and had to check in, find out where we had to go, follow the signage, and eventually board our flight. We were set to fly to New York. We arrived at the shiny new building and saw rows of check-in machines and behind those, unmanned areas where we weighed our baggage, attached our baggage labels, and sent our luggage on its way. This new automated way of working was quite alien to me, but customer service was still evident as there were members of BA staff on hand to help if we got stuck. Passing reasonably quickly through security, we found ourselves airside, with empty shops and restaurants, which were ready for real customers. Looking at the information boards to find our flight number, we saw that the terminal was divided into zones; A, B and C. We were standing in zone A and found that the European flights departed from this zone, but the flights heading further afield would leave from zone B or C. To get to either of those we had to get a monorail, which stopped at both. Our job was to time the process from checking in to arriving at our departure gate, and clearly, waiting for a monorail would add to the timeframe. The whole process did take much longer than it should have done, probably because there were a few teething problems at check in and baggage drop-off, but it was an interesting exercise and one that needed to be done. Sadly, this was only role play, so although we did board a plane and got strapped in, that plane was going nowhere

Christmas Day 1960, first career choice

Early holiday, south coast of UK

No idea how to tie the scarf, 1979, modelling my new uniform

Perfecting the art of drinking from a porron, December 1975, Majorca

Sandra - Uxbridge – 1985

Seeing parents off on Concorde, Sandra (R), Rosemary (L)

Education, Education, Education!

Educational trips are one of the biggest perks in the travel industry. These are where we are flown to a destination and are hosted by a tour operator, a destination management company, or a tourist office to experience their product. Naturally, they want to give the best impression. I have had my fair share of these so-called 'fam' trips over the years, not so many with British Airways, but plenty with Travel Counsellors.

These trips are designed for us to familiarise ourselves with a particular destination. Often the schedule is very hectic, with early starts, meeting with hoteliers, who show us around their hotels, including various types of rooms, and all the facilities they have to offer. Either some form of refreshment, a lunch or dinner is included. We would need to make notes and video clips where relevant, so that we could write a report on our return to share with colleagues. I must admit we had some fantastic hospitality, but I gained more from those trips that did not follow a tight schedule of hotel visits. After a while many hotel room types merged into others, so that it would become difficult to remember which hotel had the junior suite with a pool leading onto a lazy river, for example. For me, it was more important to see more of the resort, island or country and experience the activities people could do whilst there, or experience the scenic views, and understand the logistics and distances involved to get around. Nowadays, it is easy to get information on the accommodation, with perhaps a video link from the hotel. If you have these, the important things are to know what there is to do and see once you get there. I have always tried to repay the generous hospitality of airlines, ground handlers and hoteliers by booking clients with them after a trip away. It is far easier to sell using the emotions you felt when experiencing the destination, remembering the sights and smells, seeing the local culture first-hand, tasting the food, enjoying the entertainment and experiences. I know what it is to have aching muscles after kayaking across a lake, the exhilaration of breathing in mountain air or catching my breath when first seeing a snow-capped mountain, and a glistening alpine lake, and to watch a beautiful sunrise, or a sunset, as the sky changes colour.

Now that I was travelling to far-flung places, I decided it was about time I started collecting fridge magnets to remind me of all the wonderful trips I had been on. There is nothing like a sudden flash of a memory when you are about to raid the fridge. Both my fridge and freezer are now covered in lovely memories from all around the world.

One of my earlier educational trips did not happen though. I had been invited to join some other agents and BA colleagues to travel to Colombia, South America. I met the others at the airport and bonded over a drink in the bar, as you do Then we checked in and did a bit of shopping at duty free and made our way to the boarding gate. Shortly before they called the flight to board, I got a message asking me to call my office. It was Rosemary, trying to get hold of me before I left for Colombia. My mother had called to tell me that my father had been taken into hospital and was on dialysis. I had to make the snap decision about whether to take the flight or not. Of course, the right decision was not to go. I was escorted back through security, leaving my luggage to make the journey to South America and back. In those days, security did not dictate that if a passenger didn't board the aircraft, the luggage had to be taken off the flight. Every cloud has a silver lining though. I was allowed to keep the bottle of alcohol I had bought at duty free! I am glad I decided to travel back to Southampton as my father was seriously ill with discussions about life expectancy. He lived for another year and died aged just fifty-nine years. Some years later I was at a British Airways reunion and got chatting to a couple of people. One of them said she remembered me as she was one of the people on the trip to Colombia. She had spent the past twenty-odd years wondering what on earth had happened and why I did not get on that flight! Small world.

Down Under... Part 1

I have been to Australia several times, but the first couple were educational trips. On the first visit I was pregnant with my first daughter. Arriving in Sydney, we went to our rooms to rest. Laying on my bed, I suddenly felt my baby kicking for the first time. Tiny fluttery butterflies, but the sad thing was I could not share that moment with anyone. It was on that trip that I couldn't face eating beautiful prawns which were the size of your fingers, and of course alcohol was off limits. We did get a broad but quick experience of Australia, making eleven flights in as many days. We covered Sydney, Brisbane, Townsville, Cairns, Dunk Island on the Barrier Reef, Ayres Rock, as it was known then, and Alice Springs. More on Australia later but the abiding memory I have from that trip is I now understand why Australians wear hats with corks hanging from the brim. Around Alice Springs and Ayres Rock we were plagued with flies buzzing all around our heads. It drove us mad. Ayres Rock was magical though. We rose at sunrise, which was quite late given it was in May, and their winter. We watched the sunrise hit the Rock, reflecting orangey red hues, which contrasted with the deeper red colours at sunset. Years ago when I visited, people were allowed to climb onto the rock. In my delicate condition I did manage a few feet up, but the summit was too much. Given that nowadays it is forbidden to climb this sacred site, I am glad I didn't try and venture to the top. We flew from there to Cairns, and onto Dunk Island, a small island paradise on the Great Barrier Reef. We only had time to look around the property, but it was the first time I had landed on a grass airstrip and walk straight to the hotel reception.

The second time I visited was on another educational organised by Gold Coast Tourism. They pulled out all the stops and planned a fabulous and varied few days on the Gold Coast showing all that this region has to offer. The area south of Brisbane had a string of resorts merging along a lengthy stretch of beach. We stayed at Broadbeach and Surfers Paradise both with pristine sands, high-rise accommodation and surf. We had a surf lesson at Surfers Paradise, where I was surrounded by fit, younger colleagues, who had no problem donning their wetsuits.

I was squeezed into mine and looked like the seal in a Tom and Jerry cartoon - all shiny and black. I had never tried surfing before and did not have the central body core strength to pull myself up even into a kneeling position but had a go and enjoyed lying down on the surfboard and being swept ashore by the waves. We also had a gentle boat ride around the many canals, visited a wildlife sanctuary and sampled an exhilarating jet boat ride around the fabulous waterside homes of Brisbane. At Currumbin Wildlife Sanctuary, I held a koala and fed the kangaroos as well as viewing other indigenous animals. I have always had a soft spot for koalas, so holding one was one of my highlights. We made a couple of hotel visits on this trip, and being shown around the spa in one, I noticed a white glove which had been left on one of the benches, so as I walked past it, I said, 'I see Michael Jackson's been in'. It amused…

We spent the night at Reilly's Rainforest Retreat, high in the hills behind Surfers Paradise. The countryside here is different to the coastal areas and ideal for those who enjoy walks amongst the lush green woodland. We learnt about the flora and fauna of this area, and even spotted a possum and carpet python on our travels. Our ranger showed us a quoll whilst we were in the rainforest, a most unusual marsupial with a spotted coat. This trip made me want to return to explore Australia in more depth which I did on a holiday a few years later.

Exploring the Canaries

Another early trip for me was a two island visit to the Canaries. As I mentioned, when working for British Airways, we sold package holidays from our own branded products, namely Enterprise Holidays, for two- and three-star hotels, or Sovereign Holidays, for four- and five-star hotels and for the more discerning customer. Not an area I had previously visited, I was intrigued to see and compare the islands. We first flew to Gran Canaria and visited hotels in Las Palmas and surrounding coastal resorts, to the north of the island and then further south to Puerto Rico and Maspalomas. Nothing about Las Palmas appealed; a busy uninspiring place with high-rise hotels, although the beach was fine. I preferred the resorts further south, although they seemed no different to any of the other Spanish resorts, with high rises, 1970s style accommodation and sandy beaches, lined with bars, restaurants and general tourist tat. I had no desire to return and haven't done so. I am sure Gran Canaria has improved over the years, but that was my impression then. The Canaries weren't so commercially developed in the early 1980s and to head further south, to the bottom of Gran Canaria would have been out of the question, unless you were looking for an off-the-beaten-track type of holiday. I hoped Tenerife would be better. We flew to the northern airport and were shown hotels in the Santa Cruz area. At that time, the south of the island was less developed, and the higher end hotels used by Sovereign were around the Santa Cruz region. We had been warned that it was cloudier in the north than the south, due mainly to Mount Teide which divided the island. I believe this is the reason the southern side of Tenerife was developed for tourism, as there would be more of a guarantee of good weather for us sun-loving Brits (other nationalities too — we still had an issue with the Germans and their towels, even then!) Moving to the south of Tenerife, we stayed in Los Cristianos and were shown around the upcoming new resort of Playa de Las Americas. I must admit, there was nothing that really made me want to return. The resorts were a sprawl of buildings spreading over the coastal area, gradually merging into each other.

Many years later, we had a couple of our Travel Counsellor Gold Conferences in Tenerife, but this time we were treated to five-star accommodation. There was a new hotel near Guia de Isora further north along the coast from Playa De las Americas, called the Abama. The views across to neighbouring La Gomera were fantastic. My impression of the island had improved but I still had no real desire to return. Now there were boulevards, and more attractive apartments and hotels, with restaurants and bars interspersed amongst them.

On a later trip we stayed in a large high-end resort hotel in Costa Adeje, which was becoming recognised as a more discerning resort, just to the north of Playa de Las Americas. One of our group trips was on a catamaran from Los Cristianos, which took us out to sea and then sailed along the coast to drop anchor for swimming and snorkelling. It all sounded fun, and I had visions of lazing on the sundeck, drinking cocktails, but unfortunately as soon as we left the safety of the harbour, the sea became choppy. Most people were sitting at tables on the top deck, but I could feel the movement of the catamaran when I leaned against the seatback, so got up and went to the front railings and stood looking out to sea straight ahead. I think moving and the motion sickness tablets saved me. Gradually, one by one, my colleagues were overcome with seasickness. It was awful. It did not matter a jot if you were a colleague like me, or one of the directors, that queasy feeling was indiscriminate. There were a few who were OK, but most looked like they were dying. Colleagues helped each other, getting buckets, holding hair, rubbing backs, trying to ease their discomfort. We pleaded with the skipper to turn back, but we were too far into the trip to gain anything by doing so, so we had to endure the nightmare for a while. Eventually we arrived at a sheltered cove and dropped anchor. Amazingly, everyone started to feel better and tucked into lunch. The rest of the trip went as planned, with a smooth ride back, sheltered by the coastline. That trip is still talked about now. Never again!

Another excursion completely changed my mind about Tenerife. We took a trip up into the mountains and saw a completely different side to the island. Heading up the quiet, isolated roads showed us how the whole of Tenerife would have been before mass tourism descended upon the island. We discovered winding roads amongst the mountains, with lovely views across valleys and peaceful, tranquil scenery. Not many tourists to be seen, except those interested in the local flora and fauna. This was more my cup of tea.

There's no business, like snow business

Me and snow do not really get on, so going on a couple of trips that involved snow was a bit of a challenge. I love looking at it but travelling in it is another thing. I had been invited to join some colleagues to the French Alps and I was the only one who had never skied. I was interested in visiting the region so that I would have confidence when selling ski holidays. Prior to the trip I went along to a dry ski slope in Basingstoke and got to grips on the nursery slope, managing to keep upright and learning how to snow plough. When we got to Val D'Isere in France, we were asked what level skiers we were. I stood there listening to the others discussing black runs and realised I was completely out of my depth. I hoped I could just spend the time sampling the Après Ski, as I knew I would be an expert in that. To my relief the ski host said they would organise some private lessons for me while the others were zooming down the black runs. I met up with Serge who was older than me, but 200% fitter, who took me to the nursery slopes. I was supposed to have a three-hour private lesson but having spent much of that time flat on my back and exhausted by the effort to get myself upright, I could only manage being out on the slopes for about an hour and a half. I will never be a skier but did enjoy seeing the various ski resorts in the region and now understand the logistics of getting from the airports.

On another occasion, I was invited to stay in Verbier, Switzerland at Richard Branson's luxury lodge, which at the time was hosted by a good friend of mine, along with her colleagues, and her partner who was the head chef. I was very keen to visit the lodge as I had heard so much about it from her, with stories about past guests including royalty and members of rock bands. I also wanted to sample the fantastic food the chef produced. On both counts I was not disappointed. I could understand why guests would rate this place so highly. The lodge is a fifteen-minute stroll downhill to the centre of Verbier, and offered comfortable luxury, with a relaxing vibe. The whole concept was to make guests feel at home with shoes off at the entrance, casual attire and no need to dress for dinner. Comfy sofas surrounded a cosy log fire, with a fully stocked bar in one corner, where guests were free to help themselves. The bed was probably the most comfortable I have ever slept in. To me the staff made the whole experience special. Without exception everyone I spoke to was friendly and helpful, with nothing too much trouble. There was someone on duty twenty-four hours a day, and none of the staff would disappear until the last guest had gone to bed. They had a minibus which would take guests to the village whenever they wanted.

What made the lodge special was the food. The head chef would come and explain the menu, where the food was sourced and how each course had been made. I heard comments from other guests saying that the chef knew his stuff, and everything I ate was delicious. We could have pretty much anything we liked for breakfast. There were no fancy waiters, simply good food brought to the table in a relaxing manner. In the evening we joined everyone in the party room downstairs, where there was a 63" flat screen TV, pool table, bar, music and fun and games. We had a couple of local singers to entertain us too. The lodge had a spa, an indoor pool and an indoor and outdoor hot tub. The staff would organise a BBQ or picnic in the mountains or even accompany guests who wanted to snowshoe or go off for a hike.

There were plenty of things to do in this area in the summer and winter, aside from skiing and walking. It was possible to go paragliding, ice karting, mountain biking, or simply get a train to Lake Geneva and visit Montreux, Lausanne or Geneva. The Italian coast was only about three hours away. If guests wanted something special and could afford it, the staff could pretty much organise anything. For example, a private helicopter for a trip over mountains and valleys followed by a private picnic, surrounded by glorious scenery, prepared by the chef. The lodge offered stays on an all-inclusive basis, and that meant all the food and drink consumed at the lodge were included.

On one occasion we were all invited to ski from the lodge to meet up on the mountain for refreshments. Remembering my past skiing efforts, I knew I would not be able to join them, but instead of missing out, they suggested I went snow shoeing with one of the hosts and the lodge's dog. That sounded fine to me, and although reasonably strenuous, I did enjoy it and managed to get to the top and meet up with the others. Another first for me!

I had been on another educational trip to the Alps some years before when I had worked in the local village agency. Swiss Tourism were promoting active holidays in Switzerland, so a group of us were invited to experience what they had on offer. We flew into Zurich and connected to Weggis on the excellent rail service, getting my first glimpse of the breathtaking alpine scenery. Our first activity was to mount horses and mules and ride from the village up a nearby hill. I had never ridden before, and neither had some of the others. These animals had minds of their own, some deciding they did not want to take part and headed back to the village with their riders, who had no control over their animals. Luckily, my daughter was a keen rider and I had been taking her to lessons and had helped tack her pony, so had some idea of how to get a horse moving and make it stop. It seemed to work, and we gradually headed up the hill, with my mount stopping occasionally to feed on the undergrowth as and when it felt like it, sometimes on a downward slope. With the horse's head buried in the lush grass, the downward slope looked much steeper from where I was sitting. One false wobble and I would be rolling down the hillside. Overall, though, I quite enjoyed the experience and felt I had achieved something that day.

During that night I had an upset stomach and was feeling rather delicate the next morning with a dodgy tummy but staying in bed was out of the question as we were leaving the area to kayak from Weggis across Lake Lucerne to Lucerne. Dosed up with Imodium®, I donned a wetsuit, stomach gurgling, hoping I wouldn't have an accident whilst on the water. It did not bear thinking about. You just cannot have the squits wearing a wetsuit, can you! Kayaking is another activity I had only ever done at school, so there was every chance I would capsize. I gingerly made a start, life jacket on, stomach protesting, (noise travels on water, have you noticed?) and kayaked across the lake. It took some time to complete, but I got into a rhythm and kept up with the others. Someone said I looked very relaxed and laid back, but in fact I was unable to hold my torso upright, so found myself leaning back to support my body. The life jacket rode up and I ended up with some chafing on my chin. Thankfully, the Imodium® did the trick and I got safely across, dignity intact.

After exploring the pretty town of Lucerne, walking over the covered bridge, we headed up a steep woody hill to mountain bike down at speed. I thoroughly enjoyed that as it's much easier to go down than up! We went on boats and trains on that trip, all super-efficient, leaving exactly on time and I have promised myself that one day I will return. The whole point of going on an educational is that you can confidently sell the destination having experienced it. I find the best way to sell anything is to have first-hand knowledge and it has worked for me time and time again.

Winter in Norway

One of the many things on my bucket list was to see the Northern Lights. So, when an opportunity arose to fly out to Tromsø, in Norway and join one of the Hurtigruten ships I jumped at the chance. Hurtigruten sail up and down the Norwegian coastline delivering goods and people to all the tiny villages and ports along the way. Along with a few other colleagues, we arrived in Tromsø in the late afternoon. Tromsø is just inside the Arctic Circle, where it is the best place for the lights to come out and play. It's a very hit-and-miss affair, but we were hoping to be lucky. The plan was to join the ship sailing southbound, that was due in just before midnight. As we had a few hours to spare, we were booked to head out of the city and go on a dog-sledding trip. We had to wear snow suits, which the company provided and after some refreshments and leaving our luggage at one of the hotels, we set off at dusk. Almost immediately we could see some pale iridescent green wisps appearing and dissipating in the sky. As it got darker, we could see a bit more and then they would disappear. We were driven out to the place where they kept the dogs who barked excitedly upon our arrival, knowing they were off for a run. They were harnessed up to long, two person sledges. We got in wrapped up in our snow suits and animal skin 'blankets' and set off in convoy into the night, dogs barking and haring along at speed pulling us through the snowy scenery. We had to duck our heads a few times as we passed bushes with branches hanging in our path, as there was no stopping the dogs on their mission.

We ended up at a large tepee where we were going to have supper. There were other tourists standing around when we got there. We all went inside and sat around the edge in a circle and were offered warming reindeer stew that had been cooking in a large pot for a few hours in the centre of the tepee, smoke escaping from a vent in the top. After filling our boots, we began to wander back outside, curious to know why others already outside were shouting. The lights had returned and were a vivid green; an awesomely beautiful scene which lasted a while before disappearing again. My camera was not sophisticated enough to record the spectacle, but it is locked away in my memory as one of those special moments I will treasure. We returned to Tromsø and embarked for our southbound journey to Trondheim. The lights did not appear again, but we enjoyed visiting Trondheim with its massive cathedral, and traditional warehouses bordering the river.

As with many 'Cooks Perks' destinations, I have since returned to explore a bit more in the hope of seeing those elusive lights again. On my second visit to Norway, again with Hurtigruten, we boarded the ship straightaway before heading to the very northern reaches the country. Again, it was winter so there was plenty of snow around making very pretty scenery. We briefly saw the Northern Lights as we departed Tromsø, (blink and you miss it), but the weather was then overcast for a few days. We passed fishermen's cottages dotted here and there along the coast as we weaved in and out of the inlets on calm waters.

We had to stop at many little ports on route to deliver mail and goods but were often allowed off the ship for maybe half an hour to an hour to explore a bit. We had hoped to take an excursion to the North Cape, but the weather was against us, so we continued to the furthest point, close to the Russian border, to Kirkenes. We spent a full day in this area, visiting a snow hotel, where every room was different, each with ice carvings depicting intricate designs. The Snow Hotel was a work of art, and difficult to imagine that it had not existed a few months earlier. Surprisingly, the temperature inside was bearable, but personally, I wouldn't spend a night there. I prefer more comfortable surroundings but nevertheless, I was fascinated to visit and appreciate the work involved in creating this masterpiece. We learnt that the Russians often came over the border to Kirkenes to do their shopping, as there were many goods that they were not able to get in Russia.

From Kirkenes, the ship turned around for its journey southbound, calling in at different ports from those on the outbound heading north. We had almost got back to Tromsø when the weather turned for the worse. High winds and heavy snow stopped us from going up on deck. The sea was rough, so all we could do was sit it out in the public lounge areas. We heard a loud crash from the restaurant when the ship hit a large wave and lurched to one side. I think they lost a large amount of crockery as plates and dishes toppled over. Across from where we were sitting was a small shop with racks of clothes for sale. When the ship lurched, the racks slowly slid across the deck towards us. We were four decks up and watched as the waves crashed up onto our windows. I'm glad I wasn't dining at that time, as I am sure the soup would have been in my lap. Eventually the storm subsided, and we arrived back in Tromsø to a glimmer of the Northern Lights. We checked into our hotel which was a short walk from the port but even though it was gone midnight we did not go straight to our rooms, but instead headed back outside in the hope of seeing the lights reappear. We gave it another hour and gave it up to a lost cause. The annoying thing was, not long after we had gone back to our beds, the lights reappeared. It was almost as if they knew.

We had some free time the next day before our flight home and had planned to explore the mountain above Tromsø to watch a total eclipse of the sun due later that morning. Before heading there, we stopped at the unusually shaped Arctic Cathedral, built from aluminium and concrete and shaped like an A. The other unusual thing about this cathedral is the organ. The keys that are normally white were black and the black keys were white. I just loved the quirkiness. We were not disappointed either with the trip up to the mountain summit. A lovely clear day gave us fantastic views from the top across the whole of Tromsø. We could see the airport in the distance, and the A shape of the Arctic Cathedral below, an excellent place to get a clear overview of the city.

It was beautiful up there, ankle deep in snow, plenty of other people had the same idea, waiting for the eclipse. Gradually the light began to fade, as the moon began to cross the sun. The birds stopped singing and we all put on our sunglasses to shield our eyes. The sun disappeared, cameras and mobile phones recorded the spectacle, and it was eerily silent as we took in the extraordinary sight. All too soon the sun began to reappear, and the light returned to normal. What a lovely memory to end that trip.

Madeira

One of my earlier trips with Travel Counsellors was a visit to Madeira. I had heard it was a great place for walking and the scenery was supposed to be beautiful. We had a hairy landing on arrival at Funchal Airport as the runway runs alongside the cliff, with the sea falling away to the other side. Anything more than a breeze could make for a bumpy landing.

We stayed in a few different properties each for a couple of nights, barely unpacking, moving from a boutique hotel, to a *pousada*, to a five-star resort, all offering something different, seeing the various types of rooms and facilities each had for their guests. By the end of the trip, I felt I knew much more about the accommodation, but no idea about what Madeira offered in terms of scenery. On the day we were to fly home we had the morning free, and while some colleagues took that time to catch a few rays on a sunbed, a few of us wanted to see some of the island. We went to the hotel reception and booked a large Mercedes with a driver and asked him to take us beyond Funchal to see something more scenic. With three of us in the back of the car and one next to the driver, we first drove to a viewpoint for some photos and then to a place called the Nun's Village. This meant driving up into the mountains through a man-made tunnel, which brought us to an extinct volcanic crater that was filled with lush vegetation and the Nun's Village. Deep in the crater valley we were surrounded by mountains, and at that moment it totally changed my perception of Madeira. Prior to that point I had no real desire to return. It was pretty, but a bit uninspiring. Seeing the interior made me want to return to see more.

As is often the case, when we were at one of the hosted dinners, the proprietor gave us an invitation for three nights complimentary accommodation at his hotel. Sometime later I attended the World Travel Market in London, which is an annual exhibition at Excel, hosted by suppliers, hoteliers, tourism offices, and tour operators for the travel industry and the public. The suppliers come from all over the world to promote their businesses. While I was there, I came across the manager of the hotel who had offered the complimentary stay. I took the bull by the horns and asked him if his offer still stood, and if it could be extended to include two rooms and to stay for longer. (If you don't ask!)

We ended up having a fabulous two-week holiday as a family of four with interconnecting rooms, just paying for the extra nights. We hired a car and explored the whole island, stopping to admire the traditional apex shaped thatched houses in the north, seeing where Sir Winston Churchill enjoyed painting in the south, and even flying over to the neighbouring island of Porto Santo for a night. Porto Santo has sandy beaches, whilst Madeira is not known for its beaches. The island's hotels took me right back to Hotel Sol Piños, in Arenal in the seventies.

Hopefully Porto Santo has now come out of its time warp, as the beaches were beautiful and empty, but after a night in a 1970s hotel, we were glad to get back to the luxury of our hotel in Madeira. We enjoyed the compulsory wicker sledge ride down some steep roads, which took us down to Funchal, dodging cars that intermittently crossed the streets. We had a lovely wander around the botanical gardens and enjoyed eating at the harbourside restaurants in the capital. I discovered a liking for madeira wine, now a favourite tipple while I am preparing our Christmas dinner. The temperature in December on my first visit was the same as when we went in the summer school holidays, around 21°C, perfect for walking the levadas and footpaths that crisscross the island.

Dubai Bound

Educational trips always seemed better if you were able to travel with colleagues who were also good friends. Even if that didn't happen there was a good chance that new friendships would form, which for me happened often.

One such educational was to Dubai. I have visited this vibrant city about five times now, most of them on educationals, each time seeing the city grow. The skyline is an architectural wonder with buildings of all shapes and sizes. Flying over the Middle East and seeing large swathes of desert below, with the odd nodding donkey producing oil, is an experience in itself. One such trip started in the Emirates Lounge at Heathrow. On that occasion I was travelling with my good friend Helen, she of Danish pastry fame from our time at the village agency. Helen had joined Travel Counsellors after a chance meeting in a supermarket and having that 'How are you and what are you doing now' conversation. I told her all about Travel Counsellors and shortly after that, she joined the company. We have been on many trips together and something always happens when we are away. We are both at an age now where we need a carer to keep an eye on us, so we take turns!

On that particular trip, in the Emirates Lounge before the flight, Helen decided to go into the adjacent room where they had a few computers, as she needed to sort something out for one of her clients. It was dimly lit and appeared to be empty. Helen got settled and proceeded with the job in hand. Out of the blue, she gave a very loud belch, and thinking she was alone, said out loud, 'That's better Helen'. To her horror and embarrassment, a head popped up on the other side of the screen and glared at her. Red-faced Helen made a hasty retreat, repeated what had happened, which was met with much laughter. Only Helen!

We arrived at the sparkling Emirates Terminal in Dubai and were swiftly transported to our hotel. There are always giggles with Helen, and as we settled into our room relaxing on our beds, I glanced up to the top corner of the room. Being a bit short-sighted, I could see something large and dark up there. I thought it was a large spider, so shuddered at the thought. Helen just laughed though and told me to step nearer to it. I put my glasses on and looked closer. The 'spider' turned out to be the arrow many hotels put on the walls in their rooms pointing to the direction of Mecca!

We had a full day of hotel visits, moving in groups from one hotel to another, being shown this room type, that room type, spa areas, dining options and so on. My colleagues always present themselves in a professional manner, as we are representing the company, so it annoyed us intensely, when arriving at the Armani Hotel near the Burj Khalifa, to be greeted by an officious staff member, whose opening comment was that she expected us all to be professional whilst being shown around their hotel. This was not only insulting to us, as we knew very well how to behave, but also like a red rag to a bull. I had by that time been in the travel industry for more years than she had lived on this earth. I took an instant dislike to the hotel, as there was no welcoming reception, and staff who were supercilious. When we exited one of the lifts and saw the minimalist displays of flowers all leaning in the same direction, in a feng shui style (possibly facing Mecca?), I am afraid the mischief monkey took hold, and those flowers were moved to point in the other direction. Professional eh, we'll show you who's professional!

There is often someone in a group who rubs people up the wrong way and we had one in our group on that Dubai trip. The best remembered eye-rolling moment was when we ascended the Burj Khalifa, the tallest building in the world. We got to the top to enjoy the panoramic vista below. We could see far out over the ocean and through the haze make out The World and The Palm, both offshore man-made islands. We could also see the tiny Burj al Arab Hotel, and the Jumeirah Beach Hotel in the distance with their sail-shaped architecture. The Burj Fountains were way below us and then in the distance the empty desert stretched for miles. Our grumpy colleague's response to all that? 'There's not much of a view'! Basil Fawlty would have had a field day…

It was on another visit to Dubai with a large group of colleagues that we were booked to stay at the Atlantis the Palm Resort. We had only stayed one night, when we were advised that we all had to be moved to another hotel because a wealthy sheikh needed our rooms for his entourage. He must have had a lot of clout and brought in a lot of money to the hotel, but it didn't matter to us, as we all got to experience another hotel.

It was at the Atlantis that I was able to interact with dolphins, standing thigh high in the water in Dolphin Bay. Bottle-nosed dolphins swam right up to us, allowing us to stroke their smooth bodies. Any interaction with animals is special for me, and I never thought I would have the opportunity to do this. Later we were taken out on an evening trip into the desert. The plan was to transport everybody in jeeps over the sand dunes, do a bit of dune bashing, and end up at a camp, where we would dine and be entertained, whilst watching the sun set. I chickened out of the dune bashing part, as I did not fancy getting car sick, so instead went via the road arriving at the camp quite a bit earlier than my colleagues. There were a few green faces when the other jeeps arrived, some having to stop along the way for those who couldn't cope with the rolling movement of the jeep. We sat around in groups on cushions and ate various meats and local foods, watching belly dancers, followed by a mooch around a couple of makeshift tents.

Inside one there was a lady busy drawing intricate henna designs on our arms, hands or feet, and in the other tent, a fortune teller. For a bit of fun, I thought I would have my fortune read, careful not to give anything away, but interested to see if anything she said was true. She took my hand and studied the lines in them. Completely out of the blue she said I had three children. Well, that was not strictly true, and although no one on that trip knew, I had been pregnant three times, having lost one baby early on in pregnancy. I hadn't thought about that for some years, and it completely threw me, making me quite emotional. The other thing she said is I would be married twice. Well, that was quite a few years ago now and I am still on husband number one, so who knows!

On another trip we explored the Deira area, the older original part of Dubai which is dominated by Dubai Creek. We visited the Dubai Museum, where they have interesting displays showing traditional life in Dubai, with replicas of pearl fishermen's boats and dhows; the large boats that sail up and down the creek. All a very far cry from the glittering new developments that dominate the city now. From there we crossed Dubai Creek on traditional *abras*, which are small boats that ferry people across to the souks on the other side. We had fun bartering at the various stalls, generally starting at a third of the price asked and working up to a half. The souks are divided into different areas. The Spice Souk gave off exciting aromas, whilst the Gold Souk was full of little shops selling watches and jewellery. I managed to get a replacement watch for my husband, which looked exactly like the one I bought him when we got engaged but had died a death after years of use. I suppose the souk reminded me a bit of the Grand Bazaar in Istanbul; a busy, colourful area full of traders trying to entice you to buy. I noticed a couple of English girls wandering through the souks clad in only shorts and bikini tops. If they felt uncomfortable with all the stares from the male stall holders, they only had themselves to blame. They stuck out like a sore thumb, amongst the local women who were covered head to toe.

Ten minutes from there we witnessed skiers and snowboarders enjoying artificial snow runs in the Ski Dome, adjacent to another vast shopping mall, the Mall of the Emirates, while outside it was about 30°C. I was fascinated to see the female skiers expertly skiing but dressed in burkas, amazed at how they did not trip or get their clothing entangled with the skis. We were able to look around the iconic Burj al Arab hotel, which stands on the shoreline, looking like a tall sail, complete with helicopter landing pad on the roof. Approaching the entrance, I noticed a fleet of expensive-looking Rolls Royce cars used to transfer guests to and from the airport. We were greeted by a waiter offering us fresh dates. At that point I had only ever tried prepacked dates from a supermarket that were only ever bought at Christmas. I never liked those as a child, but trying these, was a whole different culinary treat. They were very moreish. Looking upwards from the lobby area we noticed the vast atrium, where we could see all the different floors. It all looked quite futuristic, and I remember commenting that it looked like something out of the *Jetsons* cartoon programme which we watched as children in the 1960s. Despite the regular cost of staying at this place, I personally thought the reputation of the hotel outshone the reality. I could never afford to stay there, and in retrospect, I do not think I would ever choose to even if I could.

Alternative UAE

Along with over 100 Gold Travel Counsellors, I was invited to spend a few days sampling all that Abu Dhabi had to offer. My first impression was that the city was clean, and gradually developing as a tourist destination. Not as glitzy as its neighbour Dubai, which is only ninety minutes away by car, but quite spread out, so not a place that is designed for pedestrians. We were shown around some lovely hotels, which would be suited to business or leisure. We stayed at the Fairmont Bab Al Bahr, a contemporary hotel with a fantastic view of the Grand Mosque across the water on the opposite shore, which is lit at night. Close to the mosque, we visited the Ritz Carlton hotel, which I found to be very elegant with a calm ambience.

There were a few things to do beyond relaxing at the Fairmont. A visit to Yas Island brought us to the F1 Circuit. We were fortunate enough to go behind the scenes and visit the pit lanes, then walk on the circuit itself, before standing on the winner's podium raising a trophy to record our 'win'. Ferrari World, plus a fantastic Water Park was in the same area. Ferrari World has the world's fastest rollercoaster and because all the activities are inside, is a great place to get away from the heat of the day. There were simulators and shows for those that wanted an alternative to the high rollercoaster. Ever developing, at the time of my visit, there were a few hotels in this area too, such as the Rotana, and the Yas Viceroy, which had a roof that changed colour once the sun went down.

A tour of Abu Dhabi was interesting, as we visited the Heritage Village, and the Grand Mosque. We got a good feel for the size of the city. We also crossed over to Saadiyat Island, which was only just being developed, and by 2030 there will be a Louvre and a Guggenheim Museum, plus villas and hotels. Saadiyat Isalnd is still a work in progress, but from this island, which looks out over the Arabian Gulf, the sands are pristine with uninterrupted views of the sea. We had to use our imagination, but once the development of Abu Dhabi is complete it would be a good alternative to Dubai.

Rather than just explore Abu Dhabi, we ventured further afield to Al Ain, a city some ninety minutes away. This trip was rather disappointing. We spent a total of four hours on the coach, visited a small museum, an oasis, which did not have any water, and a camel market, which was probably the highlight of the whole excursion. There is nothing complimentary to say about the camel market, a place full of smelly, noisy beasts sitting huddled together behind fenced off areas. The other 'highlight' in Al Ain was stopping at a shopping mall, which had main UK high street names, such as Marks and Spencer. I could have got the bus from home if I had wanted an M&S. The excursion was too far to travel for a limited choice of things to see. For anyone stopping over for a day or two on route to Australia, or someone on a business trip, or just a place that guarantees sunshine and no rain for a winter break, I think Abu Dhabi would tick the box, nevertheless.

To the north of Dubai is another of the Emirates, which is developing and becoming a cheaper alternative to the vast choice of accommodation in Dubai. Beachfront resorts in Dubai come at a premium, but with a longer transfer, a stay in Ras al Khaimah could be just the ticket. We had another of our Gold trips there a few years ago, organised mainly to showcase that there are now other Emirates to enjoy. The transfer from Dubai to Ras al Khaimah did take some time, about one to two hours, and dependent on the level of traffic, especially around Dubai. The route took us past scrubby desert, passing miles of emptiness, no buildings, and the odd camel grazing on the scant undergrowth. I must admit I did wonder where we were heading, but eventually we arrived in Ras al Khaimah and checked into our hotel, the Waldorf Astoria, set on a wide sandy beach. Unlike Dubai, this area was spread out with lots of space between hotels. We visited a few resorts and crossed over to neighbouring Marjan Island to look around a couple of other hotels. Both resorts seemed quieter than buzzing Dubai. Although the accommodation standards were high, the cost to stay seemed lower.

Just beyond the resorts was desert, and just as we had in Dubai, we headed there by jeep to spend an evening in a Bedouin camp. Seated on cushions around a makeshift stage, we dined on local meats, and watched displays of falconry, sword dancing, whirling dervishes, and belly dancers. I think the word 'entertained' might be stretching it a bit, when two of my more heavily endowed male colleagues were invited to show their own prowess at belly dancing. They gave the belly dancer a good run for her money, valiantly wobbling bits we would not normally see. It was, in fact, hilarious, helped by the beer no doubt. Some of my colleagues headed out on another trip to the world's longest zipline at Jebel Jais in the sparse Al Hajar mountains. Strapped into a harness, they whizzed across two valleys, the longest section of the trip, taking between two to three minutes. I'm told it was exhilarating, but better them than me.

So along with Oman, which offers similar experiences and hotel standards, the Emirates are an excellent choice for a winter destination, not too far to travel, and certainly a shorter flight than flying to the Caribbean. Living in a region which is dark and cold in winter, the thought of escaping to the sun always seems enticing.

Talking of Oman, I was reminded of an incident that happened when we were visiting the Chedi Hotel, a lovely minimalist five-star hotel in the capital, Muscat. We had just finished lunch, feeling sated, relaxed, and chatting with the others on our table, when we heard a deafening explosion of glass crashing to the floor immediately behind us. It sounded as if a gun had gone off, making us all jump out of our seats. My dear friend Katy was in the firing line. A waiter had squeezed past our table and had knocked an entire display of wine and glasses to floor. Red wine shot out in every direction; up the walls, across the floor, and over our table, covering poor Katy's white linen trousers in a red mess. It was so unbelievable that it was funny. I'm sure the copious amounts of wine we had drunk during lunch helped. No doubt the poor waiter was mortified, and thankfully no paying guests were affected. I just hope the culprit didn't lose his job because it certainly entertained us all!

Indonesia

A few years ago, I was invited to join a group of agents to explore parts of Indonesia. Hosted by Garuda Airlines, we were set to visit Yogyakarta and Bali, which would combine a mix of ancient culture and architecture with beaches and rainforests. I called my mother as I normally did to tell her I was off to the airport and would call again when I got back. Always a mother, even though I was over fifty by that time, not six, she told me not to speak to strangers; nigh on impossible given I was about to meet up with a random group of travel agents. Mothers, who'd have them!

This type of educational was much more memorable for me, because although we did inspect a few hotels as is normal, we also spent a lot of time exploring the region. The airline offered much better service than anticipated and after a long flight we arrived in Yogyakarta, where we stayed at the Hyatt Regency for a couple of nights. The city was once the capital and was still a busy, thriving place.

The reason we were there was to visit the very impressive and ancient Borobudur Buddhist Temple. About an hour from the city, it predates Angkor Wat in Cambodia by 300 years, although it is much smaller. We climbed the narrow ancient steps for a face-off with the buddhas and looked out to far reaching views of the countryside beyond. We also visited the 9th century Hindu Temple of Prambanan, which was just as fascinating, and to my uneducated eye, looked like Borobudur, but if I had been blindfolded and dropped there, it was easy to think I was looking at Angkor Wat, in Cambodia, despite being a different religion. We were the only Westerners visiting and this gave much amusement to groups of giggling schoolchildren on a day out. They wanted to have their photos taken with us, probably because we looked so different to them all. Staying a couple of nights in this region, would be enough time for a trip by jeep to one of the volcanos, and perhaps a ride on an elephant too. We saw rice paddy fields and local farming as we drove along. It was like stepping into a *National Geographic* publication.

An hour's flight from Yogyakarta was the popular island of Bali. We first visited the family resort of Sanur, which had plenty of stalls, shops, bars and restaurants immediately outside the hotels. It had a safe feel about it and set on a long 5km sandy beach, I thought it would be a great choice for an authentic Balinese beach holiday. Further south were the resorts of Nusa Dua and Kuta. Nusa Dua was protected by a security point, leading to many large resort hotels, again on a long sandy beach. Outside the boundaries of the hotels, the only place to wander was along the beach, with stalls selling tourist 'tat' peppered along the beaches. The stall holders pounced on us as we wandered by, ready to barter with anyone who wanted to buy. There were some fabulous hotels along the coast, but I felt we could have been anywhere. There was nothing particularly Balinese about this resort. For me, for an authentic experience, I preferred Sanur. We only drove through Kuta, without stopping but the impression was it was geared for backpackers and lined with tacky shops.

About ninety minutes inland from the coast was the rainforest region of Ubud, set within lush vegetation. Ubud was lined with artisan shops, bars and places to eat. The main road through sometimes got busy, but stepping into the grounds of our lodge, we found ourselves in an oasis of calm. Some of the accommodation in Ubud was within walking distance of the shops, but with many more alternatives a couple of miles out, a hotel shuttle would be required to get to Ubud centre. This area was perfect for couples and honeymooners who want to get away from it all.

We met up one morning before breakfast at our lodge for a yoga session, surrounded by rainforest, listening to the birds and monkeys calling each other. As mentioned before, I am not very bendy, so thought I would struggle with the yoga moves. I had no idea what a downward dog was. With the help of the instructor, I found I could stretch places that hadn't been stretched in years and must say I felt fantastic afterwards. There was plenty of other activities on offer in this region, such as a relaxing spa treatment, hiking, or hiring a bike. We visited the Monkey Forest, where under supervision, a macaque monkey perched on our shoulders. Slightly worrying, as they had a habit of pinching sunglasses. We were told not to carry any plastic bags, as they have learnt that some people carry food in theirs. From experience in other countries, I am now very wary of wild monkeys as they are so unpredictable. I have seen them leap on unsuspecting tourists' backs grabbing hats and bags in both Cambodia and Gibraltar.

While we were in Ubud, we had to meet our host for dinner one evening. I put on a new white, sleeveless cotton blouse and sprayed myself liberally with mosquito spray, because without it I would be eaten alive. We dined outside, sitting on chairs with dark metal arms. Unbeknown to me the staining on the chair arms mixed with my mosquito spray, so that when I brushed my arms across my blouse, a large black mark appeared, ruining my new top. It wasn't the end of the world, but the host was most apologetic, and promised to get the top laundered for me. The only issue was, we were leaving the next morning for our final night along the south coast. I thought that was the last I would see of my blouse but was most impressed when it turned up the following day at our new hotel, some two hours away, looking as good as new, neatly pressed. Now that's great service.

One evening we took a taxi to Seminyak, which is about twenty minutes from Nusa Dua. There we found numerous bars, music venues and restaurants. My impression was that this thriving area mainly attracted the younger generation and was a great antidote to the quiet resort hotels. I found the Indonesian people eager to please, offering fantastic customer service, as was proven by the blouse incident. I have sold many holidays on the back of experiencing this trip, as it is so much easier to talk about to people if you have been there.

She sells Seychelles

When I was working in the British Airways Travel Shop in Uxbridge I always enjoyed looking at the brochures with exotic beaches in far-flung places, with soft white sands and palm trees filtering out the sun, dreaming of the day when I could go in person and see these beautiful places for myself. Roll forward to 2005 when I had the chance to visit the Seychelles with about six other colleagues. We flew on Emirates changing planes in Dubai, which made a nice break midway on the journey. We landed in Mahé and immediately transferred to a boat that took us offshore to St Anne's Island, where we spent a couple of nights. I had found my beautiful beaches at last, dotted with giant granite boulders — a stunning place, perfect for a hideaway escape. I remember celebrating my birthday whilst on the island and enjoying a hosted barbeque, sitting at a long table on the beach with my colleagues — a far cry from my normal working day, sitting alone in my office.

We explored Victoria, the capital named after Queen Victoria, and as it is reasonably small, it was easy to explore on foot. We watched people ply their trade in the colourful central market, reminiscent of the Caribbean. Driving to our next hotel, the Banyan Tree, I noticed many huntsman spiders' webs on the top of the telegraph poles and along the telegraph wires. I was so glad I was in a minibus! Arriving at the Banyan Tree we walked out to see the beach and I can tell you it is jaw-droppingly beautiful. The dazzling white sand edges a deep turquoise blue ocean. I could have stayed watching this beautiful scene for hours, but we had to get ready for a Thai dinner with the hotel manager, which ranked as one of the best Thai meals I have eaten.

We next headed to the airport to board a light aircraft to an eco-island called Frégate Island. This really was a hideaway, even landing on a grass airstrip. There were no cars, so to get around we used golf carts, sharing one cart per private villa. My colleague Sue was my driver, who said that with me as her passenger, it was just like *Driving Miss Daisy*. Our villas were gorgeous, with thatched roofs, each one set behind a private gate, looking out to the sea. Each villa had a separate lounge, and then across a small courtyard to a separate thatched rondel where the bedroom and bathrooms were located. There was an additional private outdoor shower and a plunge pool. We had a few hours to relax so I took the chance to use the plunge pool. One of my colleagues did the same from her villa and had turned up the volume of the music system from her lounge so she could hear it in the plunge pool. Unfortunately, the rest of the villas in the resort could also hear the music and a paying guest complained about the noise. Oops! This exclusive hideaway had guests who had paid an awful lot of money for some peace and quiet, and within an hour of our arrival that peace had been shattered. With apologies made; the music was turned down.

We had to drive to the main building for our meals in the golf buggy, but not before driving around the island to explore the beaches, coves, forested areas, and interior. Bearing in mind this was classed as a self-sufficient eco island, we crunched over an awful lot of millipedes in our golf buggy, so we felt a bit guilty about committing wildlife murder. Part of the island interior was used as a film set for *Jurassic Park*, and we really could imagine dinosaurs roaming free millions of years ago. Near the main building of the hotel, we met the giant tortoises that roamed free. They can move surprisingly fast and kept following us. There was a lot of wildlife on the island, from stubby lizards in the thatched ceiling above my bed, to more millipedes found by my shoes in the wardrobe, to the enormous fruit bats that appeared when it got dark, (thankfully not in my room!) and the air was filled with the smell of their guano. Pretty birds such as fairy terns flew overhead.

The next morning, we all met for breakfast and were shown to a long table for our group, which was set up alongside the open windows and a verandah beyond. The table was laden with breads and fruit, and everything we needed for a healthy breakfast. There were a couple of other tables for two with guests enjoying a quiet breakfast. Our table was a magnet for the smaller birds, and they kept landing on the bread and trying to take chunks of it away. One of my colleagues, Andrew, tied a knot at the corner of his napkin and flicked the birds away. Unfortunately, he knocked one unconscious, and it landed legs up on the table. OMG, bird murderer! He became known as the Bird Twatter. We had been on the island for less than twenty-four hours and had killed a bird, squashed millipedes, been chased by a giant tortoise and disturbed the paying guests. I think the hosts were glad to see the back of us!

One final excursion we enjoyed in the Seychelles was a trip out on a boat which could be hired for overnight stays and island hopping. On board were a variety of activities to enjoy. We needed to record a video to send to our head office which would be broadcast to the rest of the staff. We thought a story board showcasing the activities onboard would be a fun thing to record. Whilst one of us did the commentary, Andrew boarded a kayak and started paddling away from the boat. There was a pirate's swing rope that another colleague swung out on and dropped down into the sea. Snorkellers had their heads down in the water, while the commentator told the story of the escape of the Bird Twatter, closely followed in hot pursuit by the pirate, with the snorkellers following on. It made us all laugh, although I am sure no one at head office had any idea what we were doing! That trip was one of the best. We all bonded and have all remained friends to this day and poor Andrew is still being reminded of his murderous moment.

Moments in Mauritius

Mauritius is another destination that I have visited a few times - on an educational and a couple of Gold Travel Counsellors' conferences. I use the word conference very loosely, as these trips were basically a big thank you from our head office and sponsored by a selection of companies that we worked closely with. They all took a similar form in that our partners were invited to join us at a cost, but at a much lower rate than they would pay if booking themselves. The reason other halves were invited was because head office wanted to acknowledge that working from home would not always be possible without the support and consideration from the family.

Unlike working in an office, you cannot leave work at the front door. Many a time I have been about to do something with the family when I have had stop what I was doing and had to make a work call or sort something out on my computer. I have been on the phone to the USA while on route to friends for dinner (husband driving!), and then while he went inside their home, I stayed in the car until the issue was sorted. We have been in supermarkets doing our weekly shop, away on holiday, travelling to see a show or band at the theatre, when a flight amendment or urgent booking would come through that really could not wait, so I would disappear and have that conversation with my client.

I think the partners really enjoyed meeting up with others and becoming friends on these Gold trips. The first trips started off with about fifty people in the group, but nowadays they split the group and give us a choice of two different trips because there are many more that have reached the criteria of becoming a Gold Travel Counsellor, based on the level of commission we have earned in a year.

My first visit to Mauritius was an educational, with only a handful of colleagues. We stayed in a few resorts and visited hotels on both sides of the island. It was at Le Touessroc on the east coast that I had my first experience of having my own butler. We were all allocated our own sumptuous villa, with a free-standing bath at one end and an enormous bed with Egyptian cotton bedding and views beyond to the turquoise sea and reef in the distance. Knowing we were staying at this luxurious resort for a couple of nights, I had packed some smart dresses, ready for the hosted evening meals.

When I was shown to my villa and my suitcase brought in, my butler asked if he could unpack my case for me. This girl was brought up on a council estate in Southampton, and the thought of someone rifling through my big M&S pants and well-worn underwear made me wince. So, I politely declined and said I could manage myself thank you very much. Not the best decision I made because when I did unpack, I found that the dresses I had thought about wearing were both creased. Not wanting to bother the butler and get them pressed, I had the bright idea of hanging them up in the shower and kill two birds with one stone. The steam from my shower would drop the creases. Job done! It did not quite work out that way though because mid shower both hangers holding the dresses fell off the hook that I had lodged them on and straight into the shower tray, that was wet through. So now I had two soaked dresses and nothing to wear. I had a rummage in my case and found some trousers and a smart top that would have to do. I was a bit underdressed for the occasion and really wished I had let the butler do his job, and instead had taken a long soak with bubbles in that lovely deep bath. Whilst at dinner, I noticed the waiter put a napkin over my jacket that I had hung over the back of my chair to protect it from any spillages. I have never seen that since in any hotel, it was that posh!

We also stayed on the other side of the island at the Sugar Beach Hotel, a colonial style resort with enormous palm trees on the lawn leading down to the beach. I felt like I had stepped back in time and half expected to see crinoline-gowned ladies with parasols taking a stroll. Linked by a walkway, the Sugar Beach led us to a more traditional thatched-roof resort called La Pirogue. This was one of the hotels I had swooned over when looking at the exotic locations in brochures many years before, so I loved seeing the actual resort with its unusual shaped thatched roofs.

On my next visit we stayed further south on our Gold Travel Counsellors weekend. Yet another beautiful resort hugging the southwest corner of the island. We explored more of the interior, which is mostly covered in sugar cane, and is quite hilly in places. We saw coffee bushes ready to be harvested and visited an area called Chamarel where we could see seven different coloured sands in a striped formation, a sort of Alum Bay (Isle of Wight) of the Indian Ocean. It was most unusual seeing red, brown, violet, green, blue, purple and yellow sand all banded together in wavy layers.

Port Louis, the capital, is typical of many island capitals. Like Victoria in the Seychelles, it reminded me of the main towns on the Caribbean islands with its colourful concrete low-rise buildings, many corrugated roofs, dusty shop fronts and an air of poverty. Tourism is one of the main industries in Mauritius and most people would visit for the water sports, diving and wonderful beaches. A year-round destination, anyone who wanted a peaceful paradise wouldn't go far wrong, although unlike my aforementioned deceased surgeon, it's important to choose the right side of the island for the time of year being travelled. Trade winds affect rainfall, and the temperatures and humidity do vary depending on the time of year.

My last visit to Mauritius was in 2019, when 100 Gold Travel Counsellors and some of their partners, together with sponsors and head office directors were guests of Beachcomber Holidays. They pulled out all the stops out for us at the Troux aux Biches Resort in the northwest of the island, the highlight being a day long pool party. All around the pool were bean bags, large tubs full of ice-cold drinks, tables of wine and spirits where we could just help ourselves, and several stalls with barbecue and finger food, spicy treats and desserts. The pool was filled with inflatables and music played throughout the day. It was a time to relax and get to know other colleagues, meet with those who had become friends, and enjoy the beautiful surroundings. I cannot think of any other company who appreciate the hard work of their staff and reward them with the type of trips and experiences that we have enjoyed.

A Glittering prize in the Gambia

Given the number of people who attend our annual conference, I would be extremely lucky to win one of the prizes donated by one of our suppliers. One year though, my name was pulled out and I won a holiday for two to The Gambia, just perfect for a winter destination. By the end of January, I was more than ready to have a break from my rabbit in the headlights, headless chicken existence. That time of year is always hectic workwise, so I really looked forward to some winter sunshine, a good hotel and maybe a bit of exploration.

The six-hour nonstop charter flight arrived mid-afternoon. As Gambia is in the same time zone as Britain, there was no need to adjust our watches. It was lovely stepping out in the warm air, dressed in summer clothing. Immigration was a breeze, but slightly chaotic collecting our bags. Who knew it was OK to walk across the baggage conveyor belt?

We had about a forty five minute drive, through the capital Banjul to our resort, passing half-built buildings, corrugated roofs on shacks, goats, donkeys and colourful locals going about their business. I noticed how lovely the ladies were, dressed in their traditional brightly coloured dresses with matching headwear. Clearly still a developing country, Gambia's people struck me as the happiest I have seen on my travels. We passed people selling fruit and local crafts by the dusty roadside.

Our hotel, the Ngala Lodge, was an oasis of calm set in beautiful, but somewhat quirky, gardens. We were greeted by Jonathan the English manager who welcomed us with a local juice drink called Wonjo, made from sorrel berries.

All the rooms were decorated in a different, but distinctly African style. We had beautiful views from our balcony overlooking the gardens, which had odd, bizarre statues and works of art in random places dotted around. It certainly made the place memorable.

There were many repeat guests, returning because of the relaxed ambiance, and wonderful staff who clearly loved their jobs. Each staff member remembered guests' names and I was particularly touched by the fact that the pool lad got our sunbeds ready for us in advance, without us knowing. Jonathan was right when he said the hotel was all about good service. Food in the restaurant was excellent and frequented by outside guests too, a measure of a good restaurant in my book.

We took a day trip into neighbouring Senegal to visit the Wildlife Reserve at Fathala. To get there we rose at dawn, (not that early, as sunrise was about seven a.m.), drove back to Banjul and took the local ferry across the River Gambia to the north shore at Barra. The ferry crossing alone was an eye opener, with a jumble of cars, trucks, people, babies and goats. We had to be careful not to have any valuables on show as tourists are targets for the local traders. The crossing took about forty minutes, as we watched the sunrise. Then we boarded an open truck and travelled to the Senegalese border, about thirty minutes away. The roads were good and straight, although very dusty. We passed waving children, more animals and more run-down shacks on the way. The border crossing was a busy place where locals had set up their wares alongside children asking for money, empty water bottles and anything they could sell on. No one was aggressive, and it all felt safe. We had to show our passports and yellow fever certificates at the border and were asked our occupations. I told them I was a travel agent, but it was clear they did not have a clue what that was!

On arrival at the wildlife reserve, we were soon rewarded with views of zebras, rhino, warthogs, giraffe and various antelope species, a beautiful bright blue bird, and a couple of monkeys. Some were well camouflaged in the dry long grass but everyone onboard had their eyes peeled. All in all, a good trip to break up the week, and a vast improvement on my animal viewing success rate from a Zambian visit some years earlier.

A Quick stop in Kalkan

Even a short trip away to experience the culture of a country helps when selling. I had heard much about Kalkan in Turkey and was interested in sampling it myself. One of the companies that sold holidays there invited a small group of us for a few days away to see the accommodation they offered and generally get a feel for what to expect. I thought this whole area in the southwest of Turkey was very scenic, with little rocky coves and pretty villages and crystal clear azure seas— just the thing for a relaxing break away. We visited a handful of pretty villas and had lunch by the harbour front, enjoying the local cuisine, including freshly caught fish.

Kalkan and nearby Kas had the sort of narrow streets you just wanted to wander along lined with tiny artisan shops, and with bougainvillea tumbling over whitewashed balconies. The only thing that nearly killed me was the walk back to our accommodation up the aptly named Cardiac Hill. I had to walk up backwards; it was that steep! That particular trip to Kalkan was short and sweet, but I saw enough to be able to sell it confidently.

Sampling a River Cruise

Not all my trips were a long way from home. I was once invited to look around a new river cruiser that was about to sail from Cologne. I had to fly to Dusseldorf, where I would be met, and driven to the River Rhine in Cologne, in the centre of the city, where the riverboat was moored. My flight and transfer were smooth, and I enjoyed a lovely lunch on board the cruiser after being shown around the cabins. Sitting up on the sun deck after lunch, we watched as new guests began to arrive for their trip. Most people were couples in their senior years, which was interesting to note, as I have a clientele who would enjoy this experience. The riverboat would be sailing down the Rhine, stopping at towns along the way, and mooring close to their centres, making it is easy to explore each place.

Sadly, I was only invited to look around the riverboat, so had to disembark, and be taken back to Dusseldorf for my flight home. Unfortunately, we hit the rush hour and our short transfer turned into a much longer one. Time was marching on, and it looked like I would miss the flight. With only hand luggage, I dashed to check in, jumped the queue at security, (my A-level German came in handy: *'Entschuldigung sie bitte!')*, and boarded the flight with minutes to spare.

I came away from that short visit thinking I might enjoy a river cruise in the future, but it would have to be with friends. For myself, there wasn't enough to do in the evening, apart from enjoying an evening meal and having a drink at the bar. With friends it could be more enjoyable, and I thought at the time it would be a few years before I set foot again on a river cruiser, but I was wrong.

It was announced that one of our Gold Travel Counsellors' trips would be on the *Scenic Jewel*, for a short cruise along the Danube between Budapest and Vienna. I jumped at the chance because they are cities I had never visited, and I would be amongst many friends onboard the ship. The riverboat was moored on the Danube almost opposite the Hungarian Parliament Building, a notable landmark and the largest building in Hungary. This was in the month of October, so it grew dark early, but it meant we saw that magnificent building beautifully lit up. There were numerous buildings in this area along the river that combine to make Budapest a World Heritage site. These include Buda Castle which sits at the southern tip of Castle Hill. Close by were the Szechenyi Chain Bridge, the first permanent crossing over the river that links Buda and Pest, Matthias Church and the Liberty Statue, holding a large, sculpted feather aloft. Budapest is one city I will return to one day to explore further.

Pausing along the Danube to restock the bar, as we had drunk them dry, we continued to Vienna, passing through the huge Freudenau Locks, one of ten locks on this section of the Danube. Living near the Thames, I have often watched from above the smaller pleasure boats and barges make their way through the locks, but I have never been down below within the lock itself. So, making our way through this larger lock system on the Danube was both entertaining and fascinating to see how it all worked from the 'inside'.

Arriving in Vienna, we headed ashore for a short taster of the city. Vienna was designated a UNESCO World Heritage Site in 2001 in recognition of its varied and historic architecture. The grand boulevard ring road, surrounding the old historical city centre of Vienna, is called the Innere Stadt. It was around this road that we passed numerous fine buildings that would not look out of place in Paris. Some were five or six storeys high, with many windows surrounded by intricately carved columns and filigree styled railings on the balconies. It all looked very grand. Tram lines criss-crossed the streets, providing an alternative way to travel, passing monuments and parks. We headed to one of the grandest buildings of them all, the Schönbrunn Palace. This was the former summer residence of successive Habsburg monarchs and was built between 1742 and 1760 with over 1400 rooms. The bit I remember most of all is that a young Mozart, aged just six years old played his first concerts here for the royal family in 1762, while Haydn went there as a choirboy to take part in a musical production. A nice gig if you can get it. We only caught a glimpse of everything there is to see in Vienna, but from the little I have seen, I think it is worth a return visit some time.

Weekends Away

Not long after I had joined British Airways, the company came up with the idea that all frontline staff selling flights should experience the onboard flight service, so we were all given a ticket to literally anywhere of our choosing. The criteria they gave us was that we could only travel on flights that had spare seats and that we had to travel out on a Friday and be back at work Monday morning. Most of my colleagues opted to travel to somewhere in Europe, on a short flight, giving them a couple of nights away, but I always liked to be different to others, so along with three colleagues, decided to fly as far as we could to somewhere we had never been.

Looking at various options, we decided we would fly to Bermuda for the weekend. We thought it would be lovely and hot, not realising that as we were travelling in November, the weather was not that warm, being much further north than the Caribbean. Our VC10 left London one Friday morning and arrived in Bermuda just after lunch, their time. We had not booked anywhere to stay so we headed to the hotel desk at the airport on arrival and they suggested a hotel in Flatts Inlet. We had no idea where that was but just went along with that idea. We only needed the Friday night there because the return flight home left Bermuda at midnight on the Saturday night, arriving mid-afternoon in London on Sunday, back in time for work on Monday! The Palmetto Bay Hotel was fine, sharing a room, to keep the cost down. The next day we awoke to rain, so we decided to hire pushbikes to explore the small island. Bermuda Airport is at the eastern end of the island and Flatts Inlet is to the west of it on the way to the capital Hamilton.

Our hired bikes arrived, which I think were built in the 1950s, as they were solid and heavy, probably made from iron, and without gears. One of my friends had never ridden a bike before but was up for the challenge. The old saying is true that you never forget how to ride a bike because for the first time in about ten years, I mounted my bike and set off without so much as a wobble. Poor Heather, who was the bike novice, wobbled, fell off, got back on, more wobbling, and gradually got used to riding. She did not use the brakes and would slow down by scraping her toe caps on the ground, ruining her shoes, and getting bruised and battered in the process. We did make progress though and cycled past some beautiful pink beaches, eventually arriving at Hamilton. We spent a few wet hours wandering around the town and enjoyed seeing the smart policemen in their white Bermuda shorts directing the traffic. We cycled back to the hotel, picked up our overnight bags and headed back to the airport. The whole weekend cost us the princely sum of £17 each!

I would often have a few days holiday to use up at the end of March, so we would often fly standby on short flights and explore places closer to home. A favourite trip was to pop over to Jersey, hire a car and drive around the island. Sometimes it could be a bit risky travelling in March as it was often foggy. On one occasion we took off from Heathrow and headed to Jersey, where we circled over the island for some time, because of thick fog. Eventually, we flew back to Heathrow, went home, and tried again the next day, this time with more success. In those early years, we often asked if it was possible to go up to the flight deck and sit in the jump seat in order to watch the descents and landings. This is one of the treats my husband in particular misses now that there is tighter security when travelling. He has fond memories of watching the take-off and landing from the cockpit of an airliner whilst travelling to Jersey. And he also says the highlight of our honeymoon to Thailand was doing the same in a Tristar, whilst I sat alone up the back. The highlight? Really? Thanks.

We bought our wedding rings in Jersey, taking advantage of the tax-free prices. We loved the beaches, especially the wild northern coast which reminded me of north Cornwall, as well as the pretty interior of the island. One moment that has stuck in my memory is a walk we took in the north of Jersey. We climbed down the rocky path to the shore and had a wander, and then slowly made our way back up to the cliff top. There was a pub at the top and we looked forward to some refreshment after the strenuous climb. As we approached the pub, we heard some unfamiliar music. Whatever it was sounded fantastic, and we both wanted to hear more. The pub was shut to customers because it was too early in the day, but that did not stop us. We needed to hear more of the music. We knocked on the door and asked if they would serve us a couple of coffees, which they kindly agreed to. We were able to enjoy the rest of the track in question and asked who was playing. It turned out the band was Genesis. I was mesmerised by the sound, which touched my soul. That unforgettable track is still one of my favourites and I still get the same feeling when I hear it. Since that moment we have become massive fans of the band, having bought all their albums and seen them perform live several times. If we had not decided to stop and do the cliff walk, we may never have discovered this awesome band. We have driven all around Jersey numerous times over the years and love the contrasting sandy south coast and the rugged north coast, along with the pretty villages, amid rolling inland scenery, while World War Two fortifications and buildings show a darker side in the history of Jersey.

One of the routes we often booked for customers was a train trip from Cologne to Frankfurt. What fascinated me was that this train was booked as a flight, on an air ticket, complete with a Lufthansa flight number. The route followed the River Rhine, so I thought it would be a fun day out to fly to Cologne, have a quick explore around the cathedral and area and then get that train to Frankfurt. It worked a treat, and as the river wound its way south, we particularly enjoyed the scenic views from the train, especially past the Lorelei, a steep slate rock topped with an amphitheatre. We were not able to stop for any length of time in Frankfurt so instead made our way to the airport for the return flight home.

Another short break in March was a quick trip to Amsterdam. I had to hold the map upside down with my finger on our location so that we did not get lost, as all the canal lined streets looked the same. We found our way to the Rijksmuseum where we were fascinated by Rembrandt's famous 'Night Watch'. We then visited a diamond factory where we learnt all about the 4 Cs of a diamond: cut, clarity, colour and carat, ending the visit with a purchase of two small perfect diamonds which we had designed into a ring on our return home. Another excursion to the nearby villages of Volendam and Marken showed us authentic Dutch architecture.

We enjoyed a day trip to Paris, getting the earliest flight out and the latest flight back. We walked our socks off, having first viewed the city from the top of the Eiffel Tower and then walked along the Seine via the Arc de Triomphe, to the Louvre and Notre Dame, before ending up at Sacre Coeur. Finally, we headed to a station to catch the train back to the airport. We struggled to get though the ticket barrier, which would not open, to get onto the platform. So I went to the ticket booth and in my best schoolgirl French said, *'Il n'oublie pas'*. This was met with a puzzled look from the ticket clerk, which I took to be completely unhelpful. Knowing the French are not exactly forthcoming when it comes to the English. I repeated it a bit louder. (That always works doesn't it.) *'Il n'oublie pas.'* I was getting more and more frustrated at the lack of help, so with a heavy sigh, we headed back to the barrier and forced our way over, as time was getting on, and it looked like we might arrive at the airport too late.

The train took an age to arrive, but eventually we arrived at Charles de Gaulle airport. By then I was in a complete panic because the flight was about to close boarding and there wasn't another that day if we missed it. I had not realised just how big the terminal was and it seemed to take an age rushing to the boarding gate, eventually arriving completely out of breath and the last to board. I cannot tell you how welcoming the steward's voice was, calmly greeting us at the door. It was only when we were seated on board and I thought about what I had said to the rail ticket clerk that I realised I had said, *'He does not forget'*. No wonder the guy looked at me strangely! I thought I was saying *'It will not open!' (Il n'ouvre pas)*. No wonder I only got an E in my GCE O level!

Of course, weekends away were not confined to Europe and we did manage a few long weekends across the pond. New York was a favourite with the family, and we visited a couple of times. We stayed close to Times Square, where we really got the feeling that the city never sleeps, as the saying goes. When darkness fell, the neon-lit adverts brightened the skies enough for it to feel like it was still daylight. Broadway was buzzing, and all the shops and theatres looked inviting. First though, after arriving during the afternoon, we checked in at our hotel and walked a few blocks south to the Empire State Building, arriving there just as it was beginning to grow dark. That way we had views from the top, 103 floors up, during daylight while gradually watching the skies turn to dusk, with the city coming to life for the evening. We could see the Statue of Liberty in the far distance to the south and the Chrysler Building with its Art Deco facades to the north. The East River and the borough of Queens were just beyond in the east with the Hudson River and Manhattan to the west.

The Empire State Building is a great place to get an appreciation of the overall perspective of this bustling metropolis.

It was possible to walk from our hotel to the Hudson River and climb aboard the USS *Intrepid*, a large aircraft carrier which houses an Air and Space Museum. We went mainly to please my husband, but it was interesting because they had a Concorde on deck, as well as numerous helicopters, military jets and a space shuttle. A few minutes further down the Hudson we boarded a boat that took us down to the tip of Manhattan, and around to the East River passing under Brooklyn Bridge, before turning round and returning to our jetty. From the river we had great views of the Manhattan skyline, picking out iconic buildings as we sailed past, such as the One World Trade Centre, the Statue of Liberty, and Ellis Island.

From Times Square we bought multi-day tickets for the hop-on-hop-off bus and used this means of transport to explore the rest of Manhattan, planning our days carefully so we did not miss anything out. We made our first stop on the bus close to the 9/11 Museum and Peace Garden. The museum was beautifully laid out and took us on a journey of that fateful day. Seeing the mangled fire trucks really brought it home. This sombre feeling continued outside in the Peace Garden, where the original twin towers have been replaced by two reflecting pools. The edges of the pools have been inscribed with the names of those who lost their lives. We also had timed tickets to go to the observation deck in the One World Trade Centre tower, but the view was blocked by low cloud, so we took a rain check for the following day. When we returned, we rapidly ascended the One World Trade Centre, with our ears popping, to the top of the 1776ft high structure, where we were afforded fantastic views of the southern end of Manhattan. We could see across to Staten Island and the lonely Statue of Liberty on its own island, and next to it Ellis Island, where thousands arrived from all around the world throughout the twentieth century to start a new life.

The walk from the World Trade Centre to Battery Point on the southern tip of Manhattan was not too far and it was from there we took a ferry across to Liberty and Ellis Islands. On reflection the Statue of Liberty was just as visible without going ashore. We could have gone on the free Staten Island ferry and still had great views. However, I think Ellis Island was worth a stop, as the National Museum of Immigration History was housed in the original colonial style building and it was easy to imagine what it would have been like in the vast immigration hall, where thousands would have queued to be admitted into America.

We walked from Battery Point, past Wall Street in the Financial District, to Pier 17 on the East River where we were able to buy discounted theatre tickets for that evening, without having to queue. Not the easiest place to find, as it is tucked away across the road from the pier, next to a children's park. Otherwise, the same 'TKTS' booth can be found at Times Square, but it is usually much busier there. We bought tickets to see a show on Broadway for that evening, and excellent stall seats we had too.

The following day, we explored the area to the north of Times Square. Our hop-on-hop-off bus took us up around Central Park, passing the Dakota Building where John Lennon was murdered, and on up to the top end of Central Park to Harlem. Here we passed the famous Apollo Theatre, where groups such as the Jackson Five played, and then continued down the eastern side of the Central Park, along Park Avenue, passing the Metropolitan and Guggenheim Museums.

Central Park is a vast green oasis in the middle of bustling Manhattan, covering over 843 acres, so it was great to escape the traffic and noise while we wandered around the park. As it was a Saturday, there were many families out at play. We passed artists with their easels set to capture a pretty scene. There were ball games, picnics, street dancers, roller skaters, people in rowing boats, others riding bikes and a few bridal groups having photos taken. It was all very pleasant. We found Strawberry Fields and an Alice in Wonderland sculpture too. Back amongst the buzz of the city, we headed to the Top of the Rock at the Rockefeller Centre to give us a final view of the city from the upper end of Manhattan, with the Chrysler Building to the south of us and the Empire State Building beyond, and Central Park in the other direction. We watched the sun set, and Manhattan slowly light up for the evening.

Our last day started off extremely wet, so we decided to keep to indoor activities. First stop was Madame Tussauds, sitting at the President's desk for a quick photo, and seeing numerous famous American faces. It was the nearest I was ever going to get to Johnny Depp and he didn't utter a word! Our next stop was a tour of Radio City Music Hall. This beautiful Art Deco building has bags of history with the interior still as it was when it opened in 1932. The domed auditorium seats a capacity audience of 6,000 and has seen many famous acts perform there over the years.

It was then time to head back to our hotel to meet our pre-booked taxi. Unfortunately, I think the hotel desk must have called Uber, as the driver, who arrived to take us back to JFK Airport, used her mobile as a satnav and for some reason we ended up having a detour around Queens, which was surprisingly nice! I am not sure she knew where she was driving but our hour-long trip took us nearer two hours, so we had to dash to check in, fortunately making it in time, but it was touch and go. Not really the time to get lost. What is it with airports and trying to get there in time? Memories of Paris and Dusseldorf came flooding back!

***

While I worked at the local travel agency, an offer to stay at the landmark Willard Intercontinental Hotel in Washington DC was made available. It was an offer too good to miss, so, leaving our six-month-old daughter with her doting grandparents, we headed off for three nights to explore the capital of the USA. I love Washington, with its grid layout, and its numerous iconic statues and memorials. It is such an easy city to explore, with the most famous buildings within 'viewing' distance of each other. Our hotel was close to the White House, so we had an easy stroll to the President's pad, viewing the exterior through the railings. This was well before 9/11, and security was not as tight as it probably is nowadays.

Across the road from the rear of the White House, it was an easy walk to the Washington Monument. Heading up to the viewing platform at the top, we had great aerial views of the city. In one direction, stood the domed Capitol Building at the end of a long wide grassed mall, with the various museums of the Smithsonian group along each side. In another direction was the neoclassical Lincoln Memorial, looking towards the White House, with the Potomac River beyond, and the rectangular reflecting pool in front of the memorial. We could see the Jefferson Memorial, looking remarkably like the Pantheon in Rome, at the Tidal Basin. Such a clear view of four iconic buildings from the top of another. The obelisk shaped Washington Monument sat on top of raised parkland and was surrounded by American flags representing the fifty states.

Having got our bearings, we explored further in all four directions, and particularly loved the Lincoln Memorial, with the great man seated behind the Doric columns, looking out beyond the Reflecting Pool to the Washington Monument and beyond. It would not be a holiday without seeing some military aircraft, so we had to head into the Museum of Air and Space along the National Mall, one of the museums here that collectively make up the Smithsonian. Seeing how flight developed, with examples of early aircraft right up to the lunar modules from the NASA space missions, showed just how far aviation has come in less than one hundred years.

Continuing along the Mall brought us to the Capitol Building, which dominated the skyline. We were able to go inside and see the interior of the massive dome. Given the architecture we could have been in Rome. Next stop was the National Archives Museum to view the Declaration of Independence, although we were not permitted to take any photographs of this historic document.

To travel beyond the central area, we used the hop-on-hop-off trolley bus, as this was the easiest way to see everything that Washington DC had to offer. Across the Potomac river we stopped at the Arlington Cemetery pausing to view the eternal flame that shines for John F Kennedy. Also here is the Iwo Jima War Memorial honouring the US marines who fought in Japan during WW2. Then we headed back across the river to the Vietnam Memorial Wall, with its inscriptions of the thousands of those that had given their lives, which I found very sobering. Georgetown was one of the nicer suburbs of the capital, with charming shops, and federal style architecture. I thought it would be a good place to stay as an alternative to accommodation in the centre of the city. The area has bags of character and is quite different to the central DC area. Having been to four major cities in the US, I can say that each one has something different to offer, and all have their own charm. It's difficult to say which I prefer, but if forced, I think Washington would be my favourite.

Exploring the Wider World
Six go to Florida

My first long journey happened about a year after I joined British Airways. Along with five other colleagues we flew on standby to Miami with the plan to spend a week in and around Orlando. At that time, when I would have been about twenty years old, it was not possible to fly direct to Orlando. One thing I remember vividly is the sun setting in Miami not long after we landed. I had never seen the sun so big. I suppose it was because we were much further south and nearer the equator than in the UK.

We had arranged to hire a car and drive the four hours north to our accommodation, but the only person who had a driving licence then was my friend Teresa who normally drove a mini. To fit us all in with our luggage, we hired a station wagon, which sat three of us in the front and three in the back. Bearing in mind we were five hours behind the UK, our body clocks felt like it was midnight. We only had the one driver, who had never driven on the other side of the road, had never driven an automatic, and felt like she was driving a bus, so we decided she should have a practise in the car park before tackling the highways. It must have looked comical driving round and round the car park before having enough confidence to take the plunge and start the journey. Amazingly, we did not get lost. (I wonder if my Majorca skills at navigation came into play!) Teresa stayed awake, probably because we chatted all the way, and we eventually arrived at our motel in Cocoa Beach on the Atlantic coast of Florida some four hours later. I had never stayed in a motel before, and it seemed strange parking right outside our rooms, just like the movies! We had us four girls in one room and the two fellas next door.

We spent the week exploring, driving north to Cape Canaveral one day and to visit the Kennedy Space Centre, where only ten years earlier the Apollo mission to the land on the moon had taken place. Another day we headed west to Orlando and to see Disneyworld. At that time, it only had Main Street with Sleeping Beauty's castle at the end of it, and beyond that, a few themed 'lands'. The most futuristic of these was

Space Mountain in Tomorrowland, a stomach-churning rollercoaster, mainly in the dark, supposedly in 'Space'. (Note to self: Do not eat a burger before trying these rides!) Elsewhere on another gentler ride, we heard the annoyingly repetitive tune, 'It's a Small World', whilst gliding along in a small boat passing dancing and singing animated dolls dressed in national costumes from around the world. If you have been, you will now have that tune going around in your head. You're welcome!

In Adventureland, Pirates of the Caribbean was one of my favourite rides, and I remember thinking how sophisticated the animatronic characters were compared to what we had at home. These all moved and sang! The only other 'land' was Frontierland, which was themed around the Gold Rush. Epcot, Animal Kingdom, Universal Studios and all of their themed rides had not been built at that time. Disneyland Paris, or Euro Disney as it was first known, did not exist either. My first experience of the USA was a very positive one. Eating burgers, the massive portions of food and two dollars to the pound, were all really good value. This was the first of many visits to Florida, and no ESTA paperwork to worry about!

We have returned to Florida over the years for various family holidays as our girls were growing up. Always big fans of Disney, I felt the need to return with them to Disneyworld, Orlando when the new parks opened, along with Universal Studios a few miles up Highway 4. On one of these trips, we were travelling with a friend and her family as I had found some bargain air tickets which were sold at winter prices, yet we were travelling in the summer school holidays. I had booked a hire car for each family as we had not planned to spend the whole holiday together instead meeting up for the occasional dinner and exchange of experiences. When we were collecting our cars, we stood next to each other at the desk, so I could hear what the car hire agent was saying to my friend. I always include everything when I quote for car hire, including full insurance, so that there are no hidden surprises when the car is collected. The guy on the car hire desk was telling my friend that this wasn't included, and that wasn't included, and they needed to pay extra for insurances.

I pricked up my ears, when I heard him say, 'Your travel agent hasn't sold you the right thing.' Bloody cheek! Excuse me! I think he was a bit shocked when I leaned over and interrupted his flow, telling him, that I, in fact, was the travel agent, and knew exactly what I had sold, which was the same as I was getting for my family. I enjoyed seeing him back down, but I wonder how many unsuspecting travellers fell for his bullshit and paid unnecessary supplements.

We have explored the southern area of Florida too, spending time on Marco Island on the west coast. From here we headed out to experience the Everglades on one of those air cushion boats with an enormous fan on the back powering us through the water in search of alligators. In this southern part of the state, we were able to see docile manatees equally happy in both freshwater lakes and salt waters. It was on this trip we had time to spend in the shallow waters on the Gulf of Mexico. However, having only been used to the freezing waters of the Solent and English Channel, the sea around Marco Island was so warm it was uncomfortable. Although I do prefer to walk straight into the sea, without shivering while bracing myself to dip my shoulders under the water, this was at another level. It was too warm! Whilst there, we experienced rain like nothing we had seen before. One evening we could see large black clouds building around Marco Island. Deciding to have an early dinner, we returned to our apartment just as the first large drops of rain began to fall. We were able to watch the storm from our balcony, and soon it was hammering down, so heavy that car alarms were set off. With thunder and lightning all around us, the noise echoed and bounced around the high rises together with rivers of rain pouring down the streets. Then as quickly as it had begun, the rain stopped and within minutes the pavements were dry. I just loved that.

Family time in Zambia and Bahrain

Back in the late seventies my uncle and aunt lived in Zambia, working and living the expat lifestyle. While I was still single, I was able to include my parents on my travel concessions. My mother had not then had the opportunity to travel abroad before. When the international travel boom started in the late sixties/ early seventies, we were still having family holidays along the south coast of England. My father's MS had affected the family's ability to explore places further afield, with finances and logistics making it difficult to travel. So, it gave me great pleasure to be able to suggest that I took my mother to visit her brother in Zambia using my travel concessions. Not only would it give her a complete break from the stress of caring for my father, but it would also allow her to see her brother and his wife while broadening both our horizons visiting somewhere so alien to us.

The direct flight from London was with British Caledonian departing from Gatwick Airport. As I lived nearer to Heathrow at that time, I took the opportunity to fly us on the BCAL helicopter service that operated between Heathrow and Gatwick. This was a short-lived service, so I am pleased we had the chance to sample it. I remember it being very noisy!

We arrived at Lusaka Airport and were met by my uncle wearing shorts, which struck me as a novelty, as men did not tend to wear those in October in the UK. Apparently, he went to work in them too! We drove to his bungalow arriving about an hour before the sun set promptly at six p.m. like a bullet. After the initial greetings and hugs, my uncle showed us to our bedroom.

The very first thing I noticed was an *enormous* spider on the wall opposite the bed, sitting just above a wall vent. It might have been a huntsman, but it was as big as a child's hand. My one phobia throughout my life was a fear of spiders. This stemmed from when I was about six years old. I was sitting at our kitchen table and had been given the job of shelling some peas, which were in a brown paper bag on the table. To reach inside the bag I had to stretch my arm up and feel inside for the pea pods, as I was not tall enough to see what I was doing. I remember feeling something in the bag that didn't feel like a pea pod but didn't think anything of it. It was only a few seconds later I realised what it was when I saw a large house spider on my lap and running up my torso towards my head. I screamed the house down and must have given my father a heart attack; he dashed downstairs to see if I was being murdered.

Anyway, seeing this monster in our bedroom in Zambia filled me with dread. I could not sleep in the room with it looking at me, so I mentioned my fear to my uncle. Always a tease, my uncle laughed and said not to worry they only come out of the vents when it gets dark and banged on the wall to frighten it so that it would shoot back into the vent. Unfortunately, his action made it scuttle in the wrong direction, and headed straight under the bed, and it did not come out. So, my first night in Zambia was spent imagining my new enemy crawling out from under the bed and onto the covers. Indeed, for the next six months, I would often wake up with a start thinking a large spider was hanging just above my face, it all seemed so real. Logically a huntsman spider should be too heavy to hang from a web thread, but it did not stop me waking up in a panic.

The next day we met my uncle and aunt's houseboy (as they were called back then) and gardener. This was not a grand house with servants, but normal for expats to have 'staff'. John, who cleaned the house, lived down the garden in a little house with his family, including nine or ten children, hoping to produce a football team, no doubt. The gardener had the unusual name of Pencil. I was told that when the locals gave birth, they named their children after the first thing they saw. I wonder if he had a sister called Placenta. My aunt and uncle also had a guard that stood outside their home. I am not sure of his real name, but he was given the name of Boots by my uncle, because he only ever wore one boot. I doubt he would have been much use in an emergency. My uncle's dogs were named Boots and Toots, so I think the guard would have got very confused when the dogs were being called. Talking of footwear, my uncle told me a story of when he had left an old pair of gardening shoes outside by the back door. When he returned to clean them, they had disappeared. He asked Pencil, the gardener, if he had seen the shoes. 'No *Bwana*,' came the reply. The next day my uncle noticed him wearing the missing shoes! Roll eyes!

We explored a little whilst we were in Zambia. My uncle and aunt drove us down to Livingstone, but not without incident. We stopped along the way at a lodge in the Kafue National Park, staying overnight in a thatched roundel. My recurring spider dream woke me up with me thinking the spider was there hanging above my face. It was pitch-black in the room, so dark I could not see my hand in front of my face. There were no spiders of course. In Kafue I did learn how dangerous hippos are, although I had never really thought about that before. While on a boat trip on the Zambezi, the guide emphasised how careful we needed to be, as they can turn boats over and move at speed. The only other wildlife I saw between Lusaka and Livingstone was a dung beetle. So much for my safari experience.

We continued our journey down to Livingstone on a long hot dusty road. About thirty minutes from Livingstone, we ran out of petrol, something my uncle had been known for whilst living in Yorkshire. When getting low on fuel he would turn the engine off and coast down hills to conserve petrol and save money, but he often misjudged what was left in the tank and would run out of fuel somewhere along the way. Running out of petrol in the middle of nowhere was not the brightest idea. My uncle, forever optimistic, told us not to worry. A few minutes later he flagged down a passing truck with about twelve locals sitting in the open back of the truck. As he joined them, we wondered whether we would ever see him again. Who were the men in the back of the truck? Prisoners perhaps? We had to keep the car windows shut while we waited otherwise we would have been eaten alive by tsetse flies and mosquitos, and whilst we had taken our malaria tablets, it would be just our luck that we would be on the menu for the little critters. We also felt that three women alone might not be safe out of the car, so we melted in the stifling heat, sweat dripping off us. No air conditioning in case you are wondering. Time ticked by and there was no sign of my uncle, but eventually the truck returned, no locals in the back, but thankfully my uncle was aboard carrying a can of petrol. Apparently, the group of men he shared his journey with were in the army, heading into Livingstone. My uncle was right; we should have had more faith!

Our hotel in Livingstone, the Intercontinental, was a welcome air-conditioned relief, spending a couple of days there to see the Victoria Falls. October was the end of the dry season, so we did not see the Falls at their fullest. However, this was only the first of the many major falls I was to encounter over the years and at that time thought these were wonderful. The Zambezi river carved its way between the Zambian and Zimbabwean border and at just over 1700m wide, plunged steeply into a chasm below. We viewed Victoria Falls from the top on the Zambian side and watched it living up to its African name Mosi oa Tunya; The Smoke That Thunders.

First trip to the Middle East

Another early holiday took us to Bahrain to stay with my cousin. This was our first visit to the Middle East. From the plane we could see the vast arid landscape below, peppered with nodding donkeys and oil fields spitting occasional flashes of flame. This of course was many years before all the development we see now. Then, there was no causeway linking Saudi Arabia and no Formula 1 circuit. We stayed secure in the ex-pat community accommodation, which had high walls, with guarded front gates and were taken out and about by my cousin. On one occasion we had a barbeque out in the desert, including cold baked beans from a tin. Driving back in an open top jeep, the wind was whipping the sand up and causing havoc with my contact lenses. My eyes were streaming by the time we got back to their pad. For part of our week's stay in Bahrain we borrowed my cousin's jeep, first going to the local police station to get an international driving permit. This enabled us to explore on our own a bit, although there were some areas that were off limits. We visited the Shaikh's Beach, a private beach, owned by Shaikh Isa bin Sulman Al- Khalifa, the Emir at that time. The beach could only be used by white westerners under strict conditions, no alcohol, and no photography. We did see the man himself briefly, who was only about 5ft 2ins. It was in Bahrain when we heard the calling to prayer at dawn for the first time. A minaret, complete with loudspeakers was only 100m or so along the road from where we were staying, and the noise woke us with a start; about 5.30am! We wondered what on earth the wailing was, but we soon got used to it, and by the end of the week, slept through it all.

A Haven in France

When the girls were small, and I was working part-time at the local travel agency, money for extravagant holidays was not available, so we had to take any opportunity that arose. We still managed to have fun holidays away though, and one such trip has stuck in my mind. I had heard that Haven Holidays were promoting their new brochures by inviting agents and partners to take part in a quiz. Haven sold holidays to holiday camps, where the accommodation was in mobile homes, or lodges, with a large communal pool and other activities available to keep everyone happy. Not the normal type of holiday we were used to, but my girls were at the right age to enjoy it all, and we loved a quiz, so thought we would join in. As it turned out we won the top prize, a week at one of their international camps. Get in! We decided to book a week in Brittany; not an area we had been to before, but from our research, it looked scenic. Rather than just go for a week, we thought it would be good to combine this holiday with a few days at Disneyland Paris. We had been there before when my elder daughter was five. On that occasion, we didn't tell her where we were going, flew to Charles de Gaulle Airport and got the transfer bus to the Theme Park. She didn't ask where we were going but took it all in her stride. The expression on her face when she first saw Sleeping Beauty's castle from the transfer bus was a picture. Worth all the secrecy.

This time for Disneyland we had booked the ferry from Portsmouth to Le Havre and then planned to drive on to Paris. The crossing was fine, though a bit choppy, but on route to the capital, the heavens opened, and we had the heaviest downfall we have ever driven in. Thankfully, the girls had dozed off in the back but driving on a multilane motorway on a river is no fun, and scary too. The windscreen wipers could not cope with the deluge, and all we could see were distorted red brake lights ahead of us. It was difficult to brake without aquaplaning, but somehow, we managed to slow our pace until the rain lifted, by which time we had arrived at the Paris Périphérique to drive around the south of the city to get to Disneyland on the other side. I spent the whole time with my heart in my mouth. I am not the best of passengers. Basically, I cannot keep my mouth shut, so am extremely fortunate to have a husband who has the patience of a saint. Anyway, we got there in one piece and spent a few happy days with Mickey and friends, the character breakfast being the highlight, posing for photos with Goofy and Donald Duck. We had to put up with 'It's a Small World' again but seeing the pleasure the girls got from all the rides more than compensated.

Travelling west to Brittany was uneventful, although much further than I thought it would be. Though the roads were clear, and we could drive reasonably fast, I had not appreciated how big France was. The campsite was good, as was our accommodation, although early on, my other half got locked in the mobile home's bathroom. Musical strains of 'Oh dear, what can the matter be', could be heard by passers-by. Well, it did amuse. Pont Aven and the surrounding area was very picturesque, and I didn't make any mistakes with my schoolgirl French. Très bien! We bought ice-creams from a local vendor, and promptly lost one of them to the pavement, but was soon replaced for free. During a day by the sea, I managed to slip off some craggy rocks on the shoreline and gouge a chunk from my finger. I still have the scar to prove it. On the same day, I bought a peach, bit into it, and took the corner of a tooth off when it hit the stone, so that was an eventful day, for all the wrong reasons. Nobody thought to rename me Goofy.

At the end of our holiday in Brittany we had to drive back to Le Havre for the ferry home, so drove to Normandy along the coast. Although we needed to get to the ferry on time we could see Mont St Michel offshore and thought it would be a good place to stop for a break. We were all desperate for the toilet but did not have much time to spare. By the time we had parked and paid for the entrance fees we had no more than five minutes to look around. Having relieved ourselves, it was time to head off again. I think we can say that was the most expensive wee we have ever had.

Hawaii -Volcanoes, Lava, and Rainforests

When I left British Airways, I chose to take severance and freeze my pension so that when I reached retirement age, I would be able to get my standby and confirmed BA travel concessions back to use for the rest of my life. That seemed like a good idea to me then, aged 32, and I'm glad I did. In 2009 they changed the rules so that we could start using the concessions from then, but only for the duration of full number of years we had worked for the company, which in my case that was 11 years.

By this time, my business had grown to be a success, and the type of trip I enjoyed booking for customers were tailormade trips to far-flung places. I now had 11 years to explore these places for myself and to also return to some of the places I had visited on my educationals. That meant a lot of travelling. My closest friends and colleagues nicknamed me Non-Dom, as I always seemed to be away. (I really wasn't!) In 2009 my daughters became eligible to travel on concessional rates too, so we took advantage of this to expand our horizons. They learnt a lot, which all added to their education, and so the fridge magnets started to mount up!

The first place we fancied was a trip to Hawaii. We managed to get four seats in business class to Los Angeles, which was quite an experience for my husband and daughters none of whom had been previously. The girls spent much of the flight pressing the button that makes the privacy dividers between the seats go up and down. A sort of in-flight hide-and- seek. Now you see me, now you don't. Arriving in Los Angeles, we checked into an airport hotel for the night, but before retiring, managed to fit in a whistle stop last minute tour of the city. In the space of about three hours, we walked on the sands of Venice Beach, and saw rollerbladers, volleyballers, and fitness fanatics exercising on the beach. Then, onto Santa Monica for a view of the old pier and the beautiful seafront homes, followed by a stop at the Hollywood Walk of Fame, a drive along Rodeo Drive and Mulholland Drive and finally a photo stop at the famous Hollywood sign. After a good night's sleep and an early start, we returned to the airport terminal to standby for the flight to Honolulu.

Travelling on a different airline — in this case United Airlines — meant we were well down the pecking order for boarding and we were unable to get on the first couple of flights. Before us, after the paying passengers, priority would be given to United Airline working staff, followed by United Airlines retired staff. If there were any seats still available after that they would look at working staff from other airlines and then retired staff, so we were at the bottom of the pile. To us it was all part of the holiday and we were prepared for this, happy to hang around all day if necessary. We were just grateful to get on any flight out.

Eventually arriving in Hawaii, we had booked three nights in Waikiki and I must say it was much nicer than anticipated. We wandered down to the seafront expecting it to be a bit tacky, but it really wasn't. Some fine hotels lined the beach, and there were plenty of inviting places to eat with many shops to wander around. We found a great picture gallery selling stunning dramatic photographs of the Hawaiian Islands by a photographer called Peter Lik. We were due to join a cruise around the islands in a couple of days, and these photos really whetted our appetite. We were in for a scenic treat. Before leaving Oahu though, we had an excursion to see the Pearl Harbour Museum. Educational for all of us and hearing first-hand from veterans what happened on that infamous day in history. I found the whole experience really moving. Standing on the USS *Arizona* Memorial, which marks the final resting place of over 1100, whilst listening to how twenty-one ships were destroyed on that fateful day, made for a very sobering moment. We obviously saw all of this from the American perspective. A few years later, my elder daughter travelled to Japan and visited the Hiroshima Peace Garden. She told us that it was equally as moving to see how lives were extinguished when the atom bomb was dropped on the city, particularly when she saw a clock with its hands frozen in time. However, experiencing things from a different perspective may not necessarily make you feel any better about loss of life.

We took a tour of the whole island, exploring the colonial buildings from the past mixed with more modern buildings in

Honolulu. Journeying around the island we saw rocky coves, golden sandy bays, and in the north, the popular Waimea Bay, passing Sunset Beach in the process, which is home to the world cup of surfing. We also had a quick stop at the Dole Pineapple Plantation and Gardens, seeing for the first time how pineapples are grown.

Our tour of the Hawaiian islands was on *Pride of America*, the only cruise ship to sail within these islands. It runs weekly from Oahu sailing arounds the main islands before returning to Honolulu. This is a great way to cover the area in the least amount of time. All other cruise ships must remain in international waters, so they sail from mainland USA, around the Hawaiian islands and back to the mainland, therefore making it necessary to cruise for longer. The ship was actually rather disappointing. With four of us in a cabin, we only had three life jackets for the entire week, despite asking for the fourth a few times. The food was at best adequate. I normally gain weight when cruising, but this time lost a few pounds. We were served coffee on our first evening at our dining table, and I watched in amazement as the waiter drizzled the coffee across all the cups, spilling the liquid across the table as he did so. Not a chance of getting a Michelin star! However, the cruise route was fantastic, and the cost was very reasonable, so this outweighed the bad service.

Our first port of call was on Maui, the second largest of the islands. More than 75% of the island is dominated by the Haleakala National Park, which is centred on the dormant Haleakala Crater. We headed up to the summit which stands at over 10000ft. The views from there were far-reaching, enabling us to compare the green lushness at sea level with the barren volcanic, moonlike landscape up at the summit. We drove along the 52-mile Hana Highway skirting the eastern coastline, much of it very winding and narrow, passing through tropical rainforest with numerous waterfalls close by. In many places we could see black lava edging the sea, while some of the beaches had black sand. We had fun walking through a lava tube on the black sand and pebble Waianapanapa Beach.

We continued cruising south to our next port of call on Big Island. Once again more lush vegetation at sea level, but we really wanted to explore the higher elevations of the interior. Mauna Kea, another dormant volcano dominates the island and at 13802ft is the highest point in the state of Hawaii. As we ascended by minibus, the vegetation became sparse, and the air became thinner. We noticed our water bottles became misshapen, and our breathing more laboured. The temperature up there was much cooler, with snow still clinging to the rocks in places. At the peak, we walked around thirteen telescopes which are funded by eleven countries, this being one of the best sites in the world for astronomical observation. The views from the top of Mauna Kea were fabulous, right out to the sea in the far distance.

The highlight of this Hawaiian holiday happened after we set sail from Big Island. In the south-eastern corner of this island are the Kilauea Lava Flows, which have fiery lava flowing slowly into the sea. It is best seen when dark, with the best viewpoint being from offshore. We departed Big Island and waited until it got dark, dropping anchor a short distance from the shore. We were then treated to one of those magical moments that I will never forget. All the lights were off up on deck, so we had a fantastic view across the black ocean to the orangey red ribbons of fire tumbling into the sea. Some of us lay down on the deck and stared up at a million stars in the inky blackness. With no light pollution coupled with the total silence on deck, I could feel the vastness of the universe and could feel how insignificant we all were. It was so dark it was impossible to see my hands in front of my face. I loved it.

From Big Island we sailed to the north of the Hawaiian islands to Kauai, known as the Garden Island. It is the fourth largest of the island archipelago. We hired a convertible for our day ashore to explore the coast and interior. We were particularly interested to see the Waimea Canyon State Park, which is like a mini Grand Canyon, but in the Pacific. The canyon is about ten miles long and up to 3000ft deep in places. It was formed after an erupting volcano collapsed forming a deep depression which filled with lava flows, and then eroded over time by rainfall. The scenery was stunning and offered numerous hiking trails. The canyon was used to film *Jurassic Park* and its sequel *Jurassic World*. The high cliffs along the northern shoreline were particularly beautiful, rising to 4000ft in places. We could see where rainfall had eroded the rocks, exposing the red earth and the green and browns of the landscape.

Returning to Honolulu on the ship, we flew to Las Vegas to spend a couple of nights there before heading home. We arrived in Vegas on one of the last flights of the day, so the airport was empty, but the Strip was buzzing. I felt like I had arrived late to a party. We loved the Bellagio Fountains and can completely understand the appeal that Las Vegas has to tourists looking for a fun break. The artificial entertainment and neon lights were a complete contrast to the natural beauty of the Hawaiian islands.

I returned to Las Vegas a year or so later, on a Gold Travel Counsellors weekend and enjoyed it more then. I decided that to see Las Vegas you need to be with like-minded people. We were shown around a few of the resort hotels, a bit like being in a Disney theme park, and watched a few excellent shows in the evening. Las Vegas is quiet during the day, so many people take trips out to the Grand Canyon, or the Hoover Dam. Others might just keep cool wandering around some of the shopping malls or relax by the pool at their resort. There was always the constant noise of the one-armed bandits being played as you walked through the dimly lit casinos at any time of the day or night. Nevertheless, I am glad I have been to Las Vegas and have seen what all the fuss is about, so I can more readily sell it as a destination, although personally I have no desire to return again.

Caribbean Escapes

I have visited the Caribbean on a few occasions over the years and each island has its own charm, but there are overriding similarities too. Scenically some are different from others. For example, St Lucia is a volcanic island, with lush green vegetation and rocky coves, whilst Antigua is flatter, but with more sandy beaches around the island. Barbados is different again, with a wilder coastline on the east coast, flatter in the south and beautiful sandy coves on the western side. All the islands have villages and townships with low rise buildings, some with corrugated roofs, an abandoned rusting car here and there, a few dogs barking at strangers passing, and most with shops and stalls set up by roadsides selling local fruit and vegetables. My favourite name for a shop I saw in St John in the Virgin Islands was Shoes 'n Tings. I wonder what they sold...? I loved repeating it to myself in a Caribbean accent. The people of the Caribbean have a very relaxed laid-back attitude, which takes some getting used to, when you have been working at 110 miles per hour. Just the thing though for a relaxing holiday. As with many countries, there are beach sellers who try and sell their wares. It can be annoying, but with the right attitude, and taking the same laid-back approach, it's easy to go with the flow. We had to learn to be patient when ordering drinks. Sometimes we were left thinking maybe they had gone off to grow the fruit or cut the sugar cane before our order was ready. A far cry from the swift service from countries further east in Asia.

Once, when on holiday in Barbados, in the early eighties, we were coming to the end and didn't have much money left to spend. One of the regular beach sellers, named Trevor, came by and had some beautiful conch shells, which we thought would be a lovely reminder of our holiday. Short of cash, we saw him eyeing up the tee shirt my husband was wearing. Trevor suggested we use the tee shirt as payment. Now I do know the phrase 'taking the shirt off my back' but never thought it would have a literal meaning. This tee shirt had frankly seen better days, and only been thrown in the suitcase at the last minute, but he wanted it because of the Adidas logo. Trevor thought it was *the* best. We made a comment that he would probably wear it when he was on the beach, but no, he said, "I'll be wearin' it to do me partyin'…" It must have been the brand name and logo that appealed, rather than the hard crusty underarms!

Our room on that Barbados holiday was right on the beach, literally stepping out onto the sand from the bedroom door. I loved that, but not however the large cockroach that appeared from nowhere in the bedroom. We tried to murder it by whacking its shell with my wooden Scholl sandal, but boy, can they move fast, and it made a beeline for the bathroom. By that time, I was sitting on the loo seat, with my legs in the air, not giving it a chance to scuttle onto me. I looked around for another weapon and the only thing I could find was some talcum powder and deodorant spray, so gave it a blast of spray and a deluge of talc, and still the bugger beat us, escaping once again, leaving a trail of powdery prints in its wake. Maybe this new fragrant model would attract another cockroach! I didn't care, so long as it was ousted from our room. Eventually, we caught it and flushed it down the loo. It's probably still scuttling about somewhere, as it seemed indestructible.

On that same trip we hired a Mini Moke, an open- topped mini jeep, to explore the whole island. Driving across the middle interior, we stopped by the roadside on a hilltop to admire the view and take some pictures. On each side of the road were acres of sugar cane. Suddenly out of nowhere a couple of locals appeared brandishing machetes. I think they were farmers, who had been cutting down the sugar cane, but we were not thinking that though when they stepped out in front of us. Time to make a swift exit! Then later, driving back through Holetown to our hotel, a lady carrying a shopping bag walked straight out in front of the Mini Moke and sauntered across the road. I'd only recently passed my driving test, after two attempts, including failing on my emergency stop. I now had to do another to avoid an accident. Luckily, I missed her, but her shopping bag was not so lucky. *Bang!* Against the front of the car. She just looked at me as if to say, 'What?' and carried on… as I say, completely laid back!

We seemed to attract locals with 'weapons'. On another holiday to St Lucia, we hired a car to explore, and pulled over to get some photos of the iconic twin volcanic peaks of the Pitons as they came into view.

We were on a remote road and no one else was about. We were just walking back to the car when a couple of dreadlocked locals appeared from nowhere. They had penknives and to us looked a little threatening. They asked us what we were doing, so slowly backing away as calmly as possible, we made a bit of small talk with them. Then they pulled a chunk of sulphur from their pockets, which had probably been lying on the ground earlier, since the geology in that part of the island was quite sulphurous. We felt almost obligated to buy it off them, and then left a bit sharpish. My husband *is* interested in geology, so we ended up keeping the piece of rock for some years after.

That experience reminded us a little of an excursion we took on our honeymoon in Thailand. At that time we were first taken to a rubber plantation where we saw rows of rubber trees, with rusty cans attached to them and white latex seeping out of the trunks into the tins. Next, we went to a sapphire mine, which was basically a reddish clay hole in the ground, where men in loincloths were standing and panning for the gems. Both experiences were straight out of the educational films we used to watch at school. From the mine we were taken to what I can only describe as a garage, where we were able to buy a couple of the cleaned and polished sapphires. I have had both made into jewellery and have had them valued. From memory we only paid about £5 for them but have since been told they are good stones.

Apart from the usual lizards and geckos that are often seen around the hotels in the Caribbean, we have also seen giant iguanas sitting on walls and strolling across roads on the island of St Thomas. More recently I stayed on Palm Island in the Grenadines with our younger daughter. We shared the island with iguanas. One morning while I was eating my breakfast in the outdoor restaurant, one determined iguana sneaked up behind me and tried to jump onto my lap to get at my food. Flicking it away, it kept trying to return but it was out of luck. I don't share my food with anyone! While we were in Barbados, we met up with some friends who were staying on the west coast. We went to their hotel and watched the sun set, enjoying a drink by the pool and some local entertainment. As the sun dropped an army of red crabs came up from the sea and spread across the pool area, forcing us to raise our legs up to avoid being snipped. There were hundreds of them! I really did not like them and was very relieved to see them disappear a few minutes later. I am not sure if it was a regular occurrence, or only happened at a particular time of year, but I was glad I wasn't staying there. I have never seen any mention of getting crabs in the Caribbean!

We took our eldest daughter to Antigua when she was only six months old. I had to use up some leave before the end of March that year, so with my travel concessions, I was able to have a week there. The biggest lesson I learnt in Antigua is not to park a pushchair under a palm tree. It might be considered a shady spot, but it is dangerous. A few minutes after moving the pushchair with our little daughter in from under the tree, we heard an almighty thud, and saw a coconut had fallen out of the tree. A few moments earlier our baby had been asleep in the same spot. I still shudder now to think what could have happened. On a happier note, we took photos of her having her first taste of ice cream and watching her facial expression change, from confusion to delight. It was a picture!

On a later visit to Antigua we were able to get a reduced rate at Sandals Grande Antigua. By this time, we had got used to more active holidays, so we weren't used to spending a week doing nothing on a beach. However, for now it was just what was needed. The resort itself was lovely, but we realised it was more suited to young couples and honeymooners. By the end of the week, I was sick of hearing mawkish love songs, being played constantly through the speakers dotted around the landscaped gardens. I think someone else had the same feeling, because we noticed some of the speakers had been kicked in or their wires discreetly removed. Lovely! I cannot abide songs like that, being more of a stadium rock kinda gal.

On our last visit to Antigua, we had another moment that amused me. We sat undercover having lunch at our hotel's beach bar overlooking the cove and sea beyond. We could see there was a thunderstorm coming but were protected from the rain from our viewpoint. Gradually the beach cleared as the rain started to fall. We watched a couple of people still in the sea, thinking it was probably a good place to stay as they were already wet. What amused us though was a few minutes after it started raining, one of them came out of the sea, dripping wet, retrieved an umbrella, and then promptly returned to the sea. They must have been British!

Canada, East and West, and New England

While our daughters still wanted to come away on family holidays with us, we decided to have a road trip taking in Ontario and New England. This was a very full and varied holiday which gave us many different experiences. In that respect it is exactly the type of trip I organise now for my clients.

We flew into Toronto and spent a couple of nights there, staying at the Fairmont Royal York Hotel because of its proximity to a car hire depot and also within walking distance to the CN Tower. We always like to get an aerial viewpoint at the beginning of a trip as this usually provides a great overview of a city plan layout. In Toronto the CN Tower gave us great views over the city, across to Ontario City Airport and Toronto Islands. There is a glass floor at the top, so we could see the ant-sized people and dinky cars far below. Leaving Toronto, we picked up our hire car and drove around Lake Ontario shoreline to Niagara Falls for another couple of nights. We saw the Falls from every conceivable angle, from above in the Sky Tower, from the water in the Maid of the Mist, from behind, up close and in the distance. Thunderous and impressive, I think the Canadian Horseshoe Falls on the Canadian side were more memorable than the American Falls. I always say I learn something new every day of my life. On that day, I learnt a new word. Funambulist. This is somebody who walks between two points on a tightrope. Apparently, there were a few people in the past who had ignored the danger and successfully walked across Niagara Falls.

We crossed the border into the US without incident and made our way across the northern part of New York state into Massachusetts, stopping overnight in Williamstown, a pretty university town midway to Boston, and full of wooden colonial buildings. In Massachusetts we visited a Shaker Village which showed a much simpler life, pausing to play at 'school' in the schoolhouse sitting at the wooden desks. To save some money, we decided to stay just outside Boston in the suburb of Cambridge, which was fortunately on the direct subway line into Boston, giving us a quick glimpse of Harvard University on the way.

Boston has bags of history, and I loved the mix of original buildings interspersed with the newer high-rise offices. We walked along the Freedom Trail, which took in some interesting historic areas of the city, including leafy Beacon Hill and Copley Square. We had a wander around Quincy Market, followed by a boat trip on the Charles River through to Charlestown and the historic dockyard where the USS Constitution, 'Old Ironsides' was moored. Just beyond the old battleship, we visited Bunker Hill, where one of the first major battles of the American Revolution took place in 1775.

Leaving Boston for our next stop further north in Maine, we took a detour west to Concord Massachusetts, with a brief stop at Orchard House, once home to Louisa May Alcott, she of *Little Women* fame. I loved everything about Concord. It was packed with grand colonial buildings and it felt like we had stepped back in time. A short walk from the central square led us to North Bridge, which, along with a small battle at nearby Lexington, was the site of the first colonial action against the British redcoats in 1775, marking the beginning of the American Revolution. There is a monument here called the Minute Man, representing the local militia who, at a minute's notice, could take up arms and defend the area against the advancing British. North Bridge is a very photogenic wooden bridge spanning the Concord River. We watched a few artists set up with their easels on the riverbank ready to capture in painting the beauty around them. It felt very peaceful and difficult to reconcile that this inoffensive spot is so important historically. From there we drove to the town of Lexington where the leaders of the colonialists would get together at the Meeting House. On Battle Green another statue of a colonialist marks the site of the battle there.

Heading back to the Atlantic coast and then northwards, we drove to Boothbay Harbor in Maine. This is a typical New England coastal resort and here we dined on clam chowder while watching the numerous fishing boats and other vessels moored in the small harbour. This part of our holiday was all about getting out onto the water. We took a trip out to see some whales, although this was not altogether successful. It was a 'blink and you'll miss it' experience, but fun, nevertheless. This area of coastline is dotted with lighthouses on rocky outcrops. We loved the totally uncommercial feel to the place as well as the unspoilt landscape, together with a general lack of tourists.

From the coast we headed west into New Hampshire and drove up to the summit of Mt Washington in the White Mountains. This 6,288ft high mountain had a sign up the summit declaring that the highest ever recorded wind speed was observed here in 1934, at 231mph. I love facts like that. A small cog railway, which was first used in 1869, still takes people to the very top of the mountain. From there we could see several states, in conditions perfect for viewing. From New Hampshire we crossed into Vermont and spent a night in Burlington. Then back into New York State via Lake Champlain and Lake Placid, before re-entering Canada again at the other end of Lake Ontario, staying a couple of nights in Kingston. Kingston used to be the capital of Canada back in 1841 for three years. Consequently, it has some fine buildings including the magnificent City Hall.

From Kingston we took a boat tour around the Thousand Islands, which are all within the St Lawrence River. Most of the islands are inhabited with only a single house. They 'lied' about the number of islands! There are, in fact, 1876 islands in all with the US/Canadian border winding through them, each island being named and numbered. Close by are a selection of forts, originally built to defend Kingston's naval harbour. After spending a little while back in Kingston, it was time to head back to the airport in Toronto, after following a circular route of nearly 2,500 miles over a two-week period.

***

A few years later we decided to explore the other side of Canada, this time just the two of us. There were a few places that had been on my bucket list, and the Rockies was at the top, along with New Zealand and Patagonia. To see towering snow-capped mountains and valleys always fills my heart with joy, and this for me this is the reason I love to travel. We flew into Seattle, in northwest USA and spent the rest of the day exploring this underrated city. It was great wandering around Pike Market, that sold just about everything. We spent the night at the Fairmont Seattle before an early start the next day, beginning with a three-hour ferry across the border into Canada to Vancouver Island. Whilst on board we booked an excursion to Butchart Gardens, prior to checking into our hotel in Victoria. Butchart Gardens are a must for anyone who enjoys wandering around beautiful, landscaped gardens. I had visited before and whatever the time of year there is always something different to see. Indeed, I would go as so far as to say they are the best gardens I have ever seen. They were created from an old quarry and have expanded so that they are now divided into different themed areas. It was all so colourful and varied. After exploring the gardens, we were dropped off at our hotel, the Fairmont Empress in Victoria, but not until we had first been given a tour of this lovely city. Victoria was relatively small, considering it is a state capital, and it also had a Victorian feel about it. There was a constant stream of seaplanes coming and going, which to us Brits was quite a novelty to watch. We spent a while wandering around the waterfront area, just relaxing and taking photos.

The following day, we had a short stroll to the coach station behind the hotel for a coach and ferry across to Vancouver on the mainland. The route took us past numerous small islands and inlets and was altogether a very pleasant way of travelling. We were dropped off at the Fairmont Vancouver, chosen because not only is the hotel central, but also adjoining it was a car hire depot, so nice and easy to collect our car when we were ready. Before that though, we spent a couple of nights there, taking the hop-on-hop-off bus around the sights, including Stanley Park, Canada Place and Gastown. I saw my first black squirrel and a family of racoons when we walked around Stanley Park. I think they must be as common as our grey squirrel, since no one else batted an eyelid, but I loved them anyway. At Gastown, we saw the world's first steam-powered clock which whistled every fifteen minutes and emitted steam, much to the amusement of passing tourists. We also had a wander around the artisan area of Granville Island, an area full of warehouses used by artists.

Then we began our 2,000 mile round trip drive, first heading north via Horseshoe Bay to Whistler, where we had our first sight of the snowy peaks of the Rocky Mountains. Whistler reminded us of the film *The Truman Show*, somewhat Disneyesque, as it is a car-free, purpose-built resort, where all roads lead you back to the main street. I am sure during the winter when the ski season is on, it would be a great place to stay, but at the time of our visit in the summer we felt it was all a bit artificial, with not alot going on other than eating and shopping, unless you were prepared to venture beyond the resort. It was really just pit stop for us as we headed northeast from there to our next stop at Sun Peaks north of Kamloops, encountering our first black bear on route. We rounded a bend on a quiet road, and out from some undergrowth strolled a black bear, which stopped right in the middle of the road, as if to say, 'Go on, take a picture!' Unprepared, I fumbled with my camera. With my husband worried another car would come hurtling around bend unable to break in time, we dared not stop long enough to get any photos. The bear became bored and wandered off, so we just carried on our way. It was a thrilling moment though. Our hotel, the Delta Sun Peaks Resort, was contemporary and served the best meal we had on the whole trip. A nice resort, which would be a great alternative to Whistler. Next day, we had a long drive north towards Jasper. The scenery was so beautiful that the time flew by with many photo stops on route.

On arrival at the Jasper National Park, we had to pay a park entry fee for the number of days we were planning to be in the region. This fee paid for the upkeep of the roads and facilities, so I was glad we had some cash to hand. Luckily, the weather was glorious, with clear cloudless views of the snow-capped Mount Robson and other mountain peaks. Our hotel, the Fairmont Jasper Park Lodge, was rustically styled, set on a beautiful lake, just a five-minute drive from Jasper itself, and again surrounded by beautiful scenery. We took the Jasper Skytram cable car up a neighbouring peak, some 7,424ft high, which gave uninterrupted panoramic views of the town of Jasper and the surrounding area. Up there we watched many ground squirrels skittering about in the rocky undergrowth and caught sight of a couple of Hoary marmots. The views from the top were tremendous, looking down on the whole of Jasper, and beyond. From our viewpoint up above the town we watched an extremely long freight train wind its way through a valley below, and when it stopped at the station, the length of it seemed to wrap around half the town. Given more time, we would have spent longer on the mountain, exploring various hiking trails. With nil pollution up there, it was also a perfect spot for star gazing. We then found Maligne Canyon with its deep ravines and plunging waterfalls, taking some great shots of Mt Edith Cavell which was nicely reflected in a nearby lake.

The highlight of our trip was the journey between Jasper and Lake Louise, which took in the Icefield Parkway. The road was easy to drive but the three-hour trip took us seven hours to complete as the scenery was so jaw droppingly beautiful. There were so many snowy peaks, glaciers, thunderous rivers and falls to take in on the pine tree lined road. Two thirds of the way along, we stopped at the Athabasca Glacier, part of the vast Columbia Icefield, and drove onto the glacier in the Ice Explorer, an enormous snow-coach, with huge, tracked wheels as high as a person. This enabled us to get out onto the glacier and walk gingerly on the icy surface — what a memorable experience that was! Continuing south, we kept stopping because at every turn there were mountains, lakes, wildlife and places to stop for a short walk. All the roads were well maintained and easy to drive. Everything was well signposted with plenty of places to pull in, complete with clean toilet cabins, picnic tables and bear-resistant food waste bins.

We arrived at our next hotel, the Fairmont Lake Louise, early in the evening to see the sun retreating behind a glacier across the lake. We splashed out and enjoyed a lake-view room, as this iconic sight was worth waking up to the next morning. We strolled around the lake, taking heed of the many 'Beware of bear' signs. Lake Louise was another image I had seen in brochures and had yearned to see in person. Standing on the lake side and looking across the turquoise water to the mountain peak beyond, I felt my life was complete. If I had died there and then, I would have been happy. The following day we drove out of town to a cable car which took us up to grizzly bear country. Unfortunately, we didn't see any, but others mentioned they had spotted some between the trees below us. When we alighted the cable car at the top, we could see right across the valley back towards our hotel with the lake and mountain beyond. Surrounded by the mountainous scenery the hotel was just a tiny speck in the distance. On route back to the hotel we detoured via Moraine Lake a few miles from

Lake Louise, and another stunningly pretty spot.

It was time then to start heading back west towards Vancouver, passing through the Yoho National Park and Glacier National Park with yet more of the same wonderful scenery on display. I would never tire of the fresh mountain air, clear blue skies and towering peaks. We stopped overnight in Revelstoke with a local family, who gave us inside info on the town as a ski resort and the local area. They recommended that we detoured on our return journey slightly to enjoy a circular trip which took us across a couple of lakes on free local ferries before arriving at Kamloops. Kamloops is probably the least scenic of all the places we visited, but the Holiday Inn and Suites were perfect for our overnight stay before our drive to Vancouver Airport and our flight home.

A Rendezvous with Russia

The same year we decided to fly over to St Petersburg and meet up with my eldest daughter who at that time was living in Moscow as part of her degree course. Our rendezvous point was the hotel we had booked just off Nevsky Prospekt, the main street in St Petersburg. She had travelled overnight on the train from Moscow and planned a few days exploring this beautiful European-influenced city with us. Normally we are confident travellers, who can make our own way around, but on this occasion, we felt it would be a lot easier if we had our own guide, given the signage at that time was completely in Russian. I believe since the Olympics in 2012 they have dual signage in both English and Cyrillic which would certainly make things easier.

I had not really known what to expect and had visions of long queues for food at grey looking outlets, so was pleasantly surprised to find St Petersburg was a beautiful city, complete with Western shopping centres. The architecture was a photographer's dream. Many buildings were painted with a pale-yellow exterior, and there were many beautiful Russian Orthodox churches with interiors embellished with gold, that put our own to shame.

The first place we wanted to visit was the Hermitage, also known as the Winter Palace. As it was a long walk from the hotel, we took a local *marchrutka* (minibus) down the length of Nevsky Prospekt to the Hermitage. Had we not had our Russian speaking daughter with us, it would have been totally confusing. We boarded the minibus, and then the fares are passed through the hands of the other travellers to the front and the driver, all in Russian. I didn't have a clue what was going on when someone handed me money!

'Pass the money to the driver, Mum!' came the response!

The exterior of the Hermitage was just as beautiful and ornate as the interior, looking like a work of art. It reminded me of a cake made from pale blue icing decorated with white piping. We knew there could be long queues to get in, but as we had arrived there early, we didn't have too long to wait. The queues can be avoided if you book on a guided tour. Once inside, we walked up an ornate staircase leading to the state rooms. All the ceilings were reminiscent of the Sistine Chapel, painted with heavenly scenes, and the walls were heavily embossed with cherubs in bright gold against royal iced white. It would have been easy to spend all day inside wandering around the magnificent rooms, marvelling at the famous artwork.

There are many buildings like this in Russia, and now having seen them first-hand, completely understand what a young student had once said to me. A few years earlier we had a Russian exchange student stay with us, and we took her out and about to show her the pretty English villages, as well as London, and places of interest close to where we lived. I remember asking her what she thought of Blenheim Palace and London after doing the tourist trail. I was a bit shocked at her rather disparaging remark that 'eets nice but not as beeautiful as in Russia'. I now understand what she meant. Our stately homes and public buildings are much plainer, no glinting gold, just understated architecture, a bit like us Brits, I think. Anyway, back to St Petersburg. Just outside the Winter Palace was a statue of Peter the Great on horseback, which was commissioned by Catherine the Great. (Why aren't our Kings and Queens suffixed with an extra title — Elizabeth the Steadfast has a good ring to it!) From the statue, it was an easy walk to St Isaac's Cathedral and then on to the Church of Spilled Blood. We couldn't help but be impressed by these buildings. Both St Isaac's with its golden dome and the onion domed Church of Spilled Blood, looking a bit like St Basil's in Red Square Moscow, will take your breath away. I particularly loved the Church of Spilled Blood. The red brick exterior was covered in ornate designs with splashes of colourful tiles on the roofs and domes. Inside, each column, ceiling and wall was covered in religious images made from mosaic tiles. It really was a work of art inside.

Our first evening meal was at a Russian chain, a bit like the Harvester, but a Russian version. My daughter wanted us to sample real Russian food. I enjoyed the borscht soup, but could not eat the beef stroganoff, presented to me as strips of meat braised in lard, on a bed of overcooked ribbon pasta, also cooked in lard, with a dollop of sour cream on top. Later in our stay we headed to a Ukraine restaurant, but the choice was no better. Presented with a menu, I turned to one page, where I could choose from a selection of lard dishes. There was Smoked Lard, Lard Ukrainian style, Lard Assorted, Lard Paste, and a long list of uninspiring choices. I just fancied something less lardy. (If lardy cake had been on the menu though, I would have had that!)

Out sightseeing, we took a metro under the River Neva to Peter and Paul Fortress. Taking the metro was an experience. We bought tokens at the ticket booth, with people pushing in front of us. Excuse me, we are British, and we queue in an orderly fashion! I just kept handing my purse to my daughter who was well versed in the process. I was just so glad she was there and made it easy for us. Peter and Paul Fortress is a citadel and home to their first prison. We walked around the preserved cells and could see who once occupied them, some with recognisable names such as Lenin's brother, along with Dostoevsky and Trotsky. The citadel is also home to St Peter & Paul Cathedral, again with a luxuriously decorated interior in pale greens and golds. The cathedral houses the tombs of the Tsars, including the last resting place of Nicholas & Alexandra and family — all very poignant. The fortress was built in 1703 by Peter the Great and provided the foundation for the city of St Petersburg. Beyond the exterior walls of the citadel, we watched locals catching the warmth of the sun on the concrete banks by the river. However, this was early April and there was still ice floating along the river. On that side of the river, a short walk from the entrance to the fortress, we came to the *Aurora*, the battleship that fired a blank shot in October 1917 signalling the start of the assault on the Winter Palace, just across the river, and the beginning of the October Revolution.

We took a train to Catherine the Great's Palace at Pushkin and again, if we had not had our guide with us, we would have been lost. On arrival at Pushkin, we had to get another *marchrutka* which dropped us off outside the palace gates. We were one of a few non-Russian-speaking tourists there, which meant we avoided having to be shown around with the official Russian- speaking guide and could enjoy the interior at our leisure. Again, the palace was a magnificent building with ballrooms decorated in blues and golds. I imagined this is where Cinderella met her prince! We had to wear blue shoe coverings to protect the floors. Well, that what they told us, but I really think it was a way of getting the floors polished! At the entrance to each room, there was an old woman dressed in black sitting and observing us all, probably making sure we did not help ourselves to any treasures. The palace was set on a large lake, which we walked around passing numerous equally ornate pavilions and summer houses.

On another occasion we took a bus to Peterhof Palace, again another impressive building, which looked out onto the Gulf of Finland. Unfortunately, we were there a little early in the season and missed the beautiful water fountain displays which were due to be turned on for the summer in May. I particularly enjoyed the gardens there, and could see that when the fountains were on, it would be even more stunning. We did return to Peterhof a few years ago as part of a cruise to the Baltics and saw a complete contrast. This, our first visit in early spring had been empty of tourists. No fountains, hardened dirty snow edging the canal leading from the dry fountains to the sea, ice floating in the Gulf, and bare of colourful flowers. Our summer visit gave us a completely different perspective. It was crowded with tourists, mostly congregated around the magnificent fountain displays with their golden statues, and pretty, floral displays all around the palace gardens. It was good to see the whole place at both its worst and best.

Leaving St Petersburg, we then took the overnight train to Moscow and checked into our Ibis Hotel. The train was a new experience, quite comfortable and I did manage to sleep, but I was conscious of the three of us sharing our cabin with a stranger who did not utter a word to us for the entire journey. Asking our daughter if she managed to sleep, she replied it was difficult given the stereo snoring from me and her dad, that reverberated around the cabin.

We had heard the Moscow underground system was worth seeing, as each elaborately decorated station had statues of military figures proudly wielding their weapons around the platforms. Our first stop was Red Square. As we wanted to see inside Lenin's Mausoleum, which is on one side of the Square, we had to leave our belongings, including our cameras, at a booth before we could go in. We filed past some famous memorials, including Yuri Gagarin and numerous Russian Presidents. At one end of Red Square was St Basil's Cathedral, not that big inside and not as ornate as the Church of Spilled Blood but nonetheless very impressive. At the opposite end sat the State History Museum, a red brick building with flags and banners erected ready for the May Day Parades taking place in a few days. Running along the length of one side of the square, which was, in fact, a rectangle, was the Gum Department store, Moscow's answer to Harrods, and selling everything you could think of. Our daughter took the opportunity here to buy some Lea & Perrins Worcestershire sauce! If I had known, I'd have brought some from home for her! Along the other side, by Lenin's Tomb, was one of the walls of the Kremlin, which was much larger than expected. We walked around the exterior walls of the Kremlin passing all nineteen of its towers, spaced evenly along the walls, which took us about forty-five minutes before we then went inside. The Kremlin was established during the 15th century by Ivan the Great. I had no idea what to expect but was surprised to see cobbled streets and a few government cars driving along them. There were a few museums and churches within the high walls along with government buildings. The exterior of these buildings were not as ornate as others we had seen, but all had their classic onion domes. We had a quick photo stop by the world's biggest bell, the Tsar Bell, weighing in at 202 tons, with a large section weighing 11.5 tons, lying next to it, which had broken off after a fire in 1737. Exploring Moscow further we visited the Space Museum and the Memorial Museum of Cosmonauts, which included an impressive 328ft tall titanium monument with a rocket at its tip, erected in 1964 as an acknowledgement to Soviet space flight. All around the city were grand monuments depicting various moments in history and achievement. We went to a city viewpoint that gave us views of some of the huge Seven Sisters skyscrapers which are dotted around Moscow, and then found our way to the Bolshoi Theatre, which was closed, so no chance to practise my 'good toes, naughty toes' ballet moves!

 Our final day took us out to one of the Golden Ring towns called Sergiev Posad which is the spiritual home of the Russian Orthodox Church and situated about forty minutes outside of Moscow. The whole place was contained within walls and comprised a variety of cathedrals and churches, each topped with their own colourful collection of onion domes and their associated buildings. The place was free of cars, too.

We watched as many visitors gathered to pray, many dressed in black with heads covered. We felt slightly uncomfortable taking photos, intruding on their privacy, but we really felt the authentic Russian experience whilst there. I think seeing both Moscow and Sergiev Posad together gave us a contrasting view of Russian life.

Eventually, we had to say goodbye to our daughter and become independent again. She showed us where we had to get the metro and where to get off so that we could walk back to our hotel and transfer back to the airport. We managed the metro and alighted at the correct station, but it had about four exits and we had no idea which one to take. We found ourselves standing on a pavement by a busy traffic-filled road with no idea which direction to walk in. Our daughter had written on a piece of paper the name and address of our hotel and the word *'Angliyskiy'* (meaning 'English'.) I stopped a couple of people passing by and showed them the piece of paper. Luckily, they spoke English and were able to direct us to the right road and we eventually found our way back to our hotel. Mr Bull (*El Toro*) would have been proud of me!

South Africa

I had been fortunate enough to visit South Africa and part of the Garden Route with some colleagues on an educational trip and was keen to explore further. This time with my daughters. Maybe it was because we were safely cocooned with our private driver on my work trip, but I felt completely safe on that first visit. I was not about to put either myself or daughters in any danger, so felt comfortable enough to travel a second time, with a mix of day trips and a hire car. Hiring a car over there is easy, as they drive on the left as we do, plus the roads are well maintained and empty so there is little chance of getting lost.

We flew into Cape Town and made a beeline to our accommodation at the V&A Waterfront, just a five-minute walk from the main waterfront tourist area. We loved the relaxed safe vibe of the Waterfront and enjoyed browsing the artisan market, where we watched the world go by in one of the many cafés. We wandered around the craft stalls, then watched some impromptu street theatre. Seals swam into the harbour, whilst hundreds of small craft were moored within the harbour walls. Boats were leaving to visit Robben Island and the surrounding bay. There was a fine view of Table Mountain which we were keen to visit. On my first trip we were unable to take a ride to the top. If it is too windy, which is often the case, they close the cable cars. I had planned our excursion so that we had a few opportunities to head up there, if our first attempt was unsuccessful. Fortunately, the following morning, the weather was just about good enough for the cable cars to remain open, so we bought our hop-on-hop-off bus tickets from the V&A Waterfront stop, with plans to head up to the mountain, then return down to see some of the other parts of Cape Town.

Not having to wait too long, we began our ascent and enjoyed seeing the city spread out below us, while the cable car gradually turned 360 degrees, giving everyone the opportunity to see the view appearing below us. At the top, we clambered over the rocks and spent time getting our photo shots in every direction. To the south, the valley below was covered in cloud, but towards the sea and the city, it was clear and calm. We could just about make out Robben Island offshore in the distance. The descent took much longer as the queue for the cable car tailed back beyond the café and toilets. Once back at the base, our bus continued through Cape Town and out to Camps Bay and Sea Point, where we got off for a wander along the beachfront, pausing for a drink. This area had a real tourist buzz and was a good alternative to stay, whilst only being fifteen minutes from the city.

The following day we joined a small group and headed south to Cape Point. The drive along the peninsula via Chapman's Peak had some great views, but unfortunately the weather was against us, and once we got to Cape Point, the rain was horizontal with accompanying gales. To be at the southernmost tip of Africa though was thrilling. We have the required photos to prove it, not with clear skies but battered by the wind and rain. We headed back up the peninsula and stopped to see the penguin colonies at Boulders Beach. There are hundreds of these cute fellas all living amongst the dunes, some protecting their eggs from the noisy swooping seagulls, others waddling along with their mates. Our view from the decked viewing area gave us a chance to capture their antics. The Cape Point tour concluded with a stop at Kirstenbosch Botanical Gardens, where we passed native plants while meandering along the paths before returning to the city. On a previous trip, I had stopped over at a beautiful hotel and winery called Steenberg on the peninsula. Not everyone wants to stay in the city, so for a quieter spot, but only about twenty minutes south of Cape Town, this might be a good alternative. It is next to a golf course and of course the requisite winery is a must to sample the wines. They will arrange a twice daily transfer to the V&A Waterfront, and it's possible to hire bikes to explore the immediate area. Boulder's Beach and the penguins are only about ten minutes away too.

We should have taken a trip to Robben Island the following morning, but the winds were too strong, and the boat ride was cancelled. At the V&A Waterfront, there was an interesting museum called the Nelson Mandela Gateway to Robben Island Glass Museum, where the tickets were purchased to board the boats to Robben Island. It had various exhibitions and recorded information, mainly as a precursor to the boat trip over to the island, but nevertheless an interesting substitute, without risking a rocking boat to Robben Island. A short walk from there we made a stop at the unusually shaped Zeitz Museum of Contemporary Art Africa. It was housed in a building that was originally a grain silo. The art was displayed on multiple floors, each with their own theme. The gallery building was a work of art itself and the views from the rooftop sculpture garden were far reaching.

After our short stay in Cape Town, it was time to pick up the hire car. We had to find our way to the pick-up point, a couple of miles beyond the waterfront, and had planned to get a taxi, but one of the staff at our hotel very kindly offered to drop us off there. I am always amazed at the kindness of strangers. I will deviate a bit from South Africa now and tell you about the friendliness of the New Zealanders and one specific occasion, some forty years ago, I have never forgotten.

On our first visit there we hired a campervan. It was 1984 on a Sunday morning and we were following a self-drive tour of Dunedin on South Island. Back in 1984, New Zealand closed for the weekend, so all the shops and offices were closed on Friday and reopened again on Monday morning. We managed to take a wrong turn and found ourselves on a residential road, which looked just like those in the UK, full of red brick houses. The previous night, we had discovered the campervan had a slow puncture, and we needed to contact a garage to get it repaired before continuing further to more remote areas. There were no mobile phones then but turning into the residential road we spotted a phone box. We parked alongside and I got out to make the call, only to discover the phone was broken. While standing outside the van thinking about what to do next, a lady came out of her house, to tell me the phone was not working, but offered to let me use her phone. My husband, still in the campervan, could not hear any of this and watched me disappear into her house. While they helped me contact someone from the local garage, they asked me where we were from. I doubt they had many campervans pulling up outside their house. We chatted for a bit, maps of the UK were produced, so I could show them where we came from, and all the while, a lovely aroma of a Sunday roast wafted through from the kitchen. They asked where we were planning to go from Dunedin, and said they had a holiday home in Wanaka, in the Southern Alps. It was a bank holiday the following weekend, and they were planning to go there. They invited us to dinner in Wanaka if we were in the area then and gave us their phone number. I returned to the campervan relaying what had happened. I could not get over how kind these strangers had been. If that had happened in the UK, there might have been some twitching curtains, but no one would have come out to offer help, and certainly an invitation to dinner would not have been forthcoming. We did happen to be in Wanaka a week later, so we called them, and they picked us up from our campsite and we had a very enjoyable evening.

I digress though, so picking up back in South Africa again, we collected our hire car, and headed out to Franschhoek for a couple of nights. We had booked a wine tour early the next morning and by nine thirty, we were sampling various wines, having had a brief history of Franschhoek and its origins first. By eleven a.m., I needed a sleep! I know you aren't supposed to swallow the wine, but it was too good to waste!

Franschhoek was a delightful town with traditional Dutch-influenced architecture and Huguenot history. It was surrounded by mountains set in a lush green valley, ideal for wine growing. Heading through the mountain pass to the Karoo region, we saw some local monkeys. The mountain pass twisted and turned giving way to some beautiful scenery and views. The roads were well maintained, empty and easy to drive. I wanted to return to Karoo and see the Cango Caves at Oudtshoorn, as they were some of the best cave systems I had ever seen. We had an early start the following day, before light, as we went in search of meerkats. It was great watching it get light in the middle of the Karoo, not a sound to be heard, and then gradually a few meerkat heads popped up from their burrows checking it was safe to head out for the day. Once they disappear, that is it. They do not return to their burrows until dusk.

We continued our journey east passing through the town of George, and then onto Plettenberg Bay, stopping on route at the Knysna Elephant Sanctuary. I had been there before on a work trip, but now with our own guide we spent a bit more time and some interaction with the orphaned elephants. Getting up close, we had the opportunity to feed them chunks of carrot and fruit, eagerly hoovered up with their trunks. We were able to stand right next to them and feel their leathery hides. I could have spent longer there, but it was a good place for an hour or so to have a break on our journey. Shortly after, we arrived at our next stop at Plettenberg Bay, in time to watch the sunset over the sweeping bay.

Early next morning, we headed to the Robberg Peninsula, which is a national park next to Plettenberg Bay. Getting there early meant we could park easily and then head off for a choice of walks. We picked the middle one which took us along the cliffs and then about halfway along the peninsula, there was a choice of continuing to the end, or cutting across some sand dunes to get to the other side of the peninsula and slowly make our way back. Choosing the sand dune option, I found it fairly strenuous, but I did enjoy the flora and fauna while watching cormorants diving into the sea. This walk took about three hours in all. By the time we got back to the car park, it was full, with many more cars parked all along the road. Just before we got back into our car, we noticed a family of *dassies*, small mammals similar to marmots, foraging in the undergrowth. Initially they looked cute, with their furry rotund bodies and short tails, but as we got a bit closer, they bared their teeth, clearly in charge and telling us that humans were not welcome.

We took time to explore Plettenberg Bay, and from a viewpoint above the bay, we could see some dolphins at play. On my previous visit, we had donned our wet gear and went whale watching, although as with many other attempts to see whales, we hadn't been very successful, but we did manage to see some penguins and a seal colony. I always enjoyed being out on the water, eyes peeled, just in case we got lucky. Maybe one day! About twenty minutes by car from Plettenberg Bay, we found a lovely Italian restaurant called Ristorante Enrico, on the edge of a small cove, overlooking the sea at Keurboomstrand. We went there twice, and it was always busy, with great food and was reasonably priced too. Sitting watching the sun go down, with the waves crashing to the shore, it was a peaceful end to a day's exploring.

On our final day we headed to Port Elizabeth Airport but stopped along the way at the Tsitsikamma National Park. There were plenty of hiking trails here, but the main reason for stopping was to take a walk over a series of suspension bridges that crossed the Storms River.

Below us, we watched a group of people kayaking in the gorge. All in all, a perfect way to spend our last few hours before we caught our flight to Johannesburg and our return home.

Down Under to Australia...
Part 2

Whilst at one of our Travel Counsellor conferences, my name was drawn to win two tickets on Emirates Airlines to anywhere on their route map. It would have been easy enough to book flights to Dubai and have a short break there, but you will have realised by now that this is not my style. Why take a shorter trip, when you can have a longer one, especially with the bonus that they would let us travel in business class on two of the journey's sectors. Time to return to Australia, I think.

I had never been to Perth before, so thought this would be a good place to start the trip. Arriving in Perth in the dead of night, we whizzed through immigration and found ourselves in our city hotel room within an hour of landing. I cannot think of an easier and quicker process to enter a country; such a contrast to our two-hour-plus wait in a long queue at JFK Airport in New York.

Our first day was spent exploring the city, which is relatively small, with the central business district clustered together close to the Swan River. We made our way to Kings Park to get panoramic views of the city skyline and wander amongst the native flora and fauna. The park is spread over 1000 acres with a mixture of grassed parkland, botanical gardens and natural bushland. At one end of the park is the Western Australia State War Memorial Precinct, comprising of the Cenotaph, Flame of Remembrance and Pool of Reflection, all overlooking Perth Water. We saw an abundance of colourful parrots flitting amongst the trees. Leaving the park, we strolled downhill to the downtown area of the city. We walked through the Supreme Court Gardens to the Supreme Court of Western Australia, built in 1903, surrounded by the modern high rises, and pausing for a quick photo of a line of kangaroo sculptures, leaving us in no doubt what country we were in. Perth is a mix of old and new and is still quite provincial in places. We noticed that when the shops closed downtown, the city became quiet, which made it quite difficult to find somewhere decent to eat in the evening within walking distance of our hotel.

Exploring further, we took a train to nearby Fremantle and found it to be a delightfully old-fashioned town. I thought Fremantle had bags more character than Perth, with plenty of traditional buildings dating back to when it was first colonised in 1829. Located right by the Swan River, we wandered around the Round House Prison, which was in use between 1831 and 1900. Life in prison, as expected, was harsh and must have been mentally challenging when the prisoners could see freedom just beyond the walls, looking across to the white sand of Bathers Beach and the Indian Ocean.

The main reason for visiting Fremantle though was to take a ferry across to Rottnest Island, because I was keen to see an indigenous creature, the furry inquisitive quokka. Rottnest is a traffic-free, white sand island just eleven miles off the mainland. The island is small at 7.3 square miles, but maybe a little too big to walk around in a day. There were plenty of local tourists taking their own or hired bikes on the ferry, and a few who had planned to stay in a selection of basic accommodation units for a few nights. Without bikes, we planned to use the bus that drove around the single road picking up and dropping off tourists at various stops along the way. Almost immediately after we arrived on the island, we spotted some of the twelve thousand quokka population. Looking a little like a small wallaby, these friendly marsupials were happy to feed from our hands and climb over our bags. The South African *dassies* could learn a thing or two from these little fellas. There was a permanent human population on the island of about 100, but the numbers swelled with the arrival of 500,000 annual visitors. No wonder the quokkas were tubby!

We gradually made our way around the island exploring the numerous white sand coves and rocky outlets. The aquamarine sea at the shoreline graduated to a deeper blue the further out we looked. Many visitors went to Rottnest Island for snorkelling in the sheltered coves. There was also a bit of history at Oliver Hill Battery and its lookout, and also a viewing platform to see seals basking on the rocks. Apart from the odd self-catered unit and a few other buildings such as the Visitor Information Centre and its restaurant, there were no other structures other than the arrival jetty. It was a complete getaway from the urban life across the water. Getting the ferry back, we decided to head back to Perth via the Swan River to give us a different perspective. We passed lots of beautiful riverfront properties, with their boats moored alongside. The Swan River wound its way out to the Indian Ocean from its source inland past Perth to Fremantle and the sea. Seeing Perth's skyline from the river, with its mix of both high- and low-rise buildings, was impressive, inviting us to explore more.

Our next stop was Sydney. Rather than stay in a large hotel, this time we opted to be slightly out of the centre, not far from Anzac Bridge, in a bed and breakfast. A gentle twenty-minute stroll took us to Darling Harbour, where we had a wander around, getting a bite to eat and to people watch. By pure coincidence we were there on a Saturday evening, when it happened to be the day of the free weekly fireworks display. What a great Aussie welcome!

Keen to return to the Harbour Bridge area, the following morning we made our way back to Darling Harbour to get a ferry around to Circular Quay. In my opinion this is the best way to approach the Harbour Bridge and the Opera House. Moving around the headland from Darling Harbour past Sydney's CBD, we first saw the wide expanse of the Harbour Bridge, with tiny midget sized tourists tied together walking along in a line up to the top of the bridge. As we sailed underneath it, the magnificent Opera House loomed nearer on the opposite shore. Such an iconic site to see. This metropolis was buzzing with tourists. Leaving the ferry behind we strolled around Circular Quay to the Opera House, taking a million photos along the way. I had been to the Opera House a couple of times before, once when we had a tour of the inside, and another at an evening reception at a Travel Counsellors conference, where we had a room and private area outside at the head of the Opera House overlooking the harbour. What a wonderful building it is. It opened in 1973 and is spread over 4.4 acres, with six different performance venues inside, having a seating capacity of 5738.

The Opera House led us onto the Royal Botanical Gardens, which opened in 1816. It covers a wide area and is the oldest scientific institution in Australia. We saw parrots and storks flying amongst the indigenous trees and shrubs. This led us on to Hyde Park, St Mary's Cathedral, built in 1821, and Hyde Park Barracks which dated from

1819. Back at Circular Quay we explored the Rocks, an historic district full of old traditional buildings dating from the 1800s, and a complete contrast to the high-rise office buildings adjacent to the area.

On a later trip to New Zealand, we stopped for a couple of days in Sydney before returning home, and on that occasion, we stayed at a hotel in the Rocks. We chose a harbour view room, which was great when we first arrived as we could see the Opera House in the distance above the roof tops. However, when we woke up the next morning and opened the curtains, the view was now blocked by an enormous cruise ship that had moored alongside Circular Quay. No one had mentioned that when researching our holiday! By the time we had returned in the evening, the ship had sailed, and the view restored, but blocked again the next morning by a new ship. We loved the Rocks, full of artisan shops and stalls, with lots of café culture to lure us too. We found it a relaxing way to spend a couple of hours.

Of course, no trip would be complete without a visit to the zoo, and to get there we had to take the ferry from Circular Quay across to the north shore. Again, we thoroughly enjoyed getting there as the view across the water back to the Harbour Bridge and the Opera House was outstanding. I knew I would never tire of it. The Sydney Zoo trip was mainly to feed my obsession with koalas. We had booked a time slot to have a 'one to one' with a few of them. I wondered if a couple of koala sleepyheads would greet us, but we were in luck and got within touching distance of them while they fed on their gum leaves. This was yet another magical moment for me. I had had a cuddle with one at the Currumbin Wildlife Sanctuary on an earlier trip, watched them up close at the zoo, and now just needed to see some koalas in the wild. I was to be rewarded later in this trip.

Any chance to see fabulous scenery and caves was always welcome, so a trip to the Blue Mountains and a visit to the Jenolan Caves there had to be on the agenda. It was a long day out from Sydney, but worth it to see the interior of New South Wales. The Blue Mountains are composed of sandstone, so to us that meant we were going to see some unusual rock formations carved by the wind. One of these, called the Three Sisters, is in the Jamison Valley at Katoomba and stands just under 3,000ft high, and is made up of three pinnacle-shaped outcrops. Legend has it that three aboriginal sisters lived in the Jamison Valley and were turned to stone by a witchdoctor. The colours change on the rocks depending on how the sun is shining on them and at night they are floodlit, which look spectacular against the inky black skies. So why is this region called the Blue Mountains? I had to look it up, but the blue gum and eucalyptus forests that make up much of this area give off a blue tinge when viewed from a distance.

Just west of the Blue Mountains in the Central Tablelands region are the Jenolan Caves. These are made from limestone and features many large chambers, which were discovered in 1860. We had a bit of a climb up some steps to the entrance and then dropped down gradually into the various chambers. The most impressive is the Cathedral Chamber which is over 160ft high, all artfully lit to show the stalagmites and stalactites at their best. Although caves systems basically consist of rocks, tunnels, stalagmites and stalactites, every single one I have been in has offered something different. In Majorca, the Caves of Drach are famous for their musical interludes, with a few musicians gliding across an underground lake in a boat taking advantage of the fantastic acoustics. In New Zealand, we have explored caves with hundreds of glow worms emitting their pin-prick lights to attract unsuspecting insects. Here the Jenolan and Cango Caves display their beauty with floodlit chambers and up lighting focused on specific rock formations. These rocks have been given descriptive names, such as the elephant's head or the gargoyle, and it is all part of the fun to try to recognise the shape from the description.

From Sydney we flew to Launceston in northern Tasmania, for a drive around the island. We collected our hire car at the airport and drove west to Cradle Mountain, a national park in the Central Highlands. Our accommodation at the Lemonthyme Wilderness Lodge took us back to nature, a complete wilderness retreat, where all we could hear was birdsong and the only visitors were the pademelons and possums, which came out at dusk to eat. The pademelon is found throughout Tasmania and looks like a small wallaby. We stayed in a rustic wooden cabin surrounded by tall gum trees. Some of the roads in this area were not tarmacked, which I cannot say I enjoyed, as we slid about a bit trying to get a grip on the surface, but despite this, the area was a wonderful place to walk and photograph.

Driving east from there we arrived at the Freycinet National Park on the coast. In contrast to the undulating scenery, we found beautiful white sand beaches and coves, edged by pine trees. My favourite, Wineglass Bay, does what it says on the tin, a perfect wine-glass-shaped cove, best viewed from above. To get to the viewpoint it took a strenuous hour or so to walk through the undergrowth on an uphill trail. I thought we were never going to get there, but I kept remembering a photograph I had seen of the bay and did not give up. We were treated to an up-close treat on route, up the steep rocky path, we came across a Bennett's Wallaby. It had a pretty face with long eyelashes and fur I just wanted to stroke. I didn't of course but was close enough to me. I just had to make do with getting a photo or ten! When we arrived at the viewpoint, I forgot all about the exhaustion to get there. We were greeted with a perfect arc shape bay, and deep blue sea, edged with a strip of untouched white sand, backed by a forest of pines. That view was well worth the effort. Not all the coast was sandy. Many of the bays were rocky and reminded me a bit of north Cornwall or the north coast of Jersey, but sadly no hostelries playing Genesis! Every beach we paused at was empty, completely natural, with no human interference. No kiosks, no beach cleaning, just completely as nature intended. We watched the sun go down overlooking Coles Bay, where the Freycinet Lodge was located. A perfect treat after a hard day's walking and photographing.

Next, we headed south towards the Tasman Peninsula. Here the coastline became more rugged, with crashing waves and carved rock formations. We paused in Swansea, a town on the east coast of Tasmania, on the northwest shore of Great Oyster Bay. Not far from there was the Devil's Corner Winery at Apslwan, which was a great place to stop on our journey south. From then on, as we headed down to the south-eastern coast and the Tasman National Park, the coastline became even more interesting. We came across a tessellated pavement near Eaglehawk Neck on the Forestier Peninsula. This rare natural phenomenon is only found in a few places on earth where rocks have fractured into blocks and look like man-made floor tiles. It looked like a builder had laid a smooth surface of rock on the shoreline, and carved irregular lines in a grid shaped pattern across the surface. Amazingly this has all been done by sea erosion at the water's edge. In this area the sea had carved lines into the rock faces, and natural blowholes and sea caves were evident. I really loved the drama of it all.

This led us to Port Arthur in the south-eastern corner of Tasmania. It was to here that many convicts were brought in the 19th century and sent to the Port Arthur Convict Settlement, which is now a World Heritage Site. The whole area was massive and was originally established as a timber station in 1830, but then used as a prison from 1833–1877. The main building where the convicts were held is now in ruin, but it was easy to see how it would have looked. Aside from the main prison building, there were ruins of a hospital and asylum, a church, law courts, officers' quarters, the Commandant's house and numerous other buildings all set in landscaped parkland, that led down to the shore and the secluded bay. Across the water on a tiny islet was the Isle of the Dead. No points for guessing what lay there. After the prison closed in 1877, the township of Carnarvon was established and small wooden houses were built, some of which still survive, with interiors as they would have been then. When tourism began to grow in the 20th century, the name reverted to Port Arthur.

Ninety minutes on from Port Arthur was the region's capital, Hobart. A small attractive city, Hobart was mainly focused on the waterfront. We strolled around and found old Victorian streets and houses that could have been on the Isle of Wight. Hobart was originally founded as a penal colony in 1803, so it was great to see some of the original buildings. These were mainly found in the Battery Point area of the city. Salamanca Place, close to the waterfront, had old warehouses that had been converted into restaurants, galleries and craft shops. We came across a sign inviting us in for coffee, epitomising the great Aussie humour. 'A yawn is a silent scream for coffee'. I love that. Hobart's harbour is the second deepest natural port in the world, and much of everyday life was still situated around the waterfront, busy with boats going about their business.

Driving out from Hobart, we headed up to Mount Wellington which overlooks the city. The views from the top were magnificent, from the whole city beneath us, to the Tasman Peninsula and over the mountains to the north. Every so often in the distance we could see plumes of smoke where a wildfire had taken hold. Thankfully, nothing serious, but it showed that even in the cooler climate of Tasmania, fires were still a problem. In our final moment in Hobart, we chuckled at another sign in the airport terminal. Written under the word 'Departures', it said, 'You are about to enter the hug zone. Come through and say goodbye!' Life is good when you read stuff like that.

Back to the mainland and onto the state of Victoria. We picked up another car and headed west from Melbourne to the Grampians area and Halls Gap, which is a centre for campers and walkers. Arriving in the early evening at our villa set in a quiet spot amongst the trees, we unpacked quickly and headed back outside to explore the grounds. Our villa was one of a few that overlooked a lawned area. Slap bang in the middle of the lawn, a large kangaroo ignored us, busy grazing on the grass. As the light faded, our quiet surroundings were interrupted by what sounded like a million cicadas. The noise was deafening. I have heard cicadas and crickets before, but never as loud as that. Thankfully when we went back inside the villa and closed our door, we couldn't hear them, and by the time it was light again the next morning, peace and quiet had returned.

We spent the day exploring the Grampians, which had plenty of lookouts, to view the deep valleys and forested floors below us and beyond to the far-reaching hills. It was an area of granite rock and cascading waterfalls, and a great region for hiking. From there we drove south to the coast and Port Fairy, about 180 miles west of Melbourne. This little town was very pleasant, and had everything: nice beach walks, a marina, quirky restaurants (we ate at Coffin Sally, formally an undertakers!) and the second-oldest lighthouse in Australia. We came across some more Aussie humour, again outside a drinking establishment, this time a sign saying, 'Drinking can cause memory loss… Or even worse, memory loss.' I cannot remember exactly where we read that! This area was the start of the Great Ocean Road, and we were about to drive its length back to Melbourne. We chose to drive it from west to east so that we would avoid the stream of day trippers coming from Melbourne.

About fifteen minutes along the coast towards Warrambool, we stopped at the Tower Hill State Reserve, which encompassed an inactive volcano and became Victoria's first National Park in 1892, finally being declared a State Game Reserve in 1961. We were fortunate to see a koala within touching distance, busily feeding on gum leaves. My first koala in the wild! I spent ages watching him just above my head concentrating on eating the eucalyptus leaves. Emus wandered by too. I was in animal heaven.

Not far from Warrambool we came to Logans Beach, home to the Southern Right Whales. Unfortunately for us we were visiting at the wrong time of year (what a surprise!) and had just missed the period when they could be seen from this viewpoint. It didn't stop us looking though, just in case. Again, another lost chance of viewing some whales. From this point, known as the Bay of Islands, travelling north to the Port Campbell National Park and beyond to the Otway Peninsula and Apollo Bay, the dramatic coastline is at its most interesting. We made numerous stops along this Great Ocean Road to view limestone sea stacks, carved rocks, natural rock arches in the sea, towering cliffs and blowholes. The Twelve Apostles are a collection of limestone sea stacks which are slowly being eroded by the sea. At the time of our visit only eight remained, four having already disappeared into the ocean.

As there was so much to see on this stretch of the coast, we had booked an overnight stay at a bed and breakfast, named 'Room with a View'. Indeed, it did live up to its name. The bungalow was accessed up a steep winding road from the coastal road, in a remote spot overlooking the Southern Ocean. Our bedroom overlooked the sea from high above, a fabulous place to wake up and see the sun rise. Moving on, our next stop was at Kennett River because I had read that there would a good chance to see more koalas in the trees. As luck would have it, we did see a few, sitting high up, and mostly were asleep, but that didn't matter to me. I was happy just to see more of my favourite animals. We noticed too there were lots of white parakeets and green parrots in the trees. We were standing amongst a few other tourists and one of them had a selfie stick. Suddenly about twenty green king parrots flew down from the trees and landed first on the selfie stick, and then onto my head and arms. I loved it; it was just so funny watching these cheeky birds using us as a perch. This is what I love about travel, enjoying the unexpected. This was the highlight of that day because between Apollo Bay, along the coast to Melbourne, the coastal scenery was not as dramatic, although there were plenty of pull-ins on the road that hugged the coast.

Melbourne's city roads were extremely busy, after the hours of driving along virtually empty roads, but we found our hotel and decided not to use the car again until it was time to return to the airport. We stayed south of the Yarra River and were glad we did. In this area, there were plenty of restaurants, street theatre and music as we wandered along the waterside, but a quick hop across the bridges brought us to the Northbank and the downtown area of Melbourne. As with many places we have visited, we headed up to a high viewing point. In this case the top of the Eureka Tower, which had fantastic panoramic city views and also gave us our bearings so we could see places that looked worth exploring further. We could see the Australian F1 Grand Prix Circuit at Albert Park, the MCG (Cricket Ground) at Melbourne Park, and also beneath us just across the river to Flinders Station. Along the Yarra River, watching athletic youngsters rowing, we strolled to the beautiful botanical gardens and parks.

Melbourne has some wide-open spaces and pretty gardens within walking distance of the central area, such as the Kings Domain Parklands, and within it, Alexandra Gardens, where Government House sat quietly amongst the trees and parkland. We found the Shrine of Remembrance, built between 1927 and 1934 as a memorial to all Australians who had served in every war and conflict around the world. Surrounding the memorial were the Remembrance Gardens. From that point looking back across the parkland we had a clear view of the Melbourne city skyline. In the evening we booked a dinner on the Colonial Tramcar, which is an old tram that took us south to St Kilda district to see the old part of Melbourne, whilst enjoying a hearty meal at the same time. A lovely way to end our holiday and see a bit more of the city before our flight home.

Brazil and Patagonia

If ever you get the chance to visit the southern half of South America, you really must go. I can think of a few moments on my couple of trips there that have given me chills with superlative experiences. I am often asked if I have a favourite place in the world, which is difficult to answer. I think the answer to that is there are certain places around the world that would be top of my list. Some of these happen to be in this region of the world. I first went to Brazil a few years ago with one of my daughters in August. Being in the southern hemisphere, August is in their winter, but it wasn't cold, and it was quieter than the more popular February/March peak time to visit.

Flying into Rio de Janeiro, watching the most amazing deep red/orange sunset below, we were met by our English-speaking guide and transferred to our hotel for the night. The traffic in Rio was horrendous. Solid multi-lane highways leading in and out of the city, often at a standstill. We watched local hawkers trying to sell their wares, weaving amongst the lanes of slow-moving traffic, taking their lives in their hands. After dumping our bags in our room, we walked down to Copacabana Beach. The beach was nearly empty as we watched the Atlantic waves crashing ashore. I had not realised how wide and how long Copacabana Beach extends, and just it beyond was Ipanema Beach. Naturally, I became very musical at that point with a bit of Barry Manilow in my head. A bit early in the trip to become the embarrassing mum and sing out loud, but believe me, it does not take much.

We would explore Rio further when we returned, but first we were ready to have a bit of beach time. We were collected by a local transfer company for a long drive to Buzios. Despite it costing less to travel this way, we found ourselves on an ancient coach, with narrow seats, squidged next to each other, and as we couldn't speak Portuguese, we could not understand anything the driver told us. We stopped midway for a short break, not having a clue as to why and for how long. The journey should have taken three hours, but due to the time collecting others and waiting around, it ended up being nearly six hours. The thought of having to repeat the journey in reverse was so off-putting that we booked the return with a private, more direct taxi instead, even though we had to close our eyes a few times while the driver 'negotiated' the traffic.

Buzios was a pretty beach area east of Rio. It had a very Mediterranean feel about it, much like Menorca. We stayed in a small *pousada* within a fifteen-minute walk of a choice of sandy beaches, and about ten minutes to the small centre with its shops, beachside cafés and bars — very much a family resort area. Having now seen what Buzios is like, I personally feel it is too Mediterranean for my liking, not that this is a bad thing, but when I have flown ten hours to destination, I want to see something different. I would have preferred somewhere like Ilha Grande as our beach stay, as it is a bit closer to Rio and more tropical.

We had a couple of nights relaxing before heading back to Rio for the next part of our trip, which involved a flight to Iguacu Falls. We spent two days exploring both the Argentinian and Brazilian sides of the Falls, both offering different views. Without doubt this was the highlight of our trip. The Falls are *awesome*! They are so good I had to return there and enjoyed it just as much the second time around on another trip with my husband a few years later. It could possibly be my most favourite place in the world. Having been to both Victoria and Niagara Falls, I can say with hand on heart that Iguacu/Iguazu knocks the socks off them both. The spelling of Iguacu/Iguazu depends on which country you are in, Iguacu being in Brazil and Iguazu being the Argentinian spelling.

Our guide took care of all the paperwork on the Brazilian/Argentinian border, and I think this is the best way to see the Falls. We could have seen both sides in one very full day, but the recommendation was to get to the Argentinian side for the first little train in the park at eight a.m. The park train took us to Devil's Throat, the thunderous waterfall at the head of the Falls. With over 1.6 million litres a second of iron-coloured water cascading down into the swirling abyss, the sound is deafening. Further along, accessed by a variety of boardwalks, there were viewpoints which gave the best perspective to see the 285 waterfalls that make up the Iguazu Falls, as they tumbled into the river as far as the eye can see. Some of these waterfalls were tiered with one beneath the other. I could have spent all day just taking in the view.

On our second trip to the Iguazu Falls a few years later in April, we saw many more beautiful butterflies all around the area than we did in our August visit. They landed on our arms and head, which I just loved. Normally I would not look twice at a cabbage white, but the vivid and varied colours of these all added to the beauty of the region. Included in the cost of the ticket was a boat trip that took us right into the spray at the foot of one of the falls, naturally getting soaked to the skin, but great fun. We were provided with a large waterproof bag to protect our own bag, camera, and shoes to keep them dry. It was like sitting under a full-on power shower! There was also another more leisurely boat trip on the quieter part of Rio Iguazu, a complete contrast to the power and noise of the Falls. Another bonus was getting up close to families of coati, with their pointed noses, furry bodies and long upright tails. They would follow each other in a line balancing along railings as they crossed a little bridge to get to some fruit and berries. In this area they were used to humans, and just like the quokkas on Rottnest Island in Australia, they have learnt that there might just be a titbit or two from us two-legged beasts.

Having had our fill of butterflies, coati and cascades from every angle, we travelled over the border into Brazil and stopped at a viewpoint for photos where three countries, Argentina, Paraguay and Brazil all meet, We then continued to the Brazilian side of the Falls, where the views were just as awesome and a must in order to experience everything the Falls has to offer. We made our way along the walkways, getting as close as we could to the thunderous water, gradually getting wet from the spray, but so worth it. From this Brazilian side, we found ourselves on the opposite side of Devil's Throat, but lower down, so that, initially we looked upwards to see the water crashing over. There was a walkway not seen from the Argentinian side, that led out into the river so that directly in front of us were the tumbling waters. Not a chance of staying dry on the walkway, but protected by waterproofs, it was thrilling to see the waterfall from yet another angle. The path from the riverbank led us up to a building that then had steps to ascend further to the top of the Falls, with our final view below us. Our driver met us from there, saving us having to walk all the way back to the entrance.

From Iguacu we flew to Cuiaba for a three-hour road transfer to the Pantanal wetlands. This area took us completely back to nature. August is their dry season, so we were able to see many more animals and birds feeding by the riverbed. Had we visited in our winter, their wet season, we would have had a different experience. We saw plenty of storks, herons, kingfishers, cormorants and spoonbills, plus a couple of hyacinth macaws and other birds which made a cacophony of sound especially at sunrise. We saw capybaras, caimans, iguanas and howler monkeys all within touching distance. We had activities included in our stay at our pousada where the staff were fantastic, very considerate and knowledgeable. The first morning there we donned our chaps to protect our legs and headed off along the dusty tracks on horseback, followed by a few hours relaxing by the pool in the 35°C heat. My last experience of riding a horse was when I went to Switzerland with my belligerent mule. Thankfully, this time I didn't venture off piste and my steed behaved himself.

Later in the afternoon, we took a boat with our guide along Rio Mutum, the main river there, where we saw a wide variety of wildlife. We watched the sun go down on the river and felt completely at one with nature. No streetlights, no sounds except the lapping waters and birds calling. The following morning, we were up early to go on a safari drive, eyes peeled for hyacinth macaws, tiny owls, and rheas among a range of other bird life, as well as gaucho farmers. We relaxed again for a few hours in the afternoon during the hottest part of the day, and then took the boat out again, but this time on the lake, in search of giant otters. The light was tremendous, with mirrored reflections in the water. As the sun dipped beyond the horizon we were invited to fish for piranha, as this was the time when the flies and insects came to the water and the fish pop up to catch them. Again, some great sunset views. We arrived back at our jetty in the dark to some waiting caimans, their glinting eyes reflecting in the torchlight, literally a couple of feet from us. They come up on land in the evening waiting for any piranhas caught that evening! Fortunately, our ankles didn't appeal to them as we hurried past. Any piranha caught was made into soup for us and I must say it was delicious!

Sometimes we must sacrifice sleep in order to get a magical memory. So, rising before dawn, we took a canoe out with a guide onto the river to watch the sun rise. For me this will be a treasured memory. Setting off in complete darkness, it was completely quiet on the river, with just a hint of light on the horizon. As it got lighter, we heard the odd chirrup of a bird, and gradually the birdsong increased. The sky turned pink as we heard the dawn chorus and gradually the roosting birds began to fly off. It is moments in time like these that I like to draw on when life is difficult.

After our sunrise excursion, we headed back to Rio for our last day. We had a full day ahead of us before our flight home late in the evening. First stop was Christ Redeemer, the 2330ft statue standing high over the city. Atop the Corcovado Mountain, the statue is often in cloud, but by using a private guide, who had already listened to the weather forecast, we were able to get there at the best time. Most of the crowds visit from about ten a.m. onwards, but we arrived there earlier, missing the masses. From the top, we had great views across to Copacabana, Ipanema and Sugar Loaf Mountain. The statue itself was very impressive and of course everyone took the trick photo shot of themselves with their arms outstretched and 'holding' Christ's hands. If the cloud cover had been too dense, there were views further down. There were a couple of ways to get to the top of Corcovado Mountain by either driving or travel as we did by a small train. After this excursion, we continued into the old part of the city at Santa Teresa, where we found cobbled streets and trams. There were some fine colonial buildings which unfortunately had been left in disrepair but could be beautiful again with some TLC. We took a tram down to the financial district, and looked around the enormous cathedral, which held around 20,000 people. Built in the sixties, to us it looked more like a large dalek, due to its unusual shape. I think our Russian exchange student would have been seriously unimpressed by the architecture! We then wandered through Lapa District which came to life in the evenings with street parties and live music.

Next, we stopped at the Selaron Steps, a stairway of 215 steps, made up of thousands of tiles from more than 60 countries; a very bright and interesting place in which to try and find a tile representing our own country. We were warned though not to venture to the top of the steps as this led directly to a favela. We later saw a few huge favelas clustered amongst the rest of the city's buildings. These ramshackle towns may house anything from 35,000 to a million people. Nearly every building we saw had been marked with graffiti, although some of it was very artistic. The traffic in Rio was manic. Lanes of traffic converging, weaving in and out, undertaking and overtaking at speed, yet with few collisions. We spent some time on Ipanema Beach and felt this area was better than Copacabana, as it seemed to have more character.

Our last stop was at Sugar Loaf Mountain. We had to take two cable cars to get to the top and the views were magnificent. We could see the sweeping Copacabana Beach and Ipanema beyond in one direction. And ahead in the distance Corcovado, with a lush mountainous area further on. To our right were other beach districts, such as Botafogo and Flamengo, while a smart marina was below. With views to the domestic airport in the distance, we watched planes land as we took in the panorama. I could have spent hours there. I found Rio to be a vibrant city with iconic views, and despite stories of crime, the obvious poverty and the mad traffic, we enjoyed our brief stay there.

***

A few years later we felt it was time to explore more of South America which started with a flight to Santiago, Chile. This was the start of an epic trip down to Patagonia and across to Argentina, ending in Brazil. For many years I had yearned to explore the southernmost region of South America, so was extremely excited to be able to plan my dream holiday. We arrived in a glorious sunny Santiago and were met by our driver who took us straight to our hotel. With nothing planned for the rest of the day, we took a taxi out to a military aviation museum, which suited my husband, and gave me a chance to see the area as we drove across the city. First impressions, were wide streets and leafy parks, lined with some lovely old European architecture. After an early night, we met our personal local guide who took us around the city using public transport, and on foot. It was a great way to see the city from a 'local' perspective. The metro was clean, comfortable and felt safe. We wandered through the local markets, which sold everything from fish, vegetables and fruit to beautiful flowers in stunning arrangements, although these were apparently mainly made for funerals. A shame the person they were for would not see them!

We headed to the city centre, walking through pretty plazas, passing the Basilica, the Post Office, which was housed in a lovely French style building, and onward to the seat of government, an area where public demonstrations were allowed. On the day we visited there was a peaceful pro-abortion demonstration. We continued to a viewpoint which gave us a panoramic view of the city, backed by the Andes. A brief but enjoyable visit left us with a good impression of this remote city.

We flew down to Punta Arenas in southern Chile, for the start of our five-hour drive north to Torres del Paine National Park, which I was really looking forward to visiting. The first couple of hours we drove through some flat and somewhat uninspiring scenery, stopping to take photos of guanaco (a type of wild llama), seeing rhea, and surprisingly, some flamingos too. After a few of hours, we stopped at an estancia (ranch) for a Patagonian lamb BBQ, some pisco sours and local wine, followed by a demonstration of sheep shearing. It was a nice way to break the journey. After about three hours, we could start to see a change in the scenery, with the mountains of the national park in the distance. We passed close to the Argentinian border, which we would return to in a couple of days to continue the next step of our adventure.

Our hotel in the Torres del Paine National Park was lovely, and it was good to know that everything including the long transfers was included. We woke to a beautiful sunrise and set off on a day long excursion stopping for numerous photographs. At every turn were stunning vistas, perfect for photographers. This was what I had hoped it would be like. Mountains with snow-capped craggy tops, which looked like they had been sculpted using a fork, just like the topping on a lemon meringue pie and dusted with icing sugar. We were surrounded by wild untamed treeless scenery, with not a building in sight. This area was a hiker's paradise and I had never seen so many fit people. Neither of us are serious hikers, although we do enjoy walking, so we took the gentler options by minibus. We still had the opportunity to enjoy every bit, but without the effort. Never far from view were the Torres del Paine, the three towering peaks which lend their name to the National Park. Whilst sitting comfortably in our minibus, we passed a few cyclists who ventured up and down the hilly roads by bikes which they had hired from the hotel. We were taken to Lago Grey Glacier, and to get there we had to walk across part of the dried-up lake, which would no doubt fill again when the rains came. It was quite strenuous walking on the loose shingle for about thirty minutes, but we kept stopping to take photos along the way. Eventually, we arrived at the lake and boarded a boat, which took us to the edge of the glacier. An enormous chunk of ice had broken off and floated on the lake along with small pieces of blue-white ice. Up close it was beautiful. It became very windy on the return, struggling to stay upright as we came back across the shingle, tiring, but well worth it. We stopped on the way back to the hotel for an impromptu picnic. It was such a lovely way to end the day, outside, with other like-minded travellers from around the world.

The following morning, we wandered around outside our hotel watching the horses being prepared for their riders' excursions, one of the options we could have chosen. Others set off on various hikes, some for a day, some for a half day, to different parts of the park. We headed to Lago Azul, the Blue Lake, which gave us another perspective with photo opportunities. Again, another lovely area, where we walked along the edge of the lake admiring the scenery all around us. We stopped to see a pretty waterfall and admired a small bird called the Torrent Duck, battling to stay upright as the waters plunged over the edge of the waterfall.

Having explored all there was to see in this area of the high Andes, it was time to take the four to five hours transfer across the border into Argentina. As we didn't leave the hotel until two p.m., arriving at the border point about an hour later, the border traffic was minimal. We had heard from others who had crossed in the morning, that the wait can be quite long. The border itself was interesting. After leaving the

National Park and all its stunning beauty, we travelled along dusty roads to the Chilean border post. It was straightforward getting our passports stamped, and after a quick *'baños'* stop, we travelled for another five miles or so in no man's land on a reasonably decent road, which abruptly came to an end arriving at the Argentinian border post which was no more than a large hut. There were no facilities, only a strategically placed sign telling us that the Malvinas (Falklands) were part of Argentina - very subtle! As we were the only two on our minivan transfer, the wait to get our passports stamped was minimal. We went back to our van and drove another mile or so, and then stopped again. We wondered what was happening as most conversation was in Spanish, but quickly realised we had to change to another vehicle and a new driver, who would continue our transfer for another three hours.

Noticeably there were no guanaco, or indeed any wildlife along the way. Scenically the long straight road cut through miles of empty brown plateau. I was glad I had my book to read, while my husband put his seat back and had a snooze. By the time we got to our destination, El Calafate, it was beginning to get dark. El Calafate, in Argentina, had grown since the airport was built there a few years ago. It was a small town, purpose built for tourism, set on the largest lake in Argentina, Lago Argentina. We stayed outside of town, on the edge of the lake, with lovely views across to the mountains in the distance, but this area had not been developed, so there was nothing else there. 'Back of beyond' I think I said at the time! On reflection I think I would recommend staying in El Calafate itself, as there were shops and places to eat. The reason for our stay at El Calafate was to see another awesome sight, the Perito Moreno Glacier. Having seen a lot of glaciers on my trips around the world, Perito Merino tops the lot. Another place high on my wish list, we took a well-organised excursion, picking up others on the way and were driven about an hour around the lake towards the mountains. This glacier was unusual in that was still advancing. It was 19 miles long and covered an area of 97 square miles. First, we travelled across the lake to our first view of the 3.1mile-wide blue tinged glacier. All the time we could hear the cracks and thuds of ice breaking off and tumbling down 558ft into Lake Argentino. Then we headed to the edge of the glacier, donned some crampons and began a mini trek up onto the glacier itself. What a thrilling experience that turned out to be. Small groups followed crudely carved out ice pathways, weaving over the crevasses. We stopped on top for a neat tot of whisky. Just the one! We needed to keep our heads, navigating all of the crevasses. After exploring the surface of the glacier, we were lucky enough to go underneath and inside it. Now that was most definitely a WOW! moment. To be walking underneath, inside a glacier was incomprehensible. The blue ice was almost transparent and smooth to the touch, yet it wasn't particularly cold. We then made our way back to the main viewing platform that gave us a panoramic view of the full width of the glacier from a series of walkways at different levels. Stretching back as far as the eye could see, this glacier was enormous and another moment I will treasure. It was fabulous.

The following morning, we took a short flight south to Ushuaia, still in Argentina, and claimed to be the most southerly city in the world. The Andes still form a backdrop this part of the world. Our hotel overlooked the Beagle Channel, with Chile just across the water. We spent the afternoon exploring the small city, but with a population of just 58,000, it felt more like a large town. We paused at the Memorial to the Falklands War on the waterfront and enjoyed the relaxed atmosphere. From Ushuaia, we headed into the Tierra del Fuego National Park. Here we travelled on the Tren del Fin Mundo (end of the world train), which cut through generally unremarkable, though undulating scenery. We then continued by road to the end of the Pan American Highway, loving the fact that nearly 11,200 miles to the north was Alaska. We could go no further south by road. As is the norm for us, we had to have a photo stop at the allegedly, most southerly post office in the world which was nothing more than a corrugated hut on the edge of the Beagle Channel, with a red post box outside and an Argentinian flag.

The following morning, we boarded a boat to sail along the Beagle Channel in search of cormorants, seals, sea lions and penguins, of which there were plenty. We paused by Martello Island to see the colony of Gentoo and Magellan penguins. We were visiting at the end of their season there, but still managed to see quite a few of these quirky birds. Although extremely chilly, we enjoyed the views and took photos of various sea life along the way. Incredibly the next proper mainland south of us was Antarctica! On our return, we warmed up with a hot lunch and another wander around Ushuaia before heading back to our lovely hotel.

That evening we flew to Buenos Aires and were met by our guide. Her welcoming remark was to advise my husband to leave his watch and camera in the hotel safe owing to the large number of pickpockets in the city. That really instilled confidence! The following morning, we were picked up and driven north of the city out into the countryside for a day of gauchos and a BBQ. A fourth-generation family of gauchos ran the estancia, so it was good to see the cultural authenticity there. Some of us opted to ride with the gauchos, and others take a leisurely ride in a sully (an old-fashioned open carriage.) We then had a traditional BBQ with wine and beer, followed by demonstrations of horse whispering and traditional dancing. I know it was all put on for tourists, but I am sure we were shown a good example of the how the life of a gaucho would be.

The following day it was time to explore Buenos Aires, so we met our guide for a tour around the city by local bus and on foot. Like Santiago, it was good to be part of the city and not cushioned by a private car. Buenos Aires is enormous. We had been warned about the traffic, normally just like manic Rio de Janeiro, but as it was the Easter break, there were less cars around. The city had a European influence, having drafted in French architects in the 18th century. Full of wide leafy boulevards, parks and handsome buildings, the central area was very attractive. The iconic Casa Rosada (Pink House), where Evita once stood on its balcony to address the masses, was covered in scaffolding, but fortunately the building work did not detract too much from its beauty. We continued to the bohemian area of La Boca, which was full of colourful buildings inhabited by artists and now a buzzing tourist area. We were treated to some impromptu tango dancing in a market area, with plenty of local handicrafts to browse, and numerous open-air bars and restaurants, although we were always mindful of keeping valuables out of sight. It was in distinct contrast to the wealthier central area, but just as interesting. We ended up in the

Recoleta district of the city and visited the mausoleum where Evita is buried. This was not what I had expected. La Recoleta Cemetery covers 14 acres, with over 6400 burial vaults set within tree lined streets with smaller pathways branching off. We heard stories of money laundering and goods being stored within the tombs, as many of them, adorned with statues, were the size of small houses. We ended our trip with a tango plus dinner show downtown, in an Art Deco theatre. We are big fans of Strictly Come Dancing, and particularly love watching the drama of the tango. It was a fine way to complete our tour around South America.

Travelling East

Apart from my work trip to Java and Bali, we have explored a bit of the Far East, although by no means all of it. The first foray east happened when we honeymooned. Still being relatively new to travelling anywhere beyond the Straits of Dover, I found out there was a 'staff' offer to either Crete or Thailand. I asked my husband which he preferred. He chose Crete, so naturally we went to Thailand. (Start married life as you mean to go on!) We spent a week in Pattaya, which at the time was rather sleazy and tacky, but our hotel was nice, and outside the main drag. We spent most of the time around the pool, and only ventured out on an excursion to see the rubber plantation and sapphire mine, that I mentioned earlier. On that trip we just had a driver and a guide in a car. When it was time for lunch, they took us to a local restaurant and asked us what we would like to eat. We had not really eaten anything deemed as 'foreign' at that time. In fact, I had only eaten my first pizza and tried spaghetti a couple of years earlier. My husband is still more of a meat and two veg man. Give him a cottage pie and he is in culinary heaven. So, we left it to the guide to choose something. It was all written in Thai, and we had no idea what to choose. I cannot remember exactly what we had, but it was served with what looked like greens. When we took a mouthful, it nearly blew our heads off, much to the amusement of our guide, eyes streaming, noses running, gulping down water to cool our mouths, we abandoned whatever it was. This was the first country we had been to where we melted in the humidity. I remember visiting an offshore island called Coral Island, and there was no shade at all. We had never experienced heat like it.

    I still love that feeling when you arrive at a hot destination for the first time, coming from an air-conditioned plane and stepping out to the shimmering heat, feeling like you are cooking on a Gas Mark 5, knowing you will not need a wrap or jumper for the next 2 weeks, even though you packed a couple extra, just in case. Talking of packing, I still pack far too much, even after all these years. Enough knickers for each day plus a couple of extra, just in case. Tops for the daytime, tops for the evening, plus dresses, trousers, and shorts in various combinations, with a plan to wear two or three changes of outfits in any one day. Realistically, for a few days by the pool, I would just need my swimsuit, sarong and a sun hat, a good book, a splash of sunscreen, and I'd be good to go. I always pack too many shoes although I am more likely to slip my Havaianas on every time. There are sunscreens, moisturisers, creams for this, ointments for that - known in our house as the bag of lotions, potions, ointments and creams. They normally stay in the bag, mostly being untouched, but packed... just in case! I have got better as I have got older but could still cut the packing by half.

More recently we have explored Malaysia, Vietnam, parts of Cambodia, Singapore and a little of Borneo. All five regions have something different to offer, culturally and historically. It has been a real eye opener, and I have learnt much on my travels.

Arriving in Kuala Lumpur, we decided to get the hop-on-hop-off bus to explore, costing only £8.50 each for the day. We often used this method of transport to explore cities, as their routes would take us to all of the popular places with an informative commentary to listen to as we travelled around. In this way we were able to see KL's highlights, first stopping at the Petronas Towers, for fantastic views of the city. We were treated to an aerial display by the South Korean Air Force aerobatic team, the Black Eagles as they flew past the Petronas Towers. The Skybridge observation deck at the Petronas is about two thirds of the way up on the 86th floor and links the two towers, which are still the tallest twin towers in the world. The views were far reaching, giving us a perspective of our day ahead. The traffic in KL was horrendous, so it took time to get to each place of interest. Our favourite area, slightly off the main road, was around the Royal Palace, called the Istana Negara with its golden domes and home to the monarch of Malaysia. The whole area covered 241 acres, and the main entrance was guarded by smartly dressed white suited guards. We then stopped at the Kuala Lumpur Butterfly Park, home to over 5000 butterflies and set in landscaped gardens full of exotic plants and ferns, followed by the Bird Park in one of the world's largest aviaries, and then onto Merdeka (Independence) Square.

On the whole Kuala Lumpur is a modern high-rise city, but dotted around, and particularly at Merdeka Square, there is evidence of the old colonial city, with turn of the 19th-century buildings dwarfed beside the skyscrapers. This area was formerly used as a cricket ground by the Royal Selangor Club, and it looked oddly out of place. Not far from there was Chinatown, bustling with traders trying to sell their wares. This was really no different to the other Chinatowns we have walked through elsewhere in other cities. The cost of living in KL was low, so our money went far, certainly much further than in neighbouring Singapore.

From Kuala Lumpur, we flew to Hanoi, the capital of North Vietnam. Lying on the Red River, it is Vietnam's second largest city with a population of over eight million. Previously the capital of French Indochina, the city's French colonial architecture is still evident today. Hanoi assaulted our senses; full of mopeds, a cacophony of car horns, bicycle bells, together with the smells of food. The first thing we learnt was how to take your life in your hands and cross the roads safely. At first the thought of trying to get from one side of the road to another was daunting, but we were advised just to step out, continue walking steadily and not to stop. The bikes, mopeds, cars and people would manoeuvre around us. Just to make sure that theory was correct, I noticed my husband always allowed me to step out before him. What a gentleman, you say! I'm not daft, I knew what he was thinking, so I made sure there was someone in front of me too!

We had a half day tour around the Old Quarter, which is an area where land is at a premium. Consequently, there are many very narrow, but tall buildings. Health and safety are not high on the agenda in Vietnam either. We saw numerous buildings overloaded with electricity cables just above our heads. I loved wandering past local traders who had set up stalls full of locally grown fruit and vegetables anywhere they could, such as from the top of a bicycle, complete with an umbrella perched above it to protect against the heavy downpours. Bikes and mopeds were a cheap way of getting from A to B, and they were used to their fullest capacity. There were whole families, some with all sorts of goods, delicately balanced, on them too - even a few fridges! I've never seen that in London! I just loved it.

We were taken to the Temple of Literature, which houses the Imperial Academy; Vietnam's first university. Within the walls are various pavilions, halls, and statues, all enclosed within five adjoining courtyards. Unfortunately, the heavens opened whilst we were there, and the sunken courtyards soon filled with ankle deep rainwater. Fortunately, we were able to take shelter in one of the courtyards that had an enclosed upper floor dedicated to the monarchs who had contributed most to the foundation of the temples and the academy. It was a shame about the rain, but it was absorbing to see a bit of history relating to ancient Vietnam. As the rain continued, we stopped at the Ho Chi Minh Mausoleum, an enormous construction of granite, guarded by a couple of white uniformed soldiers. Although deserted, it was easy to visualize the parades that would take place on the vast square in front of it. Close by was the Presidential Palace, a fine French colonial building, once home to the French Governor — General of Indochina, but now used to host government meetings. Within the palace grounds was a more modest traditional Vietnamese stilt house and another more conventional building where Ho Chi Minh lived and worked during most of his revolutionary life from 1954–1969.

There was plenty to see in the same area of Hanoi, such as the One Pillar Pagoda, an historic Buddhist temple built in 1049, and the Hanoi Opera House, which would not look out of place in the heart of Paris. We also saw St Joseph's Cathedral, the oldest church in Hanoi, and one of the first buildings of the French colonial government, opened in 1886 and looking like a mini Notre Dame. We wandered through the streets of the Hanoi Old Town which was full of tiny shops, and stalls selling street food. Right in the middle of the historic centre was Hoàn Kiếm Lake; one of the major scenic spots in the city. At the northern end, within the lake, lay Jade Island, on which the Temple of Jade Mountain stood, with a pretty, traditional red wooden bridge linking the island to the lake shore.

From Hanoi we drove to Halong Bay for our overnight stay on a junk. It took us about three hours to get there, passing rice paddy fields with Vietnamese, wearing conical hats, tending their crops, just like a page from National Geographic. We also passed an abundance of oyster farms as we got closer to the bay. I was surprised at the number of boats and junks docked ready to take tourists out into the beautiful Halong Bay World Heritage site. Some sailed out for the day, others overnight with more staying for a couple of nights. The bay consisted of dense clusters of limestone monoliths and outcrops of various shapes and sizes, spread over an area of around 600 square miles. Each islet was topped with thick jungle vegetation and rose spectacularly from the ocean. Several of them were hollow with enormous caves, some with enormous stalagmites and stalactites. A community of around 1600 people lived on floating houses in Halong Bay spread across four fishing villages. We weaved in and out around the bay, passing numerous sea stacks, while sailing under limestone arches to hidden lakes. Unsurprisingly many local vendors brought their trade out to the passing boats in the hope that someone would buy. We stopped at one island and went ashore to a cavern prettily lit so we could see the beautiful geology within. As the sun set, the rocks turned into an orangey hue - perfect for a photo or three.

From Halong Bay we returned to Hanoi Airport, and after a short flight we arrived at Danang Airport and drove to Hoi-An for a couple of nights. Hoi-An has a traffic free old town centre and is another World Heritage site, famous for its artisan crafts and tailor shops. Prominent in the city's old town is its covered Japanese Bridge, which dates from the 16-17th centuries. This historic district is a well-preserved example of a south-eastern trading port in use from the 16th to 19th centuries. It was founded as a trading port by the Nguyen Dynasty Emperor Hoang around 1595, rising to prominence in the 18th century as an important trade port for the ceramic industry. We wandered around for a few hours, exploring the numerous Chinese temples, crossing the river that runs through the old town with plenty of colourful fishing boats moored up alongside. The old town market was lined with traders squatting beside straw trays and bowls of brightly coloured vegetables and fruit, scantily protected from any rainfall by umbrellas and tarpaulin. Hoi-An has some beautiful Chinese style temples with jade-coloured tiled roofs ornately decorated with dragon symbols, many used for worship and some for communal meeting places. Strung across many of the streets were colourful Chinese lanterns adding a unique charm to the place.

After Hoi-An, we continued south to yet another UNESCO World Heritage site, the Citadel in the city of Hue. For a while the old capital of Vietnam, and once home to the Emperor and his concubines, the imperial city was built in the 19th century, surrounded by a moat and thick stone walls, encompassing the Forbidden Purple City and its palaces and shrines. The whole area was full of monuments, tombs and palace buildings, many guarded by stone statues of ancient warriors. Alongside the adjacent Perfume River we also visited the Thien Mu Temple and Pagoda, a 69ft tall pagoda built in 1844, each of its six levels dedicated to a different buddha.

From there we flew to Ho Chi Minh City, previously known as Saigon, in South Vietnam. This was an enormous city, which seemed more modern than Hanoi, mainly because of the US influence leftover from the war. I wished I had travelled to Vietnam when I was studying for my GCE O level History. I had no interest in the Vietnam War, that was then dominating the news on TV every evening. At the age of fourteen I was more interested in pop music and boys. I had heard of words such as Vietcong, the DMZ, Ho Chi Minh and people living in underground tunnels, but it was all so far away, and we had an uninspiring history teacher. He wore tweed jackets and beige desert boots, had a scraggy beard and breathed heavily behind us while we were at our desks. Frankly, I am amazed that I am really interested now in social history, architecture, and geography. Listening to our guide, I finally understood the events in Vietnam. We were taken to the Cu Chi Tunnels outside of Ho Chi Minh City to see how the Vietcong had survived the war, by using an ingenious set of tunnels. We also saw the traps they set for their US enemies, including a camouflaged pit, that hid a bed of up-turned nails, causing serious injury or death. We learnt a lot about the awful war that dragged on in the 60s/70s, albeit from a very biased old film, with a lot of talk about the American enemy. The tunnels were set in a wooded area, with narrow claustrophobic passageways leading to rooms carved from the earth. They were used as supply and underground communication routes as well as living quarters. In all there are 75 miles of these complex tunnels at Cu Chi, and above ground nobody would know they were there, save from the few torso sized entry holes in the ground, that were only revealed when the undergrowth was removed. In fact, some of them looked like a large animal had burrowed down to its lair beneath us. During periods of heavy US bombing, the Vietcong were forced to live in this underground world for many days at a time. This would have been a feat of endurance as the atmosphere below ground was stifling. We were invited to go down into some of the tunnels, but given that they were small, and it was 35c, I felt it was too claustrophobic to attempt and it would be just my luck that I would be stuck down there… too many doughnuts!

Back in Ho Chi Minh City we saw the CIA Station Building where a helicopter landed on the roof, evacuating US personnel and South Vietnamese government staff in April 1975. An incredibly famous image, it came to represent the fall of Saigon and the chaotic final days of the Vietnam War. I vaguely remember seeing this on the TV news at the time. We then walked along a beautiful boulevard with a statue of Ho Chi Minh and the French colonial styled City Hall behind it. Ho Chi Minh was a highly respected revolutionary leader and founder of modern Vietnam.   In the mid-1800s Vietnam was part of French Indochina, so consequently there are still many fine buildings from that era in Ho Chi Minh City. The Notre Dame Cathedral Basilica of Saigon sits prominently and adjacent to the equally attractive Saigon Post Office. The post office exterior reminded me of some of the buildings in St Petersburg, with yellow painted walls embellished with white sculptures. The whole area is photogenic and popular not only as a stopping point for tourists but also used as a backdrop by photographers taking formal photos of wedding couples and graduation students. The Jade Pagoda with its strong smell of incense, was another fascinating place to visit, watching the locals praying for various things, such as a better life, or a son.

We also made a stop at the Reunification Palace which is relatively modern as it was only built in the early 1960s. It was the site of the fall of Saigon, and consequently South Vietnam too, on 30th April 1975, when advancing North Vietnamese army tanks crashed through its gates. We walked through various public rooms, including the presidential reception room and conference hall, and then downstairs to the underground war office, with its primitive communications centre and early computers. The building was originally called the Independence Palace but was renamed after the end of the war. We went up onto the roof to see the helicopter landing pad, complete with helicopter, from where President Thieu, his family and staff were evacuated just days before the fall of Saigon. As I said, this trip was so educational. If I had known all of this when I was studying history at school, I am sure I would have passed with flying colours! Many of the buildings in Vietnam looked old but were in fact rebuilt in the 20th century after the French Colonial war and Vietnam war. Vietnam has seen many years of unrest in its recent history. I just hope this time of peace will last for many years.

Leaving Vietnam, we flew to Siem Reap, in Cambodia for the last couple of days of our holiday to explore the UNESCO World Heritage site of Angkor Wat and surrounding ancient Buddhist temples. The temples of this ancient Khmer city number over one thousand, with most of them located in the Angkor Archaeological Park which cover an area of 150sq miles. It was at Angkor Wat that we had another of our memorable moments. Rising before dawn, we made our way to Angkor Wat to watch the sun rise over the main temple complex. The silhouetted temples were back lit by the rising sun, turning the sky from pale green to orange, as the sun rose from the horizon. Adding to the beauty, a lake in front of the temple reflected the colours and the temple as a mirror image. The whole experience was magical and the highlight of our trip.

Each temple, built for various rulers of the ancient Khmer Empire over a period of six hundred years, show carvings and bas relief friezes depicting episodes from early Hindi, and later Buddhist, epic sagas, each telling a story. Some temples had restored terraces featuring a multitude of buddhas, including some enormous ones with smiling faces. Others had been left to nature with enormous tree roots snaking through the ruins, becoming part of the stonework. We visited a temple dedicated to women, with intricate carvings still visible on the pink sandstone columns. We only touched on this vast region briefly, but after our early start and walking around in 90 percent humidity and a temperature of 38°C, we were eventually all 'templed' out and longed for the air-conditioned room back at our hotel. Arriving back, we flopped on our beds, completely drained and did not move for the rest of the evening.

Cambodia is economically less developed than Vietnam and has a mainly Buddhist/Hindu influence. The style of the buildings in the city of Siem Reap are reminiscent of Thailand and quite different to those in Vietnam. I feel that travel here is still in its infancy, so is still a great country to visit while there are relatively few western influences.

***

One of my travel wishes was to see orangutans in Borneo, and a couple of years ago I was able to tick that one off. We flew via Kuala Lumpur for an overnight airport hotel stop and onward to Sandakan on the island of Borneo. Our guide took us to our accommodation just outside the Sepilok Orangutan Reserve, about fifteen miles from Sandakan. Sepilok was opened in 1964 as the first official orangutan rehabilitation sanctuary project for orphaned baby orangutans rescued from logging sites and plantations, as well as from illegal hunting. They are trained to survive again in the wild and released as soon as they are ready. The sanctuary currently has around 60-80 orangutans living free in the reserve. Arriving in the early afternoon, we had time to walk to the Reserve in the hope of seeing some orangutans feeding. The apes were fed at ten a.m. and three p.m. daily, and as the area was open forest, they were free to come and go. When we visited in September, we discovered it was the fruiting season, so many of the apes helped themselves to fruit in the rainforest and had no need to come into the Reserve. To get the best chance of seeing plenty of orangutans and monkeys, plan to visit between April and July when the weather is dry and there is no fruit on the trees and bushes. We only saw one large male that afternoon, which was a bit disappointing, but we had booked to visit again early the next morning.

Just opposite the Orangutan Reserve was the Sun Bear Conservancy Centre, which opened in 2008, with just seven bears. This rescue and rehabilitation facility is home to Malayan sun bears, the second rarest bear species after the giant panda. They are the smallest bears in the world and are only found in Southeast Asia. They continue to be threatened by deforestation and by illegal hunting for bear parts as well as from poaching to obtain young cubs for the pet trade. There were forty-three rescued ex-captive sun bears at the Conservancy

Centre. They lived in large forest enclosures, providing a natural environment suited to their needs and welfare and to facilitate their rehabilitation back into the wild. We saw plenty of cute little sun bears, with their yellow noses and black bodies (who remembers the Sugar Puff adverts?) They were great climbers and spent much of their time foraging in the undergrowth and high up on the purpose-built decked platforms. We could observe them from our viewing platform, giving us great views of them beneath us.

Then we walked across to the Orangutan Reserve, put our belongings in a locker and headed off to their viewing platform. Set around a large tree trunk, a decked area had been constructed where rangers left piles of fruit and other natural foodstuffs for the apes to enjoy. We had a clear view of these gentle giants delicately peeling bananas and opening husks to enjoy what lay inside them, displaying almost human characteristics. Some orangutans cuddled their babies as they ate, and other smaller, younger adolescents swung happily on ropes amongst the trees. Plenty of other apes and monkeys swung down to the platform and entertained us all with their acrobatic prowess, whilst we recorded the memories on our cameras.

After a while we moved along to the orangutan nursery, where behind glass we could view the younger members, who were outside, swinging on ropes and playing roly-poly. The nursery opened in 2014 and the babies are kept away from the older apes while they learn to be in the forest outside. The babies are aged between one and three years and need to undergo a period of 'preschool' training to give them skills essential to life in the jungle, such as the ability to climb, swing and move from tree to tree. In the wild, these skills would be learnt from their mothers, but those in captivity, deprived of their mothers, are unable to find food, build nests or even climb properly. All the animals are given a thorough health check on their arrival, followed by a period of three to six months' quarantine. When the young orangutans have totally adjusted to life in the forest and show signs of independence, they are gradually moved to the last phase of their 'survival training' where less food is offered further away from the Centre. Since the Centre was established, more than one hundred orangutans have successfully been released into the wild. I could have stayed there for hours watching them all.

Leaving Sepilok, we were dropped off at a jetty on the Kinabatangan River, which is Malaysia's second longest river. We met a guide with some other travellers joining us to start a two-hour boat trip along the wide muddy river to the Sukau Rainforest Lodge. This is an eco-lodge, which received accreditation from National Geographic in 2015 as one of its Unique Lodges of the World. The plan was to see some unique and diverse fauna along the river during our stay for the next couple of days. On the way to the lodge we paused to see a freshwater crocodile and kept a look out for various monkeys and birds along the river. On arrival at the lodge's jetty, we disembarked onto a decked pathway leading into the rainforest to the reception area and onto our own lodge. Included in the price were a variety of river excursions. On a night excursion we explored some of the main river's tributaries. In the dark it was impossible to see anything, except the river and the outline of trees and bushes, so I wondered how we were supposed to see any animals. Our guide had clearly done this before and with a strong spotlight, showed us a few monkeys high up in the trees and a few small birds hidden in the riverside greenery. How they knew where to look was beyond me. I could not spot a thing until he pointed them out! The following morning, we were up at dawn to see the animal life waking. This was quite a different experience to the one in the Pantanal in Brazil. From our eight-seater boat we had great views of saltwater crocodiles, basking on the water's edge, and a massive monitor lizard snoozing on a branch above us. Graceful egrets had their eye on the river and any tasty treats within it. We caught flashes of colour as a kingfisher flitted between the branches. With his vivid blue plumage, golden head, red beak and matching red legs, he looked quite dandy. Down one tributary we glided amongst the mangroves and beds of water lilies. Although classed as an endangered native, we saw plenty of 'Jimmy Durante' look alike proboscis monkeys grouped in families, flaunting their acrobatic abilities, leaping from branch to branch with accuracy. From our boat we watched large families of macaques on the shoreline, quite used to living near human habitation. Amongst them were a few tiny offspring that looked just a few days old, clinging to their mothers' backs, and alongside a few juveniles, eager to play and cause mischief. Looking up, we could see hornbills and eagles flying overhead. To enable the monkeys to cross the wide river, a highwire had been erected, and when we passed underneath, we witnessed a battle of supremacy between a couple of macaques. Neither wanted to give way to the other and neither fell in! A couple of funambulists at their best! One trip we decided against was a visit to a bat cave. Bats and their guano did not appeal, but others who took the trip told us that when they arrived at the car park, a lone orangutan wandered right past them. We had hoped to see more from our lodge in the rainforest, but sadly it was not to be.

We returned to the lodge just as the sun was setting. The river was still and the sky clear, turning pink, as the sun set while the treeline was a perfect reflection in the river. It was a beautiful sight.

Leaving the river lodge, we headed back down the Kinabatangan River where most of the human habitation lived in small village clusters, only accessed from the river. We took a flight to Kota Kinabalu and were met by our guide who took us to the jetty to depart for Gaya Island Resort, our home for three more nights. Gaya Island is a beautiful small eco island just fifteen minutes from the Borneo mainland. One of five islands located off Kota Kinabalu, Gaya island is only 5.7 square miles. We had a beautiful villa overlooking the sea and white sand beaches, surrounded by lush vegetation and walkways. Each island is fringed by coral reefs, so an ideal spot for diving in the crystal-clear waters, which teem with a variety of colourful fish. A marine centre was established on the island in 2013 and is dedicated to conservation programmes such as turtle rescue and coral reef restoration. Aside from diving, the island is peppered with walking trails and secluded sandy coves. A few hammocks swung enticingly between palm trees on the main beach. It was so peaceful and just the place to chill.

Before long it was time to move on and spend our last couple of days in Singapore. The best way to get an overview of the city is to head up to the Sky Park Observation Deck on the roof of the Marina Bay Sands Hotel. The view from the top of the hotel was fantastic. As we were not staying at the hotel, we were restricted to a largish area away from paying guests, but the panoramic views across the bay from the top were just as good and a perfect place to get our bearings. Singapore did not disappoint. Looking across to the Central Business District (CBD) and moving round, we could see the old Fullerton Hotel, and close by the Merlion statue, the official mascot of Singapore, depicted as a mythical creature with a lion's head and body of a fish. Not too far from there was the Singapore Flyer, a large Ferris wheel that was opened in 2008 and one of the tallest in the world. Looking out in another direction towards Singapore Strait we could see hundreds of ships offshore waiting to visit Singapore's busy port.

In the foreground we had great views of the Gardens by the Bay, a nature park covering 250 acres of reclaimed land adjacent to Marina Bay. It consisted of three main areas: the Flower Dome, the Cloud Forest Dome and Supertree Grove. The Cloud Forest Dome replicated the cool moist conditions of tropical mountain regions, with trees and plants from those areas, with an impressive 115ft waterfall as its centrepiece. The Flower Dome is the largest greenhouse in the world covering 2.5 acres. This dome was divided into specific themed areas representing each of the continents and showcasing plants, trees and vegetation unique to those regions. Singapore also has its own Botanical Gardens in another part of the city, but we were advised if time were short, the Flower Dome would fulfil any desire to see a huge variety of unusual plants. The largest tree in the conservatory was the African Baobab, whilst the tiniest plants in the dome, at under 2mm across were some of the world's smallest orchids. A magnifying glass was provided to see them properly! Outside the domes were the gardens' main feature: the sculpted trees. These tree-like structures, covered in vegetation, dominated the landscape with heights ranging from 82ft to 160ft. There was an elevated walkway between the two larger Super Trees which also offered panoramic views over the gardens by day. At night these vertical gardens came alive with a coordinated light and music show known as the Garden Rhapsody. We loved it.

Walking from the Merlion, we came across a statue of Sir Stamford Raffles by the Singapore River. It marked the spot where he first landed on 28 January 1819. It reminded us that we needed to stop off at the Raffles Hotel for a compulsory Singapore Sling. I have to say they were so delicious we had to double-check that a second one would taste as nice as the first. It did. Not far from the high-rise shiny modern architecture of the CBD was the downtown core of the city and Chinatown. The buildings there are much more traditional, and low rise. There were many buildings that date from colonial times, including many Buddhist and Hindu temples. In the heart of Chinatown, the Sri Mariamman Hindu Temple was the oldest of them all and is listed as a national monument. Chinatown had many buildings dating from the 19th century with elements of both Baroque and Victorian architecture. Following the river, we eventually came to Clarke Quay, another popular area, with a good choice of eateries and entertainment. We also found the subway system good value and easy to use.

Compared to the cities in Vietnam and Kuala Lumpur, Singapore was spotless and noticeably litter free. It puts our London streets to shame. No cigarette butts, no chewing gum ground into the pavements and orderly traffic despite being busy. I think our councils could take a leaf out of their book. I can completely understand why Singapore is a popular stopping-off point before heading to other parts of the Far East, Australia and New Zealand.

Even though we were thousands of miles away from England, home never seemed far away. We were sitting in café at Singapore Airport waiting for our flight to be called, when we saw a couple that we knew from the area where we live. We exchanged experiences of our trip over a drink, and kept saying what a small world it was, before continuing our journey. This has happened a few times before to us. Whilst on our cruise around Hawaii, we were waiting to go into dinner, when I spotted a colleague who was with her family, not believing we had travelled over 7000 miles and bumped into each other. On another occasion, we were sitting in the departure lounge at Vienna Airport, after a work trip, and we got chatting to a couple of people. It turned out that one of them was the drummer for Status Quo, and with him was another musician, who lived in our village.

Road trip around New Zealand

If I were asked to name my favourite country that I have visited, I would have to say New Zealand. When talking to prospective customers who want to know why, there is a long list of reasons. In my opinion a visit there ticks all the boxes. Being a compact country about the size of Britain, it's easy to explore the range of differing scenery. Sub-tropical golden beaches in the north, with lush rolling hills, thermal regions, crystal-clear waters and interesting landscapes. As you head south, you'll discover snow-capped mountains, waterfalls and lakes in the southernmost regions. If that were not enough, the people are the friendliest I have ever met. New Zealand offers so much more than fabulous scenery though. Māori culture is strong, particularly in North Island. There are plenty of places to visit to learn about the indigenous people and see their meeting houses and longboats. There are numerous outdoor activities to enjoy too. Hiking, skiing, extreme sports, cycling, fishing, sailing, wine-tasting and scenic flights are just some that spring to mind. Then there are the animals, and distinct lack of certain species. There are no snakes in the wild, no venomous spiders to worry about, but if you are lucky, you might see a kiwi, a yellow-eyed penguin, a kakapo, kea or takahe, all indigenous birds. Whales, seals and sealions are often easy to find along the coasts, whilst inland you are likely to see various species of deer, and up above, you might spot a falcon or a Haast eagle. The cost of living is reasonable too compared to the UK. We had not sampled some of the food choices on the New Zealand menus before, such as boysenberries and hokey pokey ice cream. I like their concept too of BYO (Bring Your Own bottle), when eating in a restaurant, just paying for corkage. It keeps the cost down when on a budget, although New Zealand wines are excellent and reasonably priced.

Our first visit was in 1984, when we hired a campervan and drove from top to toe over a three-week period. We enjoyed our trip so much that when we got home, we made enquiries about moving out there permanently. Sadly, our jobs did not count as ones that would be beneficial to their economy, and we couldn't fulfil certain other criteria.

Many years later we returned to cover the areas we missed on that first trip. One trip covered North Island and another South Island. I will take you on a trip from north to south, combining our experiences over the past thirty-five years.

To explore the area north of Auckland you need a minimum of three days, although the Bay of Islands is a great place to chill for longer and enjoy the pretty coves and sandy beaches. Starting at the very northern tip, Cape Reinga is the point where the Tasman Sea meets the Pacific Ocean. Just like at Land's End in the UK, there is a signpost indicating various distances in all directions. Surprisingly, the Equator is nearer than the South Pole. London is over 11,180 miles away. Interestingly, this is the same distance as the length of the Pan American Highway from Alaska to Argentina. You live and learn! Naturally, just as we have been to the furthest point south on the Pan American Highway and had a photo stop at Cape Horn, we had to pose by this signpost. Close to Cape Reinga is Ninety Mile Beach, which can only be accessed by 4WD or by tour bus, as the tides can be deceiving. The beach isn't actually ninety miles in length but a mere 55 miles. The wide flat sands are ideal for blokarting (land yachts), and the sea is popular with windsurfers and anglers. Close by there are sand dunes which attract bodyboarders.

Heading south along the east coast, the Bay of Islands would be a perfect place to spend a few days. If interested in Māori culture, a visit to the Waitangi Treaty House is a must. Just north of Paihia, the Treaty of Waitangi was signed in 1840 between the Māori chiefs and British Crown representatives marking the moment when New Zealand became a British colony. In addition to visiting the Treaty House, there are also Māori war canoes, a beautifully carved meeting house and a couple of museums. Paihia is a good place to base yourself to explore the surrounding islands. We took a light aircraft trip which gave us a wonderful overview of the area with a green patchwork landscape below us on the mainland. We flew over Russell which was the first permanent European settlement and seaport in New Zealand, and then onward over many of the 144 islands that make up the Bay of Islands. There are many other activities to enjoy in the area, such as boat trips, sea kayaking, diving and paddle boarding.

Paihia is only three hours from Auckland, and scenically the drive is more undulating than spectacular. Arriving in Auckland, a good place to get an overview of the city is to head to Mt Eden, a now dormant volcanic crater on the edge of the city. From this point there are marvellous views of the city, only 2.5miles away, with the harbour bridge beyond. From Mt. Eden we crossed Auckland Harbour Bridge, an eight-lane motorway stretching over Waitemata Harbour to Davenport on North Shore to get a different perspective of the city. There is a lovely marina area on the city side called Westhaven Marina, full of expensive-looking yachts. It is the largest yacht marina in the Southern Hemisphere with nearly two thousand berths and moorings. In the city itself the Sky Tower stands 630ft above the city, and from there, if you are brave enough, you can walk around the outside platform at the top to enjoy the cityscape below. There are no railings, but thankfully you are harnessed in! To escape the city and head off hiking or enjoy the local beaches, there are ferries to offshore islands.

From Auckland we gradually drove south and east, first stopping for a couple of nights on the Coromandel Peninsula. This area is very pretty with a rugged landscape, thick forests and winding roads leading to pretty, sandy coves and dramatic cliffs. We made our way to Hot Water Beach armed with a couple of spades to dig our own hot water pool, as the hot springs seep into the sand at low tide. In some places the water was so hot it burned our feet. We did not need a map when we got onto the beach to find where the best place to dig, because clustered in one area there were small groups of tourists, marking the best spots. A bit further along the peninsula is the small coastal town of Whitianga. We headed to the main jetty and booked a two-hour boat trip that took us along the coast to see beautiful rock formations, giant blowholes and huge sea caves, and in particular the spectacular Cathedral Cove. It is possible to walk from the white sand Hahei Beach to the cove, but the best way to see the pretty coastline is in a boat or kayak. The water in this area is crystal clear and so is easy to see the many small schools of fish.

Continuing along the coast eastwards, there are plenty of scenic vistas to enjoy along the way. We drove through Tauranga and dropped south to Rotorua to explore the region's geothermal area. Rotorua sits on a lake, and on arrival the air is permeated with the overpowering smell of sulphur. It reminded me of times in our school assembly when some bright spark would set off a stink bomb. Thankfully, after a while, the stench disappeared. Walking around the town there are numerous places where plumes of steam rise from the ground. Hot water bubbled up from the ground in people's gardens and on roadsides, There are plenty of places nearby to walk through thermal landscapes, taking in the hot springs, bubbling mud, and multi coloured rocks. We went to a place called Orakei Korako, which was about half an hour south of Rotorua. We had to get a small boat across a lake and follow a winding path that rose gradually to a fabulous viewpoint that overlooked the whole area. For a longer two-mile walk, we also visited the Waimangu Volcanic Rift Valley. Mt Taranaki can be seen in the distance from there. In 1886 it erupted and has left hot lakes, silica-filled rivers, steaming gas fumaroles, and mud pools for us all to enjoy. For anyone interested in seeing these thermal regions, but only had time to see one, I would suggest Waimangu as it ticks all the boxes.

The main reason people visit Rotorua is to have a geothermal experience, and perhaps visit some of the Māori meeting houses, but for a change, and especially if it's raining, a visit to the 3D Trick Art Gallery is a fun experience. We spent ninety minutes wandering through a gallery of wall paintings, but the difference was they were interactive. I have got a photo of me riding on a dolphin, having an injection in my backside with an exceptionally large hypodermic needle, and walking across a ravine on a fallen log. All I needed was a camera and a second person with me, and we were good to go. Another good indoor diversion is a visit to the Agrodome, just outside the town. Founded in 1971, it is a showcase of various farm animals with twenty-six different varieties of sheep. I did not know there were that many varieties! It was nice to watch the strong, muscled shearers demonstrating their prowess at sheep shearing… sigh.

After our detour to Rotorua, we continued east along the coast to Whakatane to spend a couple of nights overlooking the Bay of Plenty. The town's nearest beach, is long, dark, and wild, called Ohope, and is mainly frequented by surfers and locals walking their dogs. Naturally, we needed to find a place that would give us a good view of the surrounding area, so we headed up to Toi's Pa Scenic Lookout. We were the only people there, a shame because the view of the town, coastline and White Island in the distance is wonderful. The main reason for stopping in Whakatane was the chance to visit White Island, some 80 minutes offshore by boat. White Island is an active volcano and can only be accessed by boat through one company authorised to take guided tours, or by flying over it. The volcanic activity was at a high level 2, which meant we could visit under strict supervision for a limited time. We were given gas masks to wear, as the sulphur fumes could affect our breathing. Visiting White Island was the highlight of our trip to this part of North Island. It was fantastic to experience the raw power of a volcano with plumes of gassy steam emitting from the bowels of the earth, along with bubbling hot springs and sulphurous landscapes all around us. Sulphur was mined on the island from the mid-1880s to 1930 and there are still remnants of the old buildings there, which have been heavily corroded by the sulphuric gases. Much of the iron mine works had a yellow hue to it, especially where the hot gases escaped the earth. Apart from the rusting metal, there were no other buildings on the island. Looking around, I could imagine the surface of the moon to be similar: no trees, no greenery, just a grey primaeval landscape. While we were on the island we had to stay together and keep to the paths, with a guide at the front of our group, and another at the rear. Further ahead there was another group, and I noticed our guides in constant radio contact with other guides, checking that it was safe to continue nearer to the spot where the gases rose to their fullest extent, over a small volcanic crater lake. We could see rock breaking off as small eruptions split the rock, sending it tumbling into the water. I remember commenting when we heard a boom in the distance and asking if we should be worried. That might seem a bit dramatic, but exactly two weeks after we were on White Island, there was a major eruption which killed twenty-one tourists and injured twenty-six. All had been doing exactly what we were doing. The island is now closed to tourists and whether it will ever reopen again remains to be seen. I do count myself lucky that I was not in the area two weeks later, but the whole experience is one I will never forget. It really made me think about the power of nature.

Continuing east from Whakatane, the road winds its way to the most easterly point at East Cape, the first place the sun rises in New Zealand. There are plenty of lay-bys to stop for photos along the way as the road weaves through hills and around coves. There are no pretty beaches in this area, which is more dramatic and remote than I had imagined. On from East Cape brought us to an overnight stop in Gisborne, which is the first place that Capt. James Cook landed in 1769 at Kaiti Beach. There is a statue commemorating the landing, which we came across while we enjoyed a walk along the waterfront discovering the history for ourselves. Across the water, Kaiti Hill is a great spot to view the city and Kaiti Beach. Gisborne is a working city with a busy harbour. Its other claim to fame is that during the summer months it is the first city on earth to see the sun rise each day… unless it's raining, of course! The whole area, as we headed south from Gisborne, is rural, dotted with small farming communities, set amongst rolling hills. We passed through Wairoa, situated on the northern shore of Hawke Bay. Wairoa is a small manufacturing and farming town, with over 62% of the population identifying themselves as Māori. I noticed that places we visited throughout New Zealand, with a reasonable Māori population, all had buildings with distinct architecture. We also saw wooden churches and meeting houses painted white or cream, with brownish red tiled roofs, some with ornately carved fascia.

To the south of Gisborne is the delightful Art Deco city of Napier rebuilt in 1931 after a devastating earthquake. As bad as that was back then, the rebuild of the city in the style of that time means that Napier is architecturally different from most other towns because Art Deco was the contemporary style in 1931. I thought it was charming. Although the beach is rough and not suitable for bathing, there is a long wide path running its length which is used for walkers and cyclists, with plenty of café culture too, so I felt the city had a lot to offer for a couple of nights. Leaving Napier, we cut across to the middle of North Island to Taupo.

Taupo sits on the edge of an enormous lake of the same name and is a hub for tourists and water-based sporting enthusiasts. For the more adventurous, Taupo is a good place for skydiving, not something I have ever been brave enough to do. Just north of Taupo are the Huka Falls which are accessed by a gentle wooded walk. Nothing like Iguacu or Niagara of course, but the bluish-green water tumbling into the river was a pretty sight and a nice spot for a picnic.

South of Lake Taupo is the Tongariro National Park and if you are coming from the north will be the first place you are likely to see some snow-capped mountains. The Tongariro Alpine Crossing is renowned for hikers exploring the wild and sometimes treacherous landscape. There are three mountain peaks in this area, all active volcanic mountains, called Ruapehu, Ngauruhoe and Tongariro. This region covers over 300sq miles and is one of the locations Peter Jackson used to film *Lord of the Rings*. The whole area can take a few days to cover, but we just wanted to walk a small section of it, and an easy bit at that. Walking to the Taranaki Waterfall gave us a good insight to the region without knocking ourselves out.

On the northern slopes of Mt Ruapehu is a road leading up to Whakapapa Village, some 4000ft up. This area has over 78ins of rain annually, but in the summer months there is an option to view the volcanic crater lake at the top of the mountain via a chair lift, another 2227ft higher up. However, the weather can be very changeable, so the chairlift is often closed but there are still some panoramic views from lower down if the cloud base is high enough.

Heading further west, the most scenic and direct route to the coastal town of Whanganui is via the Parapara Highway, a section of State Highway 4. It closely follows the Mangawhero river valley, which runs through rugged picturesque terrain. Whanganui sits alongside the Whanganui River and from the opposite side of the river to the town there is a great viewing platform on Durie Hill. Accessed by an ancient elevator, there are wonderful views of the river and town beyond. Alongside the river is a bustling street market, while riverboat trips can also be taken. Just like Napier, Whanganui has many Art Deco buildings, although many predate this, such as the Royal Whanganui Opera House, which opened in 1899, and is New Zealand's last working Victorian theatre. Just outside the centre of the city is another sacred Māori site called Putiki Marae. Maraes are communal and sacred meeting places of the Māori and an important part of their culture. There is a meeting house, the Whare, which is decorated with intricate carvings inside and out, portraying stylized images of the iwi's (tribe's) ancestors. We found Virginia Lake just outside the centre of Whanganui and enjoyed a lovely walk around it, discovering various wildfowl, including black swans and pukeko. Just west of Whanganui is the coastal community of Kai Iwi. Notable for its good surfing conditions as well as its scenic black sand beaches, there are some great walks set against a stunning backdrop of rugged cliffs. From there the wild, untamed beach stretches far into the distance. Whanganui is a great place to pause before heading south to New Zealand's capital, Wellington some 120 miles further south.

Although Wellington is the capital, in comparison to other world capitals, it is relatively small and we found it easy to explore in a day. Wellington is the world's southernmost capital city. I love facts like that. It sits at the southwestern tip of North Island and its harbour provides sheltered anchorage from wind speeds that can exceed 100mph. The scenic harbour is surrounded by picturesque green hillsides with tiered suburbs overlooking the city. There are not many high rises in the city, except for a few distinctive buildings, with the Beehive probably being the most unusual, looking like what it says on the tin. The Beehive is the seat of government in New Zealand, where you will find the Prime Minister making her all important decisions. In the same area of Wellington is the Old Government Building, built in 1876, but now part of Victoria University. Up until 1998 it was the world's second largest wooden building. I wonder, what is the world's largest wooden building? Above the CBD, Wellington Botanic Gardens stretches up above the city, covering 62 acres. The pretty gardens feature protected native forest, conifers and various plant collections and is worth a stroll. Overlooking Wellington is the suburb of Kelburn, which borders the Botanic Gardens to the west. The best way to access these is to take the Wellington cable car, a funicular railway ascending from Lambton Quay, in the CBD. As with all our trips, we took this route in order to get the cityscape views. Closer to the sea, old warehouses have now been converted into restaurants and shops. We could have headed out beyond Wellington to visit an Eco sanctuary or visit an offshore island to discover indigenous birds and animals in their natural habitat, but time did not allow these. Having exhausted our sightseeing of the capital we had a choice of flying or sailing to South Island.

To get the full tour, take the ferry across the Cook Strait, which takes about three and a half hours. The journey is pretty, as the ferry passes a few smaller islands and rocky outcrops, arriving in Picton, a picturesque town in the Marlborough region of South Island, situated near the head of Queen Charlotte Sound. Apart from the arrival point for the cross-strait ferry, Picton is also a busy deep-water port. We spent some time watching men loading piles of pre-cut timber into neat piles, ready to be exported. If I were a little boy, I would have been in my element seeing all the monster trucks and cranes. From Picton the main state highway heads south, down the east coast to Christchurch and beyond.

Sixteen miles to the south of Picton is the wine growing region of Blenheim. We recognised a few brand names sold in the UK, whilst passing the many vineyards. No trip to this region would be complete without a day or afternoon of wine tasting. Sauvignon Blanc happens to be one of my favourite choices, and this area is noted for it. The bonus of course is to have someone pick you up and drop you off from your accommodation, so that you do not have to worry about how you are going to get home after your wine tasting.

From Blenheim heading south on State Highway 1, we made our way to Kaikoura in the hope of seeing some whales. You'll remember, so far, we hadn't had much luck with this. Kaikoura is renowned for whale watching, so we were very hopeful this time. At the time we visited, the main road was still being repaired after the devastating earthquake that hit Kaikoura and this part of NZ in 2016. Parts of the road had been destroyed and landslips still plagued the coast. The day we drove to Kaikoura the road was open, but the weather was squally, and it was doubtful that the boats to see the whales would be operating. Just to the north of Kaikoura we paused to see some New Zealand fur seals, basking slug-like on the rocks below us. In November 2016, a 7.8 magnitude earthquake struck in this area, killing a couple of people and triggering a tsunami, stranding many locals and tourists in Kaikoura. I bet the whales stayed away even then. We were out of luck with our whale-watching trip, so we spent the time there exploring the coast on the edge of Kaikoura. One area was fascinating. We came across a colony of fur seals laying on some unusual rock formations. The vast rock platform they basked on was smooth and flat, with a few cracks interspersed along its surface. We learnt that in 2016, this was actually the seabed, and the earthquake had raised it up out of the water by around 6.5ft. I could not get my head around the fact that I was standing on what had once been the seabed, but now out of the water. Again, the power of nature is just incredible.

Further down the coast will bring you to Christchurch. The city has changed in the intervening years between our first and subsequent visits after several earthquakes. The main area of Cathedral Square, where the late 19th century Christchurch Cathedral stands, had been irreparably damaged after the cathedral's spire was brought down in 2011. The cathedral is slowly being rebuilt, being just one of the many buildings that became inaccessible, and now part of a massive ongoing recovery programme. Other undamaged parts of Christchurch though still retain their charm. Hagley Park, created in 1855, is a large urban space which includes the Botanic Garden, alongside the Avon River. We could have been in the city's namesake in the UK. It is also worth exploring just beyond the city and heading out to Lyttelton Harbour and the Port Hills, where there are some good panoramic views of Christchurch. All around Christchurch the landscape is relatively flat as the Canterbury Plain stretches west towards the iconic Southern Alps.

Rather than drive southwards towards Dunedin, we decided to head west and stop at Lake Tekapo. At the southern end of the lake a small township has grown and is now a popular stopping point for travellers heading to Queenstown. Finely ground rock in the glacial melt waters give the lake a beautifully unique turquoise colour. Adding to the wild beauty, the water's edge is lined with multicoloured wild lupins, while on the far shore, the snow-capped mountains of the Southern Alps complete the scene. There is a small, isolated church on the edge of the lake which was built in 1935. The Church of the Good Shepherd was the first chapel built in the Mackenzie region. I mention it because the altar window here frames views of the lake and mountains, so you can impress people with an arty photo. A little further along from Lake Tekapo is another lake, Lake Pukaki, the largest of three glacial lakes that run from north to south. This lake is the nearest to Mount Cook, or, to give it its Māori name, Mt Aoraki. There is a road running along the length of the western side of the lake that leads to Mount Cook Village. We drove along it only in 1984, but I imagine it is still just as remote now. Then, we stopped overnight at a campsite at the foot of Mt Cook, not venturing out after dark, as the campsite was basic, needing a torch to guide you to the toilet block. The Hermitage Hotel is still there for those who want greater comfort, and although remote, the views of Mount Cook would be awesome, as this is the nearest easily accessible point to see it.

The route south from Lake Pukaki could lead you to Queenstown, or east back to the coast and Dunedin. We have driven both, but I will take you east to Dunedin and carry on around the coast to the southern end of South Island. Taking a scenic route through the Mackenzie District, via the townships of Twizel and Oamaru on the east coast we re-joined State Highway 1, and eventually reached Dunedin. It was here, if you remember, that we had to sort out our slow puncture whilst taking a self-guided drive around the city. Dunedin is known as the Edinburgh of New Zealand. Even the name is almost an anagram, its Scottish heritage visible everywhere, such as the Gothic style Presbyterian Church which is one of New Zealand's tallest structures. Dunedin's suburbs extend out into the surrounding valleys and hills and onto the isthmus of the Otago Peninsula. It's on this peninsula that you can see the rare yellow eyed penguins and cute Little Blue penguins, along with various species of albatross. Time now to head to the southernmost city in New Zealand, and the commercial centre of Southland to Invercargill. I can only speak of our impressions from our single visit there in 1984, but it was bleak and probably not helped by the weather, but I really did feel I was at the end of the world and had stepped back in time. Firstly though, as we were so close, and because we had been to the furthermost point in the north, we headed to Bluff, the most southerly town on mainland New Zealand. South of here lay Stewart Island, which at the time was not open to tourists. Now however, you can go over for a few days of hiking and enjoy the nature reserve. Bluff is one of the areas of the country where an early European presence became established in 1823. Not a lot else there, so we made our way back to Invercargill. The only thing I remember about this small remote city is going into a department store for provisions, and thinking I had walked into Grace Brothers, from TV's Are You Being Served. The décor was circa 1950, with bare wooden floorboards, and wooden counters. On our subsequent visit, I had no desire to return, instead going back to our favourite area of New Zealand, which we were headed to next; Fiordland.

The scenic drive from Invercargill took us through small rural townships, past herds of sheep and undulating scenery. We could see the promise of mountain scenery ahead. UNESCO's World Heritage area of Fiordland National Park is an area of superlatives. This is the area, along with the Southern Alps which draws thousands of visitors year-round to be enthralled by its sheer beauty. Lake Manapouri is perhaps the prettiest of all the lakes within Fiordland. The lake has four arms, North, South, West and Hope. Formed by glaciers, the lake is New Zealand's second deepest and contains 33 islands. The underground Manapouri Hydro Electric Power Station on the western arm is the largest of its kind in New Zealand. In 1984 we were able to make a visit there as part of a boat trip, but in 2018, it was closed to visitors. Crossing the lake brought us to Wilmot Pass, a 2201ft high pass on the main divide of South Island connecting West Arm of Lake Manapouri to Doubtful Sound. From the highest viewpoint, the view down into the Sound was spectacular. It reminded me of the Norwegian fjords. Doubtful Sound is technically a fjord, about 25miles long and up to 1381ft at its deepest. The nearest habitation is about 31miles away. The reason this region is so lush is because of the enormous amount of rainfall, between 120 and 240ins per year. The vegetation on the mountainous landscape surrounding the fiord is dense native rainforest. So where did Doubtful Sound get its name from? When it was discovered by Captain Cook in 1770, he did not enter the inlet as he was doubtful it was navigable. He missed a trick, didn't he.

A few miles further north is the small town of Te Anau, which is known as the gateway to Milford Sound, possibly the most famous and most photographed area of New Zealand. Te Anau is situated on a lake of the same name, which is over 40 miles in length. The lake is edged with distinctive blue gum, or eucalyptus trees, their tall, mottled tree trunks are unforgettable looking like someone has painted them. At one end of the Lake Te Anau is the Fiordland Bird Park, a place active in protecting endangered species. Across the other side of the lake from the town, we visited some caves to see an underground glow worm grotto. The caves are pitch black when you enter them, but your eyes soon adjust to see thousands of pinprick lights hanging from sticky threads produced by the glow worms. These lights attract flying insects within the caves, which soon become the main menu for the glow worms. There are similar caves on North Island, south of Auckland called Waitomo Caves. Beyond Te Anau is the gateway to a wilderness area famed for hiking and spectacular scenery. The Milford Track takes days to walk and can sometimes be quite treacherous. On both occasions, when we have visited this region, we have taken a coach, rather than drive ourselves. The 74-mile-long road is sometimes subject to closure, and many times there have been landslides, cutting off the road. Indeed, our trip in mid-November was unseasonably cold, and as we progressed along the only road to Milford Sound, the weather closed in, and snow began to fall. The normally lush green undergrowth and surrounding mountains were gradually dusted in icing sugar snow. Whilst having a short break on the journey, we paused for photos. Towering mountains and sheer cliffs surrounded us, covered from top to ground level with snow. It was freezing. I think at that point I had several layers of clothes on under my waterproofs, and on my head, a woollen hat, my hoodie, and waterproof hood. 'Three Hats Robinson' took in the surroundings and loved every freezing moment. We were over 3000ft up, just outside the Homer Tunnel, which is a one-way traffic tunnel through a mountain, that emerges at the western end of the Cleddau Valley. The road then descends steeply to the valley floor for the last ten miles before arriving at Milford Sound. We saw a cheeky Kea, the world's only alpine parrot. They are known for stripping the rubber from windscreen wipers, another reason for not driving ourselves!

Milford Sound runs over nine miles inland from the Tasman Sea and is surrounded by sheer rock faces rising to 3900ft or more on either side. The most famous and most photographed island in the south is Mitre Peak, which rises to over 5,500ft. The best way to see the sound is to take a leisurely boat trip that takes you past Mitre Peak, past a couple of permanent waterfalls and near to temporary falls that appear as soon as it rains, cascading down the sheer cliffs. This is one of the wettest places in the world, so count yourself lucky if you happen to have clear weather when visiting. The boat trip takes you out to the open sea, before returning inland to the head of the sound and the jetty.

There is only one road from Te Anau that will bring you to Queenstown, famous as the main tourist centre for this region. With a backdrop of the Remarkables mountain range, and sitting on the edge of Lake Wakatipu, Queenstown is picture perfect. A place to people-watch, take a paddle steamer across the lake, or simply walk around the peninsula, there is plenty to keep you occupied. Some of the buildings bear names from the gold mining era. Crossing the lake, TSS Earnslaw, an Edwardian vintage coal fired steamship, will take you to Walter Peak. To get the best views of the town, take the Skyline Gondola. There is a restaurant at the top, and if you pay a supplement, they will seat you by the window for those panoramic views. We first ate at the restaurant when it was a carvery, with a choice of roasted meats and delicious local desserts. We could sit anywhere and enjoy a clear view down to the town, across the lake and to the Remarkables beyond.

Fast forward thirty-four years, and this time we had to prebook, and decide if we wanted to pay extra to sit by the windows. As it was doubtful that we would ever visit again, we thought we would do just that. All good ideas do not always go to plan. We arrived at our allotted time, but the weather was against us. We had paid extra for a misty cloud filled view of nothingness! The menu had changed though and now not only included a carvery, but also other dishes from Asia, seafood, pasta, various salads and of course those delicious desserts. As there were no views to enjoy, we filled our plates, and refilled them until we were stuffed. I am a great believer in getting value for money!

Further out from Queenstown the scenery continues to be jaw-dropping. We drove up to Coronet Peak in the Remarkables, a nearby ski resort. The resort was closed as it was too late in the year for skiing, but we went up there because from various points along the hairpin bend road, the views below into the valley are spectacular. The Shotover River runs along the valley floor. It's along there that the brave can bungy jump from the Kawarau Gorge Suspension Bridge. We watched a few take their life in their hands. Better them than us. In the same area on the Shotover River, other adventure activities are on offer, such as jet boating and white-water rafting. Further along we came to Arrowtown, once a centre for goldmining. The old goldrush buildings, dating from the 1860s, have been restored and the town now attracts thousands of visitors each year. A nice place for a spot of lunch and a wander.

    For a scenic route to get to Wanaka, head through the Cardrona Valley and up across the Crown Range. The road is only open when it's not snowing, but the views from the top are worth the 3,580ft climb. Wanaka is a very picturesque town and the gateway to Mount Aspiring National Park. As with many other of New Zealand's towns in the region, it sits on a lake with towering snow-capped mountains beyond. Arriving in Wanaka again brought back memories from our first trip when we arrived in our campervan and met up with the friendly locals from Dunedin who invited us for dinner. On this earlier trip, what I haven't told you is that the following morning we had set off from Wanaka to travel along the Haast Pass westwards towards the coast, but unfortunately whatever we had eaten the previous night had not agreed with me. We drove along in our cumbersome campervan, with snowy roads, and me with the runs and only a Portaloo™ for comfort. I couldn't appreciate the awesome scenery because all I could think of was controlling my innards. So, all these years later, on our second trip I really wanted to revisit probably one of the best roads in the whole of New Zealand and enjoy the journey. This time the roads were free of snow, we were in a much easier to drive car, and could stop every so often to take photos. I really cannot emphasise enough the beauty of the Haast Pass from Wanaka. I would rename it Mount Inspiring National Park. Much of the route runs alongside a couple of deep blue lakes, with clumps of wild lupins on the shorelines, and beyond the lakes, soaring craggy mountains simply take your breath away. If you need to find a place with the WOW factor, this is it. The Haast Pass is one of three passes to cross the Southern Alps and is the most southerly. As we approached the west coast, we crossed the Haast River Bridge, which is the longest single lane bridge in New Zealand. From just beyond you can see the rugged coastline wind its way north. This western side of the South Island reminds me of the north coast of Cornwall and Devon.

Travelling north along the coast for a few miles brought us to our next stop at the townships of Fox and Franz Josef. One thing we wanted to do was a scenic flight over the Southern Alps as this had been the highlight on our first visit. Back then we took a small Cessna ski plane and landed on the Tasman Glacier. The sky was cloudless and landing on the virgin snow of the Tasman Neve (or snowfield), 10,000ft up, we were able to get out and walk on the glacier, listening to the pistol like crack of ice fracturing around us. Mt Cook's peak was almost within touching distance, towering above us at 12218ft. I remember feeling completely overwhelmed by the beauty of it all after that flight. I could not speak - an unusual thing for me, as normally, I cannot stop the chatter. Sadly, it's no longer possible to land on the glacier, but we wanted to relive the highlight of that holiday. Now, there is a choice of seeing the area by plane or, with more limited range, by helicopter. None of them landing on the glacier though. We chose to do the scenic plane flight because it covered the whole area and flew much higher than the helicopters. This trip is weather dependent, so we had to see if the flights were operating. The sky might be clear, but the thermals high up in the mountains might make flying dangerous. We had allowed ourselves a couple of days to try and make the trip happen. It wasn't possible on the first day, so instead we headed off early to Fox township, where just outside is Lake Matheson. If you get there early in the morning, and the skies are clear, there is every chance you will see Mount Cook and the Alps reflected in the lake's surface. For anyone interested in photography, this is the perfect spot to capture the magnificent view and be cleverly arty at the same time.

There are two glaciers in the area: Fox and Franz Josef. We had helicoptered over Fox Glacier and walked up to its base on our first visit, but there had been landslips prior to our second visit and the road up to the glacier was closed. No matter, we were still able to revisit Franz Josef Glacier. The walk from the car park now took a lot longer than it had thirty-four years prior because the glacier had shrunk back over the intervening years. There were distance markers along the path showing where the glacier front had ended over the previous forty years. When we eventually arrived at the base, we found it was impossible to get right up close to it, so had to make do with photos from behind a fenced off area. In truth, I was rather underwhelmed. All we could see was an area of grubby ice and lots of scree. Compared to the mighty Perito Moreno Glacier in Argentina, this really wasn't worth the long walk from the car park. I suppose if you have never seen a glacier before you might have a different impression. I hoped we would get a better view if we were able to take that scenic flight the next day.

We were in luck. We spent an hour or so in the air flying over the highest mountains of the Southern Alps. The pilot made sure everyone on board got uninterrupted views of Mt Cook and Mt Tasman, with fantastic views below to the various glaciers and alpine landscapes. We could see the helicopters flying over the glaciers far below us. Both Fox and Franz Josef glaciers looked far more impressive from our new perspective, seeing their full length as they descended towards the lower slopes of the mountain range. Every so often we could glimpse a hidden turquoise lake in a valley amongst the mountain peaks. The Southern Alps are over 300 miles long and include seventeen mountains that are over 9,800 ft high and over 3000 glaciers. Where the mountains end, the land gradually became flat and green as it reached the coast. That flight was just as thrilling as the first one, and highly recommended if the budget allows.

Continuing north from Franz Josef we made a stop at Hokitika, a small town about halfway up the west coast. The town is a mixture of turn of the century and Art Deco buildings, with a large ornate clock set in the centre of the town, built to commemorate King Edward VII's coronation. There are some good views of the Alps to the east, while the wild west coastline continues in both directions north and south, dotted with untamed beaches. North of Hokitika is the town of Greymouth where there are some unusual rock formations at nearby Punakaiki, known locally as the Pancake Rocks. These are heavily eroded limestone stacks with pancake like layering. When the sea is rough and the tide is high, the sea bursts through several vertical blowholes. The nearest thing we have in the UK is the Giants Causeway, but these rocks are much flatter, and looking at them side on, they look like pages from a book. Not too far from this area it is possible to cut back across the island to get to Christchurch, but we continued north until we could go no further. All the coastline near to Westport is wild and rugged, but there are some scenic walks, leading to views of the Cape Foulwind headland, where there are colonies of seals.

Turning inland from Westport the road follows the Upper Buller River and Gorge and eventually comes to the Abel Tasman National Park on the north coast. Specialized crops such as hops, orchards and small vineyards are grown in this area, but the area is better known for its scenic beaches, although these were deserted when we stopped there. Abel Tasman National Park is the smallest of New Zealand's national parks. The whole area is popular with walkers, and the traffic free coast has secluded coves which can be accessed by kayak, or small boat. This top end of South Island has lush green valleys and is more undulating than the mountainous south. On the eastern shore of Tasman Bay is Nelson, the oldest city on South Island, established in 1841. Like many of the other cities in New Zealand, most of the buildings are low rise, and many are made of wood. South Street, New Zealand's oldest street, is worth a visit as all the cottages, dating from the 1860s, are a great example of colonial style architecture, with weatherboarding, painted in various colours. Dominating the centre of Nelson is Christ Church cathedral, which is largely constructed in marble and has an unusual 115ft bell tower. The drive back to Picton takes you on a scenic route along Queen Charlotte Drive, a winding road, along the edges of Pelorus and Queen Charlotte Sounds, the largest of several sounds that make up Marlborough Sounds group in the northeast of South Island.

Back to where we started our journey around South Island in Picton, we took the ferry back to Wellington and returned home from there. I am not sure we will ever get back to New Zealand, but I would go back in a heartbeat.

The Seventh Continent

After two years of Covid 'lockdown' and travel withdrawal symptoms, constantly feeling disgruntled and unsettled, I could finally see a light at the end of a very dark travel tunnel. With so many restrictions in place, forms to complete, tests, and affidavits, travelling abroad had been extremely stressful, if not impossible. The fear of contracting the virus and being hospitalized began to diminish as the vaccination programme became successful. Sure, the virus hadn't gone away, but the realization began to dawn that we were all going to have to live with it for some time to come. Gradually restrictions from each country began to be lifted, and thoughts of getting away began to take hold.

The one continent we hadn't visited and had thought we would never get the chance to explore was Antarctica. It had been on the bucket list wish list for many years but knew the cost and the likelihood of ever getting there was slim. Had it not been for the pandemic, the opportunity to explore this remote region would never have materialised. I heard of an offer through my work for a trip on a six-star 'super' yacht that would be sailing from Ushuaia, in the far south of Argentina, across the Drake Passage, and on down to the Antarctic Peninsula. This trip would normally have been full of guests from around the world, but due to travel restrictions, it wasn't possible for some nationalities to leave their country. Consequently, these sailings were operating at half full occupancy. The cruise company needed to start operating again after the lockdown years, and Antarctica was a great route for them, since there hadn't been any covid cases there. Despite the cost to experience this trip, we decided to bite the bullet, justifying the trip with thoughts of all the moments in the past two years where we couldn't celebrate special birthdays, our ruby wedding anniversary and other occasions, where we were stuck at home, banned from mixing with more than six people.

Preparing to travel was straightforward enough. The first hurdle was to take a PCR test within seventy-two hours of our departure. We headed to the local testing station and were shown to our own cubicle ready to have a long cotton bud stuck down our throats and rammed up our nostrils. I found the best way to suffer this was to hold my breath. Apparently, this method wasn't one used by my husband in the next cubicle, as I could hear him retching, and subsequently muttering on his exit that he wasn't going to do that again.

After hearing we were clear to travel, we had a few forms to complete and upload, prior to setting off on our adventure. Apart from the compulsory mask wearing, it felt normal at the airport. Our flight took us via Sao Paulo in Brazil, where we dropped off some travellers. The usual rush to get off the plane where everyone stands in the aisles as soon as the flight lands, was not permitted. For those of us continuing to Buenos Aires, we had to stay on board the aircraft, identify our hand luggage for a security check, and watch the cleaners come on board to vacuum, clean the toilets, and remove any rubbish, all within a 12-minute slot. Impressive.

We overnighted in Buenos Aires, staying in the Recoleta area. Having only visited there in 2018, we weren't bothered about exploring far from the hotel. Within walking distance, we revisited the huge and impressive Recoleta Cemetery, where Evita was still slumbering in the same plot. Up early the next day we flew down to Ushuaia to join our ship. We had only cruised on larger ships with 2000 plus people, so it was a real treat to have less than one hundred guests, and as many crew on board to look after us. Although we had our own butler, the only times we needed his services were to open a bottle of wine for us, as we struggled with the corkscrew and to help me get into our suite when my key wouldn't work. It was lovely to have some luxury, and to be greeted by your own name everywhere you went — in the restaurants, the spa, in the theatre. How do they do that? I've forgotten someone's name as soon as I'm introduced!

As we left Ushuaia and sailed along the Beagle Channel to the open sea, we decided to attend a presentation in the ship's theatre to hear about the upcoming trip. First came the advice to start taking motion sickness tablets, as we would soon begin to cross the Drake Passage. This is a vast stretch of water in the Southern Ocean where the Atlantic and Pacific Oceans meet, so is notorious for rough seas and very strong winds which cut across from west to east. As it would take two days and nights to travel to the Antarctic Peninsula, it was wise to heed the advice about taking anti-sickness tablets. The departure from Ushuaia was delayed as a massive storm tracked ahead of us. But even delaying the departure by 12 hours, the ship still rocked violently back and forth. All the guests began to walk like toddlers taking their first steps, staggering from side to side, impossible to walk in a straight line. Even when we were laying down in bed, our bodies rolled back and forth, while we watched the horizon move from the bottom of the balcony door to three quarters of the way to the top. The curtains swung out towards us and in again. We had to concentrate when getting dressed as it was impossible to stand on one leg whilst putting on socks and trousers. We had to sit down or lean against a wall to keep upright. Although the motion sickness tablets worked, it was still quite tiring lurching about. I'm just glad we were sober.

Once we arrived in the calmer waters of the peninsula, the rough passage was soon forgotten. We awoke to clear skies, placid waters, snowy cliffs and sea ice all around us. It was everything we had hoped for. The ship offered various ways to enjoy the scenery. Subject to the weather conditions there were two helicopters on board for scenic flights. and a mini submarine, to take a few guests at a time beneath the clear waters, The ship also had several kayaks and zodiacs to explore the surrounding area on the water. To be on a kayak, meant you could be at one with nature in solitude, quietly reflecting the peace and tranquillity on the pristine waters. No engine sounds, no Wi-Fi - just the sound of water lapping against the chunks of ice floating by, and the call of terns and skuas flying above.

Each morning we would awake in a different bay and spend a couple of hours ashore on an island or on the Antarctic mainland, in search of penguins and seals. We were taken ashore by zodiac, which was an adventure in itself clambering aboard and shuffling along the edge of the small boat to our seating positions. There was a set procedure to getting back on from the shore. With the zodiac moving to the swell of the water, we had to perch on the rim at the front, facing towards the back, swing our legs over, then shuffle along. I tried this by swinging one leg over the rim, but not quite managing it. Some kind soul decided to help, by lifting said leg higher, but that only made me tip back further, ending up feeling like one of those Weeble-Wobble toys, that never remain upright. I could feel myself slipping but was saved from more embarrassment with another helping hand. My husband, who was next in line, made some derogatory remark about a beached whale. When it came to his turn, he was so concerned about protecting his camera from sea spray, that he too slipped, and inelegantly fell into the zodiac splashing water up his back. Oh, how we laughed! Karma strikes again. That'll teach you to laugh at me sunshine!

We had to tog ourselves up each time we left the ship, with layer upon layer of thermal wear. My record was four layers on the bottom, four on top plus two hats and chunky thermal gloves. We were provided with fisherman style waterproof rubber 'muck' boots which had to be scrupulously cleaned each time we boarded the ship. There were strict rules about cross contamination between landing sites. Every time we returned to the ship, we had to clean our boots on a machine with multiple brushes that at the press of a button, whizzed around cleaning in between the grooves on the boots' soles. When this was done, we then had to step into a tray of disinfectant. Once back in the boot room, there were a selection of small brushes and picks on hand in case there was still a stray piece of grit, or penguin guano trapped on the sole. Life jackets removed, and a gradual stripping of our layers made it more comfortable, until it was time to repeat the procedure for our next trip out.

If we were landing ashore, there were plenty of crew around to give a helping hand as we stepped onto the snow or ice. Expedition leaders and assistants would go ashore earlier with flags to mark out safe routes for us to follow. Any area that had a treacherous overhang, hidden by the snowy surface, was marked with two flags angled as a cross. Most of us chose to use ski poles to help our balance. Snow-covered trails were either ankle deep in snow, or slippery. It was important too to keep to the marked route because criss-crossing our path were tracks made by the penguins as they made their way to their family groups. Penguins always had right of way. Unused to humans, it was clear they had no fear, as they waddled past us, sometimes tripping up and sliding on their bellies. All around us we could see individuals and clusters of various breeds.

Amongst the different species of penguin we recognised the Gentoo with their red lipstick beaks, matching red feet and white 'headphones' on their heads, ready to head off to a penguin party. On other islands there were large families of Chinstrap penguins, recognisable by their black and white heads with a line of black under their beaks, looking as if they were wearing little black hats. On one island Chinstraps could be seen as far as the eye could see, perched on hillsides. The noise was deafening. Amongst them hungry skuas searched for any tasty eggs or chicks. One fearless skua wandered right up to us, curious to see if we were worth a peck. Thankfully we weren't skewered by a skua! On the shore, groups of penguins followed each other into the sea, coming up for air every so often, porpoising over the water.

Penguins weren't the only wildlife on land of course. We saw a variety of seals, either perched on rocks, or laying in a sluglike heap on the shore. The smallest were the fur seals, who ambled along using their strong tail flippers, warning anyone who would listen that they meant business. The largest we saw were elephant seals, named for their size rather than for any resemblance to an elephant. We came across a large group of them on one island flopped together in a blubbery heap, farting and groaning while they snoozed. A random Gentoo, dwarfed by their size, waddled past them. Weddell seals with pretty little faces congregated in small groups on other islands.

On many of the islands we came across old huts, built out of old timber and even tea chests, to be used as a refuge for anyone in need of shelter. Some had a flag outside for the country of ownership. A ragged Union Jack flew outside one particular old hut, nearby a refuge built by Argentina. We were able to go inside the British hut which had basic sleeping bunks, an old table, and some ancient dry provisions on shelves. A former stopping off place for scientific expeditions, it hadn't been used since the 1990s.

Using our ski poles, we were able to hike up to some higher points here and there to get great views across the water to mountains and glaciers beyond. Nearly everywhere on the Antarctic Peninsula was covered in deep snow except for one island, in the South Shetlands Island Group, which was volcanic, with no snow at all. The shoreline here had black lava sand, and as we walked up to higher ground, the lava became mixed with penguin guano, making it slippery under foot. The views however were worth the climb. Looking back towards our starting point below we could see the wild black landscape with a hint of green lichen visible amongst the hordes of penguins. Ahead of us, we looked down onto a black bay, with lava rock arches. This was quite different to some of the other islands we had seen before where there would be groups of huts close to the shore used by research scientists. On this volcanic island we came across a small group, who were looking at plant fossils, and using a drone to assist their research. We had to steer clear of them, and not interact because of the covid pandemic, even though none of the guests on our ship had tested positive. Across the water from this island we sailed into a flooded caldera, with just the one way in and out, and with sheer black lava coated walls all around. That was a first for all of us, I think.

The weather also gave us different perspectives. On some days we would have heavy snow and low cloud, but despite this it didn't deter us from going ashore. There's no such thing as bad weather, only bad clothing, to quote a well-known saying. In some bays the sea looked like it was on the point of freezing as small and large chunks of ice moved slowly together. In a few weeks these waters would be inaccessible. It all added to the raw beauty of the region.

It was just as interesting when we were out on the smaller zodiacs moving between icebergs in search of wildlife. Every day we were able to go out for a couple of hours with our binoculars and cameras, with our expert guide steering us, on the lookout, and staying in touch by radio with other zodiacs, getting reports of seal or whale sightings. I particularly loved the bright sunny times when we were on the millpond waters, moving past chunks of blue-white ice that had broken away from the icy cliffs. Some of the icebergs were spectacular, soaring high above us, and dwarfing our ship moored at a safe distance. A few of these had large holes and shapes carved into them, looking like art installations. We couldn't get too close to these because icebergs have oxygen trapped within the ice, which can make them very unstable and topple completely over upside down.

On a few floating ice platforms, we spotted basking seals or cormorants taking a rest. This was the first time we came across a crabeater, a pretty silver-grey coated seal. The most abundant species though were leopard seals. They can grow to the length of a zodiac and can be dangerous. We saw a few basking on the icy platforms, and came up close to one that followed us as we were heading ashore on one occasion. What a treat to be so close. It was fine if the wildlife chose to come up to us, but we were not allowed to approach, having to maintain a distance of five metres. This particular seal swished down beneath the zodiac, and up to each side, almost within touching distance, it's mottled coat clearly visible beneath the water. He'd pop his head above the water and swim a bit alongside us, and then dive down again. For myself this was one of my highlights.

This wasn't the only encounter with a leopard seal, however. On a separate occasion we watched a Gentoo penguin swimming and porpoising across the water, but then realised it was being chased by a leopard seal. Unfortunately for the penguin, its time was up as the seal expertly snatched at the penguin's wing and held it fast in its jaws. The next thirty minutes were spent watching the seal tenderise the penguin, by whacking the poor penguin against the water surface, and dragging it down beneath the water, only to repeat the action time and time again. At first, we could hear the penguin's squeals, but eventually this ceased. As the penguin disintegrated, the seal was joined by terns who flitted to the water's surface to steal a few morsels. I felt like I'd stepped into a David Attenborough documentary.

Another highlight for me was the chance to see some whales. As you will have gathered, we haven't been very fortunate with our attempts at whale watching, but this time, on our first morning in the peninsula we were rewarded. While out on the calm waters, our guide got a message over the walky-talky that a pod of humpbacks were feeding further out across the bay. We headed out in their direction, shutting off the zodiacs' outboard engines, gliding quietly along, some distance from where they were. We were rewarded with a group of six humpbacks breaching the water, then diving below. We watched for the tell-tale sign of their waterspouts as they moved along, only to surface again a few minutes later. It was a magical sight. Mostly whales do not show their tails. They tend to do this when they are about to make a deep dive, and then disappear for around forty minutes. Again, luck was on our side, as we watched one flip its tail, or fluke, and then make its dive. The fluke on a humpback is as individual as a human fingerprint, with the underside being unique to each whale.

Now that I'd got my wish to see whales, I wished we could have been closer. My Fairy Godmother must have been listening because a few days later we were out in the zodiac again, engine off, just floating and enjoying the sculpted icebergs while on the lookout for seals, when a humpback glided alongside about 10ft away from us. We watched as it breached the surface. Much quiet excitement in the zodiac as we all stood up to take photos and videos. Another fabulous memory to store away.

This brings me onto the guests. We met some lovely people whilst on board the ship, all keen to enjoy everything that Antarctica had to offer. We met one American chap travelling alone who got beside himself when seeing this particular whale up close alongside. There were only a handful of people in the zodiac, and the unwritten rule is to remain quiet when close to wildlife. In his excitement, our American friend forgot himself, blocking the view of us others, with loud whoops and a Whoa! at the sight of this humpback. That didn't go down well with those who were trying to video the scene, and who will no doubt have a soundtrack of loud exclamations to accompany their recording. 'Mr America' made friends with 'Ten Past Two', another guest, whom we had nicknamed and who suffered from verbal diarrhoea. We gave him the name of Ten Past Two with reference to the guides on the zodiacs, who when pointing out something of interest, would indicate the position by referring to a clock face. (As in, 'Humpback ahead at 12o'clock'.)

We first heard Ten Past Two when we were in Buenos Aires at our hotel. He sat with some others, who he had only just met, and proceeded to tell them his life story, in a loud voice. Every time we saw him on board the ship, we could hear more snippets of his life, while watching him chat to anyone who would listen We decided to avoid him, but when we saw him looking our way, I said, 'Quick, Ten Past Two'. Glancing in that direction we knew he was close by and made our retreat. Unfortunately, on our return flight from Ushuaia to Buenos

Aires, he was seated right behind us, so for three hours we heard more of his life story. (On the plane, he'd moved from Ten Past Two to Five Twenty-Five!) Back on the ship we had noticed 'Mr America' sitting opposite 'Ten Past Two' one morning at breakfast, neither of them listening to each other and neither of them pausing for breath. I love people watching!

Another whale highlight came one evening. It was beginning to get dusk, and most people were in the various ship's restaurants having dinner. A message came over the speaker system, from the bridge, to say they had spotted three separate pods of Orcas ahead of us. There was a mass exodus out onto the freezing deck, while staff quickly found jackets for some of the guests to put on. The whales were too far out to get any decent photos, but guests and crew alike became very excited to see this uncommon site. Their fins were clearly visible and there must have been about thirty or more of them. I feel so privileged to witness these beautiful creatures.

We had two further days at sea heading back across the wild seas of the Drake Passage, but thankfully the crossing this time wasn't as violent as before. I remember sitting in the ship's lounge, listening to some beautiful music, and thinking that after two and half years of being unable to travel, and the uncertainty with my business, this trip was truly an antidote and worth every penny. I will never forget the experiences we had on the seventh continent in Antarctica.

Antarctica - Crabeater Seal

Antarctica – Flandres Bay

Australia – Ozzie humour

Australia - Quokka, Rottnest Island, WA

Australia - Human perch -parrots, Kennett River, Victoria

Australia - Worth travelling around the world to see this fella.

Canada - Jasper & Alberta beyond

Canada – Lake Louise, Rocky Mountains

Canada - The stunning Butchart Gardens, Vancouver Island

Malaysia - Sepilok Orang Utan Sanctuary, Sabah

Cambodia – Buddha face off

Malaysia - Sun Bear, Sepilok, Sabah

New Zealand - 'Three hats' Robinson freezing near Mitre Peak, Milford Sound, South Island

Norway - Found some trolls. Hornindals Vatnet

Russia - Grand Cascade, Peterhof, Nr St Petersburg

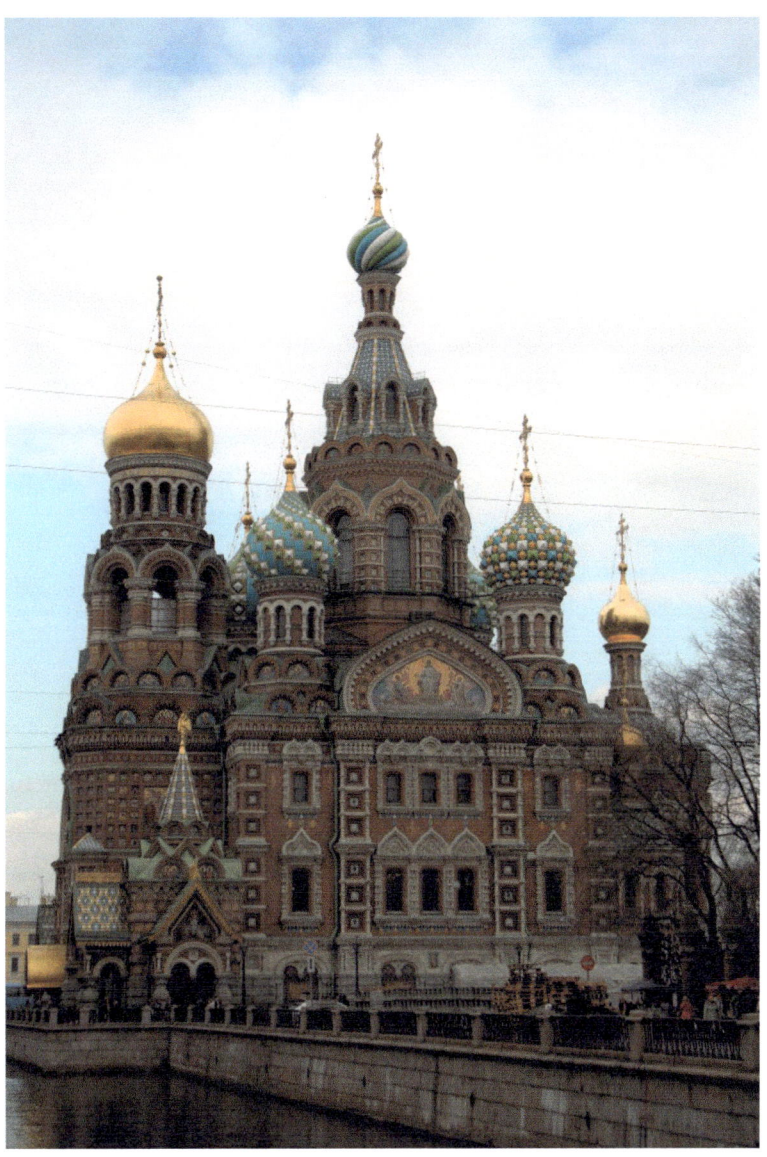

Russia - Church of Spilled Blood, St Petersburg

Russia - The Pavilion Hall, The Hermitage, St Petersburg

AT LAST! A whale -Fjords Wilderness Area, Alaska

BACK WHERE IT ALL STARTED

After I had a taste of cruising in 1972, I could not really see myself ever wanting to experience it again. As I had never sold the product, I wasn't familiar with any of the cruise lines. Growing up in Southampton, I was aware of large cruise liners that arrived in the port and remember visiting the docks to see RMS Queen Elizabeth and RMS Queen Mary in the 1960s with my parents. I never went on board, but just remember that the former had two funnels and the latter had three funnels, and to me they looked enormous. By the late sixties both ships had been retired, and the Queen Elizabeth sailed off to Hong Kong, only to be irreparably damaged by fire, whilst the Queen Mary headed off to Long Beach, California to become a floating hotel. This was followed by the new and modern looking QE2, which continued to provide luxury cruising to the affluent. It was only in the early 2000s that cruising for the masses began to take off.

My only experience of being afloat was of dormitory styled rooms, shared bathrooms, not particularly inspiring food and was more like camping at sea. I do remember though waking with excitement and looking out of our porthole windows to see where we had arrived each morning, but that was tempered by screeches from the girls in their nightwear, trying to shield themselves from the view of local fishermen who could see us all from their eye level view straight into our portholes. So yes, I did have mixed feelings about cruising. Liking the destinations, but not enjoying the advances of swarthy Mediterranean men, and not impressed with sharing our dorms with cockroaches. Some years later the cruise industry seemed to be expanding, so along with other colleagues in the travel industry, I thought I would take the opportunity to look around a brand-new ship, that had just arrived in Southampton, to see if my doubts could be expelled. The ship was Royal Caribbean's Explorer of the Seas. I was completely blown away by the size, the décor, and the activities available on board. Now these type of ship visits often entailed an overnight onboard, so we could sample everything the cruise had to offer. On arrival we would make our way to the buffet and enjoy a magnificent lunch, and then take a self-guided tour around the ship, where several different cabin types were available to view, ranging from inside cabins to Owners Suites, complete with a self-playing grand piano and a butler. We would wander around the public areas and in this case watch a very professional ice show on the skating rink performed by ex-champions of ice dance. Then we would wander down the Boulevard, a wide shop lined street in the middle of the ship, and then watch people outside on the rock-climbing wall. We would meet up later in the champagne bar for pre-drinks, before going for our four-course dinner, followed by a production in the theatre. We would roll into bed in the early hours, forgetting that we would be woken up early by the ships announcement system to get ready for breakfast and disembark.

I wondered then if I would ever get the opportunity to take my own family on a cruise, something that none of them had ever considered. From that point on whenever there was a ship visit, I always tried to go, so that I became familiar with the different brands and the client markets they would suit. I concluded that there was a cruise for every type of person and every interest. Cruising was, and still remains, not just for people above a certain age. It wasn't boring and there was enough to do on board to keep even the most restless engaged. There were cruises suited to families, activities and clubs for children, talks on various subjects, lots of sporting activities, theatre, various musical interludes, quizzes, photography, art auctions, spas, gyms, bingo and casinos plus lots of areas where you can get away from everyone and quietly read a book. There were smaller ships, where fine dining was key, party ships, and ships designed for exploration to sub-zero locations.

I did get the opportunity to book us as a family about a year after my Explorer of the Seas visit, and cruising has now become one of our favourite types of holidays. I think it is a great way of getting an introduction to a country or city. Many a time we have visited somewhere on a port of call, been impressed, and decided to return for a longer duration and explore the area in more depth. There is nothing better than when you spend a day exploring, particularly when the heat is oppressive, knowing that there is an air-conditioned ship and a choice of restaurants with an extensive menu, waiting for you at the end of the day. You do not need to keep packing and unpacking and can wake up each morning to a new destination.

Some of the places we have sailed into, or out from have been iconic. To stand up on deck and sail out of Venice, passing all the familiar ancient buildings is just fantastic. Sailing under wide, expansive bridges, with barely enough headroom, as you approach a new destination is thrilling as you arrive full of anticipation of what is ahead. I remember this feeling particularly when ducking my head unnecessarily under the Verrazano Bridge leading to New York. Or the 25 de Abril Bridge, crossing the River Tagus in Lisbon and the Askøy Suspension Bridge in Bergen. Many ships can dock within walking distance of the centre of a destination, making it easy to disembark and immediately set off to explore. There is often no need to queue for a transfer bus to get you out beyond the confines of the port. All the Alaskan and Norwegian ports are like this and other places too such as Puerto Rico and Vancouver. Some ships, however, must drop anchor in deeper water, so that to get ashore, you must take a tender, which is normally in one of the lifeboats, as we did in Guernsey and Haiti. Then there are other ports which are so large that you must get a transfer bus to the port entrance and then a further transfer to get to the nearest city. Rome, Pisa and Florence were just a few like this.

The way cruise lines make much of their money is by offering numerous shore excursions. These are very well organised and take the pressure off having to find your own way about. The bonus to this is if the tour bus is delayed, and arrives back late, the ship will not leave without the guests on the tour. If you opt to do your own thing, you really do have to make sure you are back on board with plenty of time to spare before the ship departs for the next port. Be in no doubt, they will go without you. When we have cruised, we have done a mix of official cruise excursions and independent shore days. Some of the cruise line excursions can be expensive, especially if there are more than one or two people or a family to pay for. We were always mindful of the cost when planning our trips, and on one such occasion, we had arrived in Villefranche, in France, in between Nice and Monte Carlo, and thought it would be cheaper to make our own way to Monte Carlo by train. There were the four of us, and the plan was to take a detour up into the mountains above the coast, and visit Eze, and then head down to Monte Carlo. We caught the train without issue, and then took a local bus up to Eze. It was the time of year when there were a lot of forest fires up in the hills, and I remember watching helicopters flying overhead carrying large containers of water to release onto the flames.

We continued to Monte Carlo and followed a stream of people who seemed to be heading up to a viewpoint. We found ourselves next to the Palace, overlooking the city, with fabulous views looking down onto the marina with its jaw droppingly expensive yachts moored there. We took a tour around the Royal Palace and had a good wander around the narrow streets in the vicinity. We bumped into another family we had got speaking to on board our ship, who were taking the cruise organised excursion. They mentioned that their tour bus had plenty of spare seats. 'You ought to come back on the coach', they said. Time was getting on, and we still had to make our way back to the station and then wait for the train that would take us to Villefranche and the port. Looking at the time we had, I was beginning to think we might have left it too late. Not to worry, we decided to travel back on the same coach as the other family. The only problem was we had not paid for it, so we kept our heads down, thinking it would be fine because we had been told the coach wasn't full. Our girls sat up the back with the other family, and me and my husband sat a few rows further forward. The coach began to fill... and fill. I couldn't see any spare seats and began to worry that there would not be enough for all the people that had paid. Meanwhile we could hear one of our daughters chatting loudly and enthusiastically about our earlier adventures watching the helicopters, clearly having been somewhere where no one else on the coach had been that day! For God's sake, be quiet! The tour party leader did a head count, and then another head count, and then asked if anyone was on board that shouldn't be? 'What shall we do?' whispered my husband. It was far too late to get the train back now, so I whispered back, head down, 'Just sit tight', hoping no one else was listening to my daughter's conversation. The other passengers were beginning to get restless, and then comments like, 'Let's just go' were heard. The tour leader was worried that someone was on the wrong coach and even commented that this was the first time they had ever had more people on board than there should be! Normally, if anything, there were people missing. Thankfully, they made the decision to leave, and we arrived back at the ship without incident, but for a moment my heart was banging.

I think the most embarrassing moment when cruising happened when we were in Hawaii. We had booked a cruise excursion on one of the islands, getting on and off the coach at various points of interest. It was a time when I was menopausal, and for those women who haven't experienced it, it can take you unawares, and without being too graphic I ended up walking like a cowboy, but without his horse. Returning to the ship after this excursion I walked with my bag hiding the damage to my trousers at the front and a cardigan shielding the back. Unfortunately, when boarding the ship, we had to put the bag through security, so my damaged trousers were exposed. I pulled the cardigan round me as much as I could and got my husband to walk in front of me, not looking at anyone. I couldn't get back to the cabin quick enough.

On another occasion, we were in Iceland and had taken a cruise ship excursion inland around the Golden Circle, which took us to geysers, waterfalls and the only place where the North Atlantic and Eurasian tectonic plates meet on land. It was fascinating and amazing to think that you could be standing astride the North American and European continents. When we got off the tour coach to explore on our own, we were told to be back at the coach by a certain time, so they could get back to the ship on time. Everyone turned up, except one person. We waited and waited, but she didn't appear. Other guests were trying to remember who she was and what she looked like. The guide set off in search of the missing person and we must have waited over an hour on the coach. Eventually the guide returned with a woman in tow. I don't know what was going on in her head, but there was no apology for keeping us all waiting… not a word. I can only assume she did not understand the request to be back on time. Had she not been on the organised tour, the ship would have left without her, and in fact, as we were the last group to return, the ship sailed off immediately.

Most of the cruise ships we have sailed on are quite large, but even with their modern design and size, you can still feel the swell of the ocean on occasion, if the sea is rough enough. We have been on larger ships that have a theatre at the front and been fascinated watching a chandelier swing to and fro above the stage, whilst dancers or acrobats have tried to stay upright. It has never been so bad though that we have felt ill, until that is, we went on a much smaller sailing ship, the Star Clipper. It was early in the year, in April, and we were taking advantage of an offer for travel agents of a four-day trip from Athens around a few ports in the Aegean Sea. Star Clipper is a four masted wooden tall ship that sails around the Med and Caribbean, just 360ft long, with room for 166 guests. The traditional interior has teak decks and polished brass metalwork. We were shown to our cabin, which was on the lower deck. It was small, with the bed right up against the outer side of the ship, and a porthole just above it. If we looked out of it, the sea was just below our sights. Later on, there was a knock on the cabin door. A steward had come to warn us to keep our porthole closed as 'there is big storm tonight.' Thanks for that!

We spent the night being rolled around in our bed. I have never felt my innards sloshing about before. When we woke up, I felt OK, but thought I would keep myself horizontal. I did peek out of the port hole and was horrified to see we were under water. The swell of the rough sea was higher than our cabin. Meanwhile my husband got up to use the bathroom, but then found he couldn't leave it. Poor chap. I decided at that point to take some motion sickness tablets, and stayed put in bed, waiting for them to work. We then called for the onboard nurse, who came armed with a patch to put behind my husband's ear. This releases medication to help with seasickness and I must say it's marvellous. After a while he felt better, and we staggered like drunkards up the steps to the breakfast area. The crew told us to eat apples and not to drink water, as that hinders rather than relieves. Ginger also helps. If all else fails, just stay put in bed. The original plan was to take part in all the water activities on offer, such as snorkelling and kayaking from the back of the ship. However, the weather was so bad, we had to abandon that idea. It was even impossible to put the sails up. The large main sail had been badly torn away by very strong winds. We were supposed to moor up in Mykonos but couldn't because of the high winds. We did stop in Samos though, which was an unexpected treat with its pretty, whitewashed buildings and tumbling bougainvillea typical of other islands in the region. And of course, another unexpected fridge magnet to add to my collection.

Our clipper cruise did not put me off, and a year or so later I saw another offer with the same company. My husband didn't want to go, so I went with my friend and colleague Mandy. You might remember Mandy from my days with British Airways, in the Uxbridge shop. When we all went our separate ways, after the shop closed, Mandy went off to work at Heathrow Airport on the ticket desk, helping travellers amend their tickets and offer last minute advice. Eventually she left BA, and we only kept in touch by the annual Christmas card. I hadn't been with Travel Counsellors long when I got a 'what I have been up to' letter in with her Christmas card. She had been through a messy divorce and was struggling as a single mum in a job she hated. It sounded so awful that I phoned her to see if she was all right. We got talking about my new job, and running my own business, and I said, I thought it might be a good option for her. Not long after that she joined the company and began a successful career. Consequently, we saw much more of each other, at conferences, or on educational trips. We knew this new Clipper sailing trip offer would be fun and a great chance to catch up. On board we met up with another couple we knew, a work colleague and her husband, and so spent the evenings together filling the quiet time with laughter. On one such occasion Kam, the husband, told us of his entrepreneurial ideas to make money. We had had a few to drink by then. He told us of his first idea, 'Curry in a Box'. Not sure about that one! Then, a more lucrative brainwave. There were plenty of men, who casually slung a jumper over their shoulders, tying the sleeves loosely around the neck. 'Well,' he said, 'why not have a jumper *sewn* onto the shirt. Instantly 'cool'!' Snorts of laughter. It'll never take off Kam! The funny thing was when we disembarked in Rome to spend another night there, Mandy and I wandered past a menswear shop, and in the window was a model with a jumper slung over a shirt. You missed the boat, Kam!

Mandy and I walked all around Rome, and with swollen feet we returned to our hotel. Mandy had a bright idea of lying on the bed, with our bottoms squidged against the headboard, and legs stretched up against the wall, to try and get rid of the swollen cankles. Well, imagine if you can, a beached whale. I managed to get in the right position, but my legs had a mind of their own. They gradually veered to one side, which caused me to slide off the bed into a heap on the floor, and I was too weak with laughter to get back up.

Amusing things do seem to happen to us when we are away. After cruising around the Med with the family one time and finishing in Barcelona, we stayed another day in the city, before flying home. We needed an early night as we had to get up for an early flight the next day. Not worth unpacking, we left our suitcases on the floor in our bedroom. We settled down for the night, and gradually all drifted off to sleep during the evening. We were staying in a small hotel on Las Ramblas, with our room up a couple of floors near the top. We were woken, after what seemed hours, to the sound of running water. My husband got up and was confronted with about a three inch depth of water on the floor. Outside our room, water was running down the walls, along our corridor and into our bedroom. Swiftly heaving our cases onto the bed, and waking the girls, my husband grabbed some shorts and dashed down to reception to warn them of the disaster upstairs. As we had been sound asleep we thought it was about four a.m., so upon flinging the door open to reception, he was amazed to see a bar full of revellers enjoying a drink. What they thought of a wild-eyed bare-chested man dashing in, I do not know. It was only midnight by the way! Unfortunately for us the hotel was full, so they could not move us to another room, so we had to sleep with suitcases on the end of our beds. Apparently, someone in the room above us had left the tap running in the bath and it had overflowed. Not the most comfortable way to end our holiday, but funny nevertheless.

Cruising is renowned for a constant stream of food throughout the day. There is a never-ending choice of food in the buffet to suit all tastes, and grazing opportunities if you feel peckish; a light snack, a slice of pizza or an ice cream, followed by a wide choice for evening dinner, all served by impeccable waiters and knowledgeable sommeliers. After all that, if you have room, you could have room service, or head back up to the buffet for a midnight snack. I always imagine there must be a lot of food waste.

On one particular cruise we stopped off in Haiti for a beach day.

The cruise company leased an area of beach which was blocked off from the locals. Everything that was needed for a fun day out was brought from the ship, including inflatables, towels, water bikes, and water slides. We were taken by tender to the beach and left to enjoy our day. I noticed some jellyfish in the water, so instead spent a few hours lazing in the hammocks that were hung between palm trees rather than go in the water. We discovered there were a few stalls set up in some open buildings at the back of the beach, where a few locals, who had a license to sell, were allowed to set up stalls and sell their wares. The Haitian locals were clearly very poor and the standard of the goods they had for sale was rather shoddy, but anything they sold would help feed their families. I wouldn't normally buy any old tourist tat, but I really felt we would be helping them if we bought something. So, I bought a poorly made chess set and a scary looking china doll, which my younger daughter had taken a shine to. I kept thinking about the difference between us on the ship with access to all that food and the few locals who were permitted to come onto our closed off bit of beach, struggling to make a living. It just did not seem morally right. Anyway, back on board and we went up on deck. From our raised viewpoint, we could see hundreds of jellyfish below us in the sea, floating like empty plastic bags. Later that same night, after a filling dinner, we went back to the restaurant to look at the artistic flair of the patisserie chefs, who had creatively carved sculptures from chocolate. I could not eat another thing after dinner, but having seen the poverty earlier that day, it sickened me to see other guests piling their plates so high with chocolate treats, they couldn't possibly get through the mountain on their plates. Maybe those jellyfish with their nasty stings were karma's way of showing us all that we should think about others more, because every time I think of jelly fish now, I see those poor Haitian people scraping a living from the fat cats onboard the cruise ships.

We've often combined cruising with a further week ashore, to get a real feel for a country, which gives us a varied and interesting combination. On one such trip we spent a week in Italy, followed by a cruise down the Adriatic. Instead of heading to the popular area of Tuscany, we decided to book a cottage in an Agrotourism farmstead to the southeast of Tuscany in the Marches region. There are fewer overseas tourists there, and indeed we were the only non-Italians in the village where we stayed. Marches is very pretty, mainly agricultural, with wonderful views as we drove around. In the distance we could see a hillock and an ancient village with its church perched on top. The houses with their terracotta roofs appearing to tumble down the hillside. I loved the layout of the fields, some with neat rows of crops, others a vivid green, some being tended by a tractor and plough, with tall Italian Cypress trees that dominate the region dotted around. This is just how I used to draw pictures at school, when trying to show a scene with depth. Moving on from here, the roads northwards to Venice were easy enough to navigate and within a few hours we arrived in Venice.

Compared to my first visit, the whole place was buzzing with tourists, some spending a king's ransom on a Bellini in one of the cafés that surround St Mark's Square. I particularly enjoyed getting around on the waterbuses that crisscrossed the Grand Canal. Normally, I wouldn't bat an eyelid if I saw a police car, or a delivery lorry on one of our roads back home, but seeing the equivalent on the Grand Canal, or seeing a boat delivering beer barrels to a bar, or an ambulance boat speeding along the water fascinated me. Returning days later from our cruise down the Adriatic, the Grand Canal was even busier as it coincided with the annual Regata Storica, which takes place on the first Sunday in September. That day also happened to be my 50th birthday. Wasn't it good of them to put on a regatta just for me! There were hundreds of boats on the water with teams dressed in brightly coloured outfits and flags denoting who they were, all getting ready to compete against each other. It was a birthday treat to remember.

So where have we been on our cruises? What ports of call have we explored? Maybe I should become a lecturer in Travel and Tourism and set homework to find and learn about all the places on a map of Ports of Call. There's a thought! The following places are worth a visit, even if only briefly.

Guernsey: This is much smaller than Jersey, is easy to get around and takes no time at all to circumnavigate the whole island. I was particularly taken with the Little Chapel in the Les Vauxbelets valley, Saint Andrew parish. It is tiny at only 16ft long by 9ft wide, and decorated in seashells, pebbles and broken china. It was built in 1914 and enlarged from its original size of 9ft by 4.5ft because a visiting bishop could not get through the door. Guernsey also has plenty of scenic pathways for coastal walks, some still showing signs of the Second World War.

Lisbon: Aside from the beautiful old pastel houses and the Old Town, a visit to the 16th century Belem Tower is a must, as it was the point of departure and arrival of famous explorers. Next to the tower is the Monument to the Discoveries, which commemorates the death of Prince Henry the Navigator who discovered the Azores, Madeira and Cape Verde. Across the River Tagus, in Almada, there is a great view of Lisbon from the Sanctuary of Christ the King. This statue was inspired, unsurprisingly, by Christ the Redeemer in Rio de Janeiro.

Gibraltar: If you can tolerate the apes that live on the Rock, the views across to the Mediterranean and mainland Spain are far reaching. The apes can be worrying though. One minute you are walking along, minding your own business, and the next seeing an ape leap on an unsuspecting walker's back. They are after food and any plastic bags will attract them. It certainly mars the enjoyment, as you are constantly worried that they will pick on you, but when up there, a trip into the cave system is worth the hassle. The other bonus in Gibraltar of course is there's tax free shopping.

Seville: This is quite a long day out from the southern port of Cadiz, but once there, this Spanish city epitomises our image of Spanish architecture, with typically Spanish tiled roofs and whitewashed buildings, beautiful tiled plazas, complete with orange trees, flower beds, benches and small fountains. The city also boasts some iconic buildings such as Giralda Tower, the Cathedral and the Real Alcázar of Seville. A beautiful city full of history and culture.

Valencia: Another Spanish city of tree-lined plazas, the cathedral here is supposed to house the Holy Grail, the cup that Jesus drank from at the Last Supper. Unlike many Spanish cities, Valencia sits close to some great beaches. For anyone interested in history, a trip out to Peniscola to see the medieval castle built at the time of the crusades and Knights Templar is a must. There are some great views of the town and the sea from here too. Peniscola has also been a film location for *Game of Thrones* and the film *El Cid*.

Barcelona: You need more than a quick port of call stop, but you can still see a lot in a full day, and the metro makes it cheap to get around. Head to Parc Guell, an amazing place full of sculptures and colourful tilework created by Antoni Gaudi. Another project also by him is the massive Sagrada Familia, the iconic, still unfinished Roman Catholic Basilica. The old Gothic area is a great place to wander, through the medieval streets full of trendy bars, not far from Las Ramblas.

Marseilles: It's easy to get from a ship to the Old Port, worth spending a few hours wandering along the harbourfront, full of small boats and yachts. Also spend time people watching from the many cafés and restaurants. It's not too far from Notre Dame Cathedral, and an easy walk from there around the back streets to get an authentic feel.

Villefranche: A pretty harbour, with the town climbing up the hillside behind, it is worth wandering around. It's also easy to visit Nice or Monte Carlo by train or head up to the hills at Eze.

Genoa: Birthplace of Christopher Columbus, this medieval city is packed full of history. Wander through the maze of cobbled alleyways to the main square or make the steep but short walk up to the Spianata Castelleto platform where you can get 360° views of the city and port below.

Livorno: This port of call is the gateway to Pisa and Florence, which are an easy train ride away. From the station at Pisa, you can walk for about twenty minutes until you get to the famous leaning tower, and practise trying to push the tower upright with a trick photo. Florence really needs longer, but you can see quite a bit in a day. The best place to get a view of the city is from across the river at Piazzale Michelangelo. From there are excellent views of the terracotta rooftops, the Duomo, the Arnolfo Tower of the Palazzo Vecchio and the Uffizi Gallery. Crossing the Ponte Vecchio will lead you to the towering Duomo Cathedral that dominates the city. Michelangelo's Statue of David is nearby, or you could spend your time exploring the many art galleries.

Civitavecchia: This is the port for Rome and is some distance from the city, so either take a taxi or get a train. Rome is another city that most definitely needs longer than a day, but here is what I would suggest for a full day. Get off the train at San Pietro station and walk about half a mile or so to St Peter's Square, in the Vatican City. Getting there early means beating the crowds, so hopefully time to go into St Peter's Basilica if the queues are not too long. Then head around the back for a short, easy walk to the Sistine Chapel. From there, take a taxi across the river and get dropped off at the Spanish Steps. Walk down Via Condotti to Via del Corso and you come to the Trevi Fountain. They say if you throw a coin into the fountain, you will return one day. I have returned three times (I still cannot find the coin I threw in the first time!) and never tire of the city. Walking through the ancient streets, you feel you are amongst living history. From the Trevi Fountain, the next place of note you come to will be the Pantheon. Allow time to go inside as it is one of the best-preserved buildings in Rome, dating from 126 AD. From there, down a narrow street, you will come to Piazza Navona, where there are three fountains designed and sculpted by Bernini. Around the edge of the Piazza are plenty of places to pause and get refreshments. Leaving from a corner of the Piazza, you then have a walk along a busy road that leads you to Piazza Venezia, with its huge monument, and from where Mussolini addressed the nation. To the right of the monument are some steps to Campidogli, lined with statues of Romans on horseback. Up the steps, head to the far left and you will see statues of Romulus and Remus sitting on top of their own columns. Walk alongside these and you will get a birds-eye view of the Forum which for centuries was the centre of the Roman Empire. You will be able to head down into the Forum and walk through the many ancient Roman ruins here. This brings you to the Via dei Fori de Imperiale, which leads to the Colosseum. Not too far from there is the main railway station. One other way to get around, and the less strenuous option is to buy tickets for the hop-on- hop-off bus, which covers all of these sights.

    Naples: Conveniently, there is a booking office here, next to where you disembark your ship, to buy tickets for other places along the Neapolitan coast. One suggestion for a day ashore is to buy a ticket to Sorrento on the local ferry, explore Sorrento on foot, and then catch a slow train back to Naples, stopping off at Pompeii. The station is right next to the entrance to the ruins. Arriving back in Naples, its best to get a taxi to the ship, as the area around the station looks a bit salubrious, and you would have to walk along the dockside roads that lead you back to the port.

Dubrovnik: Surrounded by ancient, fortified walls, the Old Town is a UNESCO Heritage site. Within thick medieval walls, paved streets, which are worn and shiny with age lead on to restaurants and souvenir shops. Dubrovnik is a place to explore and people watch.

Venice: Use the waterbus to get around and take a street map to help you navigate narrow streets and canals, that all look the same beyond the Grand Canal. Head over to the seven mile long barrier island of Venice Lido, for a completely different feel, where a fifteen-minute walk will bring you to the beach area of the island. It costs less to eat on the Lido too. Take a waterbus to other islands such as Murano to see the world-famous glass.

Corfu: One of the Ionian Islands, full of pretty pine clad coves and beautiful beaches. On a day excursion from the ship there is time to hire a car and head up to the northwest of the island, driving around the top through Paleokastritsa, Sidari, Roda and Kassiopi, almost within touching distance of Albania, just across the water. Head back down the east coast via Nissaki, Dassia and Ipsos to Corfu Town, where you can explore the Achilleion Palace and visit the Old Town.

Kefalonia: Not a port of call as such, but just mentioning it as an aside, as a place that has sandy beaches along the south coast. As you head to the north of this island, the beaches become crystal clear with large, rounded pebbles. There are pretty harbours lined with tavernas, where flotillas of yachts drop anchor and the crew come ashore for a local meal and to watch the sun go down. It is idyllic. It was here that my daughter aged just five swam out beyond her depth. She had only had a few swimming lessons at home and could swim with floats, but seeing her older sister floating with her snorkel, she wanted to do the same. We could see her going further out, but she was so engrossed with the fish beneath her, that with her own snorkel, she forgot she couldn't really swim. We all know how sound travels, and it did this time, as we heard a small voice, telling us, 'There's a fish. There's another fish', talking through her snorkel tube, so relaxed and absorbed, that she didn't need her floats again after that.

Athens: Home to the world-famous Acropolis, which includes the Parthenon amongst other monuments, temples and statues. When you are all 'Acropolis'd' out, head to Plaka, where there are shops, restaurants and tavernas to recharge your batteries. Also in Athens of course are those high kicking guards at the Tomb of the Unknown Soldier

Istanbul: The city at the gateway to Asia, has bags of history. Visit the Blue Mosque or Hagia Sophia, and the Topkapi Palace to see the priceless diamond there and then try some bartering in the Grand Bazaar.

Kusadasi: This is a busy beach resort on the Aegean Sea with plenty of opportunities to shop for leather goods, jewellery and Turkish carpets. It is also the place to stop to see Ephesus, the ancient Roman city, where you don't need to use much imagination to see how the ruins were once beautiful buildings. Walk along the Arcadian Way and imagine you are back in time when Cleopatra and Mark Antony rode along there in procession.

Santorini: Known in our house as Donkey Island, because of the option to ascend from the port to the top of the cliffs by donkey. This is a volcanic island, the majority submerged under the sea, having been devastated by an eruption in the 16th century. The centre of the volcano collapsed, leaving a steep-sided caldera. In the centre of the caldera is the still active volcanic core, while around the caldera rim, a string of villages sit along the top of the cliff, with their pretty, whitewashed buildings and cobalt blue roofs. A great place to wander with fabulous views from there of the sun setting to the west.

Mykonos: Another of the Greek Cyclades Islands, Mykonos has a reputation for being a party island, but it is also charming, with narrow streets, whitewashed buildings typical of Greek architecture, with tumbling brightly coloured bougainvillea cascading from balconies. There are four 16th-century windmills sitting on a hill overlooking Mykonos Town, which have become an iconic symbol of the island.

Rhodes: The largest of the Dodecanese Island group was home to one of the seven wonders of the ancient world, the Colossus of Rhodes, which allegedly stood over the entrance to Rhodes Harbour. The city of Rhodes is well preserved and surrounded by medieval walls. Head south to Lindos, which has a sweeping sandy bay with a hillock at one end. Sitting on top of the hill is an Acropolis, with the whitewashed village sitting beneath it. A steep walk, but the views from the top are worth the effort.

Crete: The largest of all the Greek islands, and the most southerly in the Mediterranean, Crete oozes history. One of the oldest places of note is the Palace of Knossos. For anyone interested in ancient history and the Minoan civilization, it should be on the agenda. There are numerous beaches and coves to enjoy all around the island, among them Venetian Harbour at Chania. There are several gorges criss-crossing the island for hikers.

Malta: Another island that has bags of history. The fortified towns and cities are home to baroque churches and deep harbours. Boat trips are popular for exploring Valetta's historic harbour and to see the various caves and caverns peppered along the coast.

Corsica: The cruise ships call into the port of Ajaccio, but the island is too big to explore in a day. For longer trips there are three airports to choose from depending on which part of the island you want to explore. Ajaccio, the capital is the birthplace of Napoleon. There are full day tours available to learn about the city and its place in history, or simply watch the world go by around the pretty harbour front. More likely though, you will want to return to explore the island in full.

Palma: The capital and gateway to the ever-popular island of Majorca, the city is worth a mooch around. It has a fabulous marina which is a short walk from the Old Town and the Gothic Cathedral that dominates the area. The whole island is home to many pretty beaches and coves, and there is something for everyone on the island. The most scenic area, however, is to the north and east. The scenery in the mountains will take your breath away, while hidden away are pretty villages, lost in time. In my opinion, the most scenic stretch of coastline is along the north coast to Formentor, and along to Pollensa. Along the east coast interspersed amongst the beach resorts are some impressive cave systems at Arta and Drach, which are well worth a visit. With so many different things to see on Majorca, it's easy to return time and time again.

Menorca: Again, not a port of call as such, but a great place for a quiet family holiday with gentle shelving beaches. I particularly loved the fact you could find some totally isolated beaches with no facilities and more importantly no people, and that was at the height of summer, although that was quite a few years ago. Our three-year-old seemed to be impressed with Binibeca, a small town full of narrow streets and whitewashed villas on the south coast. No idea why, but on our return home, she insisted on playing 'Binibeca' with her Grandad, that for some reason entailed sitting on the stairs, with shopping bags, and teddys.

Stockholm: Passing many tiny islands to reach Sweden's capital, you can maybe see the island where Benny and Björn from ABBA wrote most of their hits. The main waterfront at Strömmen Harbour is full of small watercraft, and from there the city is spread across fourteen islands. The Old Town area, Gamla Stan sits on one of the islands, and dates back to the 13th century. Here you can wander past centuries old buildings such as the Royal Palace, the Royal Swedish Opera House, the Riksgatan and Parliament House. Not to be forgotten, is a visit to the ABBA Museum, which for any ABBA fan is a fun trip down memory lane. When we visited, I found myself on stage singing my rendition to one of their hits with holograms of Anni-Frid, Benny, Björn and Agnetha dancing behind me. It made me realise I should not give up my day job!

Helsinki: There is perhaps surprisingly plenty to see in Finland's capital and largest city. The oldest part of central Helsinki is Senate Square, home to the University of Helsinki, Government Palace and Helsinki Cathedral, which has a distinctive Russian looking green and gold dome. The City Hall is near the waterfront, next to Market Square, adjacent to the harbour and ferry terminal. This area is busy with market traders, trams and tourists. Further afield, a stop at the Sibelius Monument, in the district of Tooli, dedicated to composer Jean Sibelius, is worth a visit. Looking a little like a church organ, it is made from 600 hollow steel pipes welded together in a wave like pattern, I suppose to represent sound waves. Another unusual building worth a stop is the Temppeliaukio Church, which has an easier to pronounce, more common name of the Church of the Rock. It is a Lutheran church that was built by excavating rock, so that the walls are roughly hewn from the circular pit that was created. The church is topped with a central copper domed roof and a skylight that brings in natural light. Its modern design is unusual and stylish.

Tallinn: Just fifty miles south of Helsinki is my favourite European city to date. Tallinn's Old Town is one of the best-preserved medieval cities in Europe and is listed as a UNESCO World Heritage Site. The Viru Gate is the main access point to the old town within medieval defensive walls. This whole area makes you feel as if you have stepped into the pages of a fairy tale book. Pretty, colourful buildings line the ancient, cobbled streets, opening onto quiet cobblestone squares. There are circular stone, former watchtowers dotted around the walls, with tiny, slatted windows high up and topped with red tiled triangular roofs. I'm sure I saw Rapunzel peeking out from one of those windows, looking for her prince. The Lutheran churches are plainer looking than their Russian Orthodox counterparts, having only tall dark spires and white towers. Some of the buildings in Tallinn are tall and narrow, like those seen along the canals of Amsterdam. I particularly like Tallinn's Town Hall Square, still cobbled and surrounded by the same pretty buildings. It is the hub where people meet. Market traders ply their wares, and you might hear a group of musicians playing. The Town Hall itself dates from 1322 and is the plainest of all the buildings in the square, but it has the distinction of being the oldest town hall in the whole of the Baltic Region and Scandinavia. There is some Russian influence still remaining on Toompea Hill, overlooking the Old Town, which adds to the overall charm. The cathedral here is Eastern Orthodox, richly decorated with domed roofs, and with eleven bells that were cast in Saint Petersburg. Toompea Hill is where you will find the Parliament of Estonia, adjoining Toompea Castle, an ancient stronghold in use since at least the 9th century. You certainly get a real feel of history walking the streets.

Riga: We felt this Latvian capital was less commercialised than its Estonian neighbour, although similar with narrow cobbled streets and the same style of architecture in the Old Town area. Another UNESCO World Heritage Site, Riga has the added attraction of having some Art Nouveau architecture as well as original 19th-century wooden buildings. It's easy to imagine yourself in a horse drawn carriage trotting past the pale yellows and ochres that many of the buildings are painted in. The oldest complex of private houses is the Three Brothers, dating from the 15th and 17th centuries, looking just like those narrow Dutch canal side houses in Amsterdam. The Old Town, or to give it its proper name, Vecriga is protected by a surrounding medieval wall, although only parts have been restored. One of the most recognisable landmarks is the cathedral in Dome Square. When compared to the ornate golden domes and fancy fretwork of other countries close by, this red brick Lutheran Cathedral appears very austere. Just as Tallinn has its town square, Riga has the same, although by comparison, the atmosphere seemed much more subdued and quieter for some reason The overall impression of Riga is of an authentic Baltic city, which has not been damaged by over tourism.

Stavanger: Located in southwest Norway, Stavanger is the third largest city in Norway. Like many other ports of call, Stavanger has its old town, known as Gamle, with over 250 small white wooden cottages, many restored from the 18th and 19th centuries and inhabited. Walking through the narrow streets will give you an impression of what Stavanger would have looked like then. The waterfront is busy and attractive, and the city centre has wide precincts, with many buildings that look like they date from the 1960s.

Bergen: In my opinion, a bigger and better version of Stavanger. Bergen is surrounded by mountains and the best views of the city and waterfront are from Mount Fløyen, accessed by a funicular railway. The oldest part of Bergen is conveniently situated around the central harbour in the city centre. More cobbled streets and white painted wooden shops and houses add to the attractiveness. The waterfront known as the Bryggen is lined with old Hanseatic merchants' buildings, dating from 1350, which were used when Bergen developed into an important trading centre. These old buildings have now been converted into restaurants and artisan shops. When we visited it coincided with the arrival of the Tall Ships, so the harbour area was buzzing with locals and competitors. At the entrance to the harbour is Haakon's Hall, a medieval stone hall constructed in the middle of the 13th century set within Bergenhus Fortress. From the same period located within the fortress is the Rosenkranz Tower. This is so close to the harbour and the Bryggen, it's worth a gentle walk to the edge of the harbour to see this bit of Norwegian history.

Flåm: There are only about 350 inhabitants in this picturesque village at the head of Aurlands fjord, Norway, but the numbers swell when 160 cruise ships visit each year. The famous Flåm Railway begins it journey through the mountains to Myrdal and is one of the steepest railways tracks in the world. Heading inland the real beauty of the Norwegian fjords is revealed. Following steep sided valleys, with single drop waterfalls cascading down the mountainside to the valley floor, the train passes tiny villages, with perhaps a single wooden church. The fjords are deep and surrounded by mountains that still have snow on their peaks, while some still retain glaciers, even in the height of summer.

Alesund: Situated 147 miles northeast of Bergen, and adjacent to Hjørund and Geiranger fjords, Alesund is noted for its concentration of Art Nouveau architecture. The town is located on two islands and all the buildings are clustered together shoulder to shoulder. Originally built mostly from wood, practically the whole town was destroyed by fire in 1904, and was rebuilt in stone and brick, between 1904 and 1907, hence the Art Nouveau style of that period. Above the town is a hill with accessible, but steep pathways to the top, for fabulous views of the whole area.

Andalsnes: Another small Norwegian town visited by many cruise ships. One of the main reasons for stopping here is to drive along the serpentine mountain road. A steep sided twisting route, with eleven hairpin bends climbing up the Trollindene mountain range. The views are spectacular. Along the same route is the Trollveggen (Troll Wall), a mountain range in the Romsdelen valley. It has the highest sheer vertical rock face in Europe, at about 3600ft, making it popular with climbers and BASE jumpers alike. You are unlikely to see any trolls though...

Trondheim: Once the capital of Norway during the Viking age, Trondheim has the largest university in Norway. Nidaros Cathedral dominates the city centre and is the second largest in Scandinavia. It reminds me a little of Wells Cathedral in Somerset. The old town area of the city is to the east of a wide river, with the now familiar small wooden houses, and old converted warehouses running alongside. The Old Town Bridge, reconstructed in 1681 after a fire, is an unusual construction, painted in ochre red, a colour that is frequently used throughout Norway on their buildings.

Tromsø: Known as the gateway to the Arctic Circle, I have described Tromsø in greater detail earlier in the book when we visited during winter in search of the Northern Lights.

Honningsvag: The most northerly town in Norway and well within the Arctic Circle, it is the stopping off point for the North Cape, the northernmost point in Europe that can be accessed by car. The ice-free ocean here provides rich fishing grounds, as important to the town as tourism. To get to the North Cape, you need to cross Mageroya Island, which is in the extreme north of Arctic Norway, bordering the Barents Sea. It features a bleak, barren tundra covered landscape, devoid of any trees, with steep cliffs along the coast and dramatic mountain scenery. It's here you are quite likely to see reindeer grazing on the scrubby undergrowth. North Cape itself sits on a 1000ft high plateau. It is not, as some would say, the northernmost point in mainland Europe. That accolade goes to a point on an island in the Norwegian Sea further north. At North Cape there is a sculpture of a globe sitting on top of the plateau, where the obligatory photo stop is in order. Being more creative, you can take a photo further away, with the globe far enough away so that you can 'hold the world' in your hand.

Kirkenes: Located in the extreme north-eastern region of Norway, near the Russia-Norwegian border, This marks the end of the route for Hurtigruten ships. Extremely bleak in the winter months, a snow hotel is built annually and is a place where you can go husky sledding and visit the adjoining reindeer farm. Many road signs this far north are in both Russian and Norwegian, as many Russians visit the supermarket there to stock up. Each month a 'Russian market' takes place in the central square of Kirkenes where traders from Murmansk sell their merchandise; everything from matryoshkas, linen cloths and handicrafts to Russian crystal and porcelain dishes.

Akureyri: Gateway to northern Iceland, the town of Akureyri is the stopping off point to explore Lake Myvatn and Godafoss Waterfall, an area with geothermal landscapes, hot springs and wild beauty. If you are lucky (unlike me, it seems), you will have a good chance to see some whales from a whale-watching trip in Eyjafjörður fjord or go horse riding on the unique Icelandic horses.

Reykjavik: Capital of Iceland, the city is easy to get around. This is a good place to head out to the Golden Circle, to see bubbling geysers, waterfalls and Thingvellir, (mentioned earlier) the only place on land where the North American and Eurasian continental plates are visible. A trip to the Blue Lagoon for some thermal bathing is only forty minutes away, and as I write, people are flocking to see the erupting volcano on the Reykjanes Peninsula just to the south of the city. To get an overview of this fabulous, wild country take a simulated flight at Fly Over Iceland, in Reykjavik. This is a ride that takes you on a 'flight' over the country giving a birds-eye view through the seasons. So good I have done this twice. It is an expensive place to stay, but for a few days, there is a lot to see from Reykjavik and surrounding area.

Anchorage: For many a starting point for cruising in Alaska. Before boarding though, a trip into the Denali National Park is worth a visit. If weather permits, you will see the towering mountains, including Mt Denali (formerly McKinley) at over 20,000ft, and maybe a moose in the distance. Anchorage is set out grid style, so easy to find your way around. There's also visible evidence of a relatively recent earthquake on the coast. The other place I enjoyed there was a trip to the zoo, as they have indigenous animals which might be elusive in the wild such as polar bears, black and grizzly bears and porcupines.

Glacier Bay National Park: Not a port of call as such, but a place where the ships drop anchor, up close to some of the best glaciers on earth. The cruise ship gradually turns 360° to give everyone a chance to see the enormous ice falls that crash into the sea. Large chunks of blue-grey ice float away, some with seals on board getting a free ride. The occasional sea otter floating on its back in the cold seas.

Skagway: A gold rush town, with buildings to match, looking like a set from a cowboy movie. From here you can take an excursion into the Yukon and get a stamp in your passport to prove it from the post office in Carcross. The 'cities' in this region are no more than sparse, spread-out villages. You almost imagine the tumbleweed rolling down the street, passing a rusting car here and there. The landscape is of tundra, with the odd pine tree sprouting here and there.

Juneau: The capital of Alaska. Not a great amount to see in the immediate vicinity, but whale-watching trips are possible, or head up on the cable car to a viewpoint above the port for some great views, and good areas to walk. Juneau is also the place to stop to see the Mendenhall Glacier, half a mile wide and up to 1800ft thick. You can view the glacier from land, looking across a lake, or you can kayak quite near to the front of the glacier. There are hiking trails that take you on a loop to see a wider area.

Ketchikan: Known as the Salmon Capital of the world, at least that's what it says at the entrance to the town. The low-rise buildings are mainly centred around the harbour with a backdrop of mountains and pine trees. It was from Ketchikan that we *actually* saw a tail fluke of a whale, without going on a whale-watching trip. *Yes!* Ketchikan's streets are full of Native American totem poles. In fact, it boasts the largest number of totem poles in Alaska. There is a Totem Arts Centre which houses a large collection of native artifacts, including several ancient totem poles, and other beautifully hand-crafted works of art. Heading out beyond Ketchikan, the Misty Fjords Wilderness area will take you back to nature with pine clad mountains, where the air smells so fresh and clean. At every port of call along the inside passage we saw numerous sea planes coming and going. Obviously the best way to get about in this remote part of North America.

Victoria: Capital of British Columbia, on the south of Vancouver Island, it boasts Victorian period architecture and a busy harbour filled with both boats and seaplanes. To the north are Butchart Gardens which I have mentioned previously. You also have another chance here to go whale watching, take a boat out, or book a seaplane for sightseeing. Victoria has plenty of green spaces and gardens to sit and enjoy too.

One final thought: After all the years of booking flights for people, I realise I've become a bit of a nerd. I surprised myself recently, when checking my cabin number for an upcoming cruise, which was shown as being Cabin BA702. My husband commented that it sounded like a British Airways flight number.

'I wonder where that goes,' said he.

'Oh, somewhere like Vienna I think,' I replied. Out of curiosity, I checked where BA702 flies to, and lo and behold, it does indeed fly from London to Vienna. Get in!

NOT DONE YET!

So where to next? There are still a few places I would like to visit. I would love to tour China, to see Tiananmen Square in Beijing, walk a small section of the Great Wall of China, just to say I've done it, and to visit the Terracotta Warriors at Xian. I would have to include a trip to Chengdu, to interact with the baby pandas. I think my heart would melt, as they are up there in the cutey stakes with koalas. To the north of Chengdu is an area I have long been intrigued by called the Jiuzhaigou Valley which is an especially scenic area in the Minshan mountains of northern Sichuan province. Although only seen on film, this area includes several high snow-covered peaks and alpine meadows with the most incredible lakes I have ever 'virtually' seen. These waters range in colour from a pale turquoise to a deep blue, with mirrored reflections on their surfaces of the pretty surrounding scenery. If I could, I would also love to see the ice carvings at the Harbin Ice and Snow Carving Festival in Northern China.

Something else on my wish list is to take a road trip covering the National Parks in Arizona, Utah and Colorado, particularly to include Antelope Canyon. This trip was on the list for 2020, but sadly, plans had to be put on hold. Also, in the US I'd like to visit Yellowstone National Park, explore the Californian coast, head north to see the more northern states, and then maybe another trip to the Carolinas and Georgia. Costa Rica appeals too, to see the diverse variety of animals and birds. I would also like to head back to South America, but this time explore Peru, particularly Machu Picchu, and possibly the Galapagos as well. I think a tour of Japan would be enjoyable, especially when the cherry blossom is in bloom, but to also explore the culture, history and scenic areas. So still many new places to explore while we are still healthy and willing. There are so many beautiful and interesting places in the world, still so much to learn about the history and culture of these countries. While the fire is still in my belly, while our health remains sound and while funds allow, I truly hope that it will be possible to explore the world further.

In the meantime, we are also enjoying our own beautiful country.

We are lucky to live in an area which is easy to explore without having to stay overnight. We are just two hours from London, two hours to the south coast, two hours to the Midlands and two hours from Bath. We have the River Thames on our doorstep, the Cotswolds within an hour, and the historic 'dreaming spires' of Oxford just up the road. A couple of years ago we spent a week in the Yorkshire Dales, with superb weather enjoying the numerous walks and stunning countryside, with its pretty villages, babbling brooks, and pub lunches. More recently we revisited the Isle of Wight after a period of about thirty years. Nothing has really changed there, as it is still in a time warp, with Victorian houses, traditional British seaside resorts, some of which are rather tired looking and in need of a lick of paint, but with others moving with the times. We found some fabulous walks on the island, particularly along Tennyson Down in the east, leading to the Needles, avoiding the commercial area that has been built there, but using the National Trust pathways for some fabulous views. We've strolled around West Cowes, using the old chain ferry from East Cowes, and wandered through the traffic free streets lined with local shops and cafés, to the marina and a lovely promenade with views across to Calshot Spit and the mainland. Just sitting and watching the world go by while we enjoy a 'compulsory' ice cream. I revisited Carisbrook Castle, which must be fifty-five years since my last visit, but the only thing I remember from childhood was a donkey walking within an enormous waterwheel in the Wheelhouse. The donkeys are still there, but fortunately they aren't being worked anymore. Osborne House, a favourite haunt of Queen Victoria, was as I remembered it, and still as grand and opulent as ever.

Over the years we have had breaks in other parts of the UK. We have had the standard seaside stays in Cornwall and Devon, and in North and West Wales, as well as holidays to Scotland and Southern Ireland. We have visited much of Northern England too, yet there is still many other places to explore further. Unfortunately, our weather can make a huge difference to the enjoyment of a trip. If we could guarantee good weather, some of our regions are up there with the best in the rest of the world. Our Lake District, Peak District, Derbyshire Dales, and the Western Isles of Scotland all the way south to the Isles of Scilly, all have something unique and beautiful to offer.

So, yes, I have been all over the place, but who would have thought that the £77 my parents paid all those years ago for a school trip, would be the start of my journey around the world, and what a journey it has been.

Oh, and I never did become an air stewardess!